ADMINISTRATIV

The multiple crises emerging in 2020–2021 have presented both challenges and opportunities for change in four-year residential colleges and universities. Evidence indicates that the historic structure of administrative and student services is increasingly mismatched to the needs of a diverse and stressed student body born in a digital age. Inspired by his leadership in a university-wide initiative that focused on how students' interactions with both academic and professional staff affect their success and well-being, Scott A. Bass presents fresh insights on the inner workings of traditional nonprofit four-year degree residential institutions. The book describes the influences of history, tradition, and internal and external pressures on the American university, highlighting its evolution to its staid and fragmented structure; it distills voices of students, faculty, and staff; and it explores how successful organizations outside of higher education deliver services, with potential applicability for the academy's ability to meet students where they are.

SCOTT A. BASS is Professor, Provost Emeritus, and Director of the Center for University Excellence at American University.

ADMINISTRATIVELY ADRIFT

Overcoming Institutional Barriers for College Student Success

SCOTT A. BASS

American University

CAMBRIDGE
UNIVERSITY PRESS

CAMBRIDGE
UNIVERSITY PRESS

University Printing House, Cambridge CB2 8BS, United Kingdom

One Liberty Plaza, 20th Floor, New York, NY 10006, USA

477 Williamstown Road, Port Melbourne, VIC 3207, Australia

314–321, 3rd Floor, Plot 3, Splendor Forum, Jasola District Centre, New Delhi – 110025, India

103 Penang Road, #05–06/07, Visioncrest Commercial, Singapore 238467

Cambridge University Press is part of the University of Cambridge.

It furthers the University's mission by disseminating knowledge in the pursuit of education, learning, and research at the highest international levels of excellence.

www.cambridge.org
Information on this title: www.cambridge.org/9781316514917
DOI: 10.1017/9781009091312

First published 2022

A catalogue record for this publication is available from the British Library.

Library of Congress Cataloging-in-Publication Data
NAMES: Bass, Scott A., author.
TITLE: Administratively adrift : overcoming institutional barriers for college student success / Scott A. Bass.
DESCRIPTION: Cambridge, United Kingdom ; New York, NY : Cambridge University Press, 2022. | Includes bibliographical references and index.
IDENTIFIERS: LCCN 2021056085 (print) | LCCN 2021056086 (ebook) | ISBN 9781316514917 (hardback) | ISBN 9781009094030 (paperback) | ISBN 9781009091312 (epub)
SUBJECTS: LCSH: Student affairs services–United States. | College students–Services for. | Universities and colleges–United States–Administration. | BISAC: PSYCHOLOGY / General
CLASSIFICATION: LCC LB2342.92 .B38 2022 (print) | LCC LB2342.92 (ebook) | DDC 371.40973–DC23/eng/20220110
LC record available at https://lccn.loc.gov/2021056085
LC ebook record available at https://lccn.loc.gov/2021056086

ISBN 978-1-316-51491-7 Hardback
ISBN 978-1-009-09403-0 Paperback

... the great force of history comes from the fact that we carry it within us, are unconsciously controlled by it in many ways, and history is literally *present* in all that we do.

—James Baldwin, "The White Man's Guilt"

Contents

Figures and Tables

Figures

Tables

Acknowledgments

The creation of this book has been more akin to the production of a feature-length film, with the credits to prove it. Over four years, a team at American University (AU) assessed and explored different approaches to develop a more student-centered university. The book rests on those early efforts.

First, I want to express my gratitude to AU's president, Neil Kerwin, who hired me in 2008 as provost and gave me unflinching support to strengthen AU. His commitment to the improvement of the university in every respect provided the energy and enthusiasm necessary for establishing a thoroughly modern research university deeply committed to the undergraduate experience. The board of trustees, its chair, Jack Cassell, and the chair of the academic affairs committee, Arthur Rothkopf, supported this leadership. Other board members who were particularly influential during this time included Tom Gottchaulk (who reviewed sample chapters, provided detailed feedback, and pushed my thinking about the student-centered university), Jeff Sine, and Janice Abraham. The board's support has been remarkable.

I am appreciative of Earl Lewis and Eugene Tobin, who administered the "officer's grant" from the Andrew W. Mellon Foundation that provided the initial proof of concept for the Reinventing the Student Experience initiative at AU. Members of the AU leadership steering committee included (title at the time of service) Sharon Alston, vice provost for undergraduate enrollment; Nana An, assistant vice president, University Budget and Finance Resource Center, Office of Finance and Treasurer; Fanta Aw, associate vice president for campus life, later interim vice president for campus life; Bethany Bridgham, acting general counsel; Mary L. Clark, senior vice provost and dean of academic affairs; Larry Engel, faculty senate vice chair; Violetta Ettle, vice provost for academic administration (chapter reviewer); Teresa Flannery, vice president for communications; Karen Froslid-Jones, assistant provost (chapter reviewer),

Office of Institutional Research and Assessment; Gail Hanson, vice president of campus life; Doug Kudravetz, CFO, vice president and treasurer; Raina Lenney, assistant vice president, alumni relations, Office of Development and Alumni Relations; Doug McKenna, registrar; Beth Muha, assistant vice president of human resources; Jeffrey Rutenbeck, dean, School of Communication (chapter reviewer); Kamalika Sandell, chief information officer (chapter reviewer); Peter Starr, dean of College of Arts and Sciences (chapter reviewer); Courtney Surls, vice president, development and alumni relations; David Swartz, vice president and chief information officer (chapter reviewer); Jessica Waters, associate dean, School of Public Affairs, later dean for Undergraduate Education and vice provost for academic student services (chapter reviewer); and Lacey Wootton, faculty senate chair. Bridget Cooney provided crucial administrative support on the project and faculty member Kelly Joiner served as a recorder of the initiative.

Peter Starr played a significant leadership role throughout the experience, assisting with the Mellon grant and leading the effort to revise the general education curriculum. Further credit goes to Cynthia Bair Van Dam and Jessica Waters for building campus support that resulted in the AU Faculty Senate's unanimous vote of approval for the new core curriculum. Their support and the support of everyone mentioned above were critical in bringing forward the ideas recorded in this book.

I want to thank the dean of the School of Public Affairs, Vicky Wilkins, and Vice Provost Violetta Ettle, who helped provide a comfortable and cheerful workspace for me to write portions of this book. Vicky Wilkins also lent additional administrative staff support during my transition to faculty via Emily Phipps. Cynthia Miller-Idriss provided sound counsel for the book and now is my close working colleague and director of research of the center I now lead, the Center for University Excellence.

The university librarian, Nancy Davenport, made sure I had enough library assistance, and for this I am grateful. Mitchell Stevens, a gracious host at Stanford, provided a stimulating environment for me to write and think during my sabbatical. I am most appreciative of Max Paul Friedman's comments on my draft book proposal as well as the insightful comments provided by William LeoGrande. My colleague in the AU School of Public Affairs, Anna Amirkhanyan, graciously reviewed four chapters. Neil Kerwin and Kai Drekmeier provided feedback on later chapters, Chris Silvia commented on other text, student affairs expert Chris Moody reviewed Chapter 5, and academic IT expert Jack Suess reviewed Chapter 7 and a subsection of Chapter 10. I also want to thank

William DeLone for introducing me to several leading IT executives who have transitioned their organizations to a more integrated set of business processes, as well as for his willingness to review a book chapter. The tables and figures were prepared by Laura McMahon Fulford, with the preliminary design for Figure 7.1 by Emily Phipps. Finally, editor Danielle Bendjy assisted in the editing process, including technical formatting and providing consistent sage commentary; editor Patrick Breslin served as an essential touchstone throughout, helping guide my thinking about the book; and editor and critical reviewer of the manuscript Audra Wolfe provided insightful feedback and invaluable guidance. However, it was David Repetto, executive publisher (New York) at Cambridge University Press who saw the potential of the manuscript and supported this effort. His encouragement made this publication possible. Final copyediting for the publisher (UK) was undertaken by Penny Harper. To them, and to the hundreds of others who were influential in the AU experience, I am most appreciative.

I would also like to acknowledge the impact of the late community psychologist, Seymour B. Sarason, has had on my thinking about the powerful influence that institutions have on individuals and the complexity of the process of change.

Finally, I note that the title of this book, which focuses on the administrative operations of the university, recognizes the widely acclaimed book by Richard Arum and Josipa Roksa, *Academically Adrift: Limited Learning on College Campuses*, published in 2011 by the University of Chicago Press.

Administratively Adrift is the result of many drafts, and I alone am responsible for the content and any errors or misunderstandings.

Preface

Administratively Adrift is a work that has been years in the making, tinged with personal experiences from a long and successful career in an institution I love – the university. The capacity of colleges and universities to transform lives is, in a word, awesome. However, like all institutions, it can and must evolve in order to improve. And in order to improve, it needs to assess its weaknesses, embrace its limitations, and make the necessary adjustments to respond to the community of students it welcomes. Hopefully, this book will foster further dialogue about necessary change.

The United States and its universities are facing near-Biblical upheavals – seismic disruptions that I refer to in the book as "crucible experiences." The effects of these crucible experiences have been profound for American society at large and devastating for today's generation of college students, often referred to as Generation Z. The chapters that follow draw upon multiple sources of information about colleges and universities, their history, their organizational evolution, and their interactions with students. Some of the sources are anecdotal, told through case studies of student encounters that highlight the unintended consequences of interactions with administrative offices, systems, policies, and practices. Other information comes from sources such as institutional databases and records, captured from the unique vantage point I have had as a chief academic officer at American University. Still other sources include US databases, national surveys, and previous research. In each case, the data about the problems that *Administratively Adrift* chronicles have continued to evolve since the manuscript was initially completed in July 2021. Even in the time that has elapsed since then, disconcerting new data have emerged revealing increasing numbers of students self-reporting depression, anxiety, and other struggles with mental health. Suicide among young Americans has reached unprecedented levels, as has opioid addiction. Other new indicators from the sources that I detailed in *Administratively*

Adrift identify further unwelcome findings involving today's generation of college students and the circumstances they confront.

The problems I highlight in *Administratively Adrift* have only continued to escalate, reaffirming that students are being harmed by these troubled times and, for some, the way they are treated when attending a residential college or university. The cascading events and mounting evidence have served to prove even more the urgency of one of the book's central points: today's students need colleges and universities that are equipped to meet them where they are, appreciate their point of view, support them as a whole person, and prepare them to better meet the increasingly dire and complex array of personal and societal challenges that they face. Despite the mounting challenges and escalating polarization that surround us, I remain optimistic that once academic leaders do the hard work to assess and identify their areas in need of institutional improvement, they will find and test administrative strategies designed to overcome its barriers to student success and well-being.

Scott A. Bass
February 2022

CHAPTER I

The Gap between the Student Experience and University Operations

Maurice, an eighteen-year-old first-year undergraduate student at a private, nonprofit four-year university, has a chronic medical condition that requires daily treatment at the campus health center. He is also dyslexic and entitled to additional tutoring outside of class and extra time for assignments. While the university does provide such accommodations, it also requires that students present written authorization from a doctor and a statement describing the specific services needed. Living away from home for the first time, and focused on making friends and obtaining his medical treatment, Maurice neglects to file the required academic accommodation request.

This seemingly minor lapse has serious consequences. As Maurice falls behind in his classes, no one reports his declining academic performance. Any of his professors can issue an "early warning" notice alerting his academic advisor that Maurice is struggling and possibly in need of assistance, but none of them do. Overwhelmed, Maurice decides to withdraw from classes and start over the following term with the proper support. His academic advisor agrees to this plan, completes the form withdrawing him from the university, authorizes a partial tuition refund, and informs Maurice he will be able to register the following semester in good standing.

Assuming all is in order, Maurice stops going to class. Later, when his mother calls the Office of Student Accounts about the refund, she is told Maurice is still enrolled. She calls several university offices; they all say that there is no record of Maurice's withdrawal and that if he is not attending classes and completing coursework, he will face academic dismissal. She finally reaches Maurice's academic advisor, who is surprised to find that the withdrawal petition is indeed missing from the record. But now that the semester is almost over, full payment is required, and the advisor says he lacks the authority to withdraw Maurice.

Maurice's mother works her way up the chain of command; staff members at each level are powerless to help, as the problem involves several different administrative jurisdictions. She finally reaches the dean, who eventually agrees to have the registrar retroactively adjust the official record. At long last, the accounting office, with the support of the registrar, issues a partial refund of Maurice's tuition.

Having resolved his academic and financial situation, Maurice can now register for the following semester. By this time, it is late in the registration process; afternoon classes are already full, and morning classes conflict with his daily medical treatment. After more frustration and anxiety, Maurice's mother again contacts the dean, who once again intervenes to clear the administrative hurdles. Maurice ultimately gets the schedule and the academic accommodations he needs.

Had Maurice's mother not checked on the delayed refund, Maurice would have inadvertently failed all his courses and been academically dismissed. Several different things involving different parts of the university had gone wrong: Maurice failed to request an accommodation; all five of his instructors and his advisor missed opportunities for early intervention; somehow his withdrawal form went unrecorded; and administrators at different levels and divisions lacked the authority to resolve the issue because it crossed the jurisdiction of their individual offices.

Maurice's story is not an isolated event – thousands of students at American universities face similar situations each year. Nor is it merely an unfortunate accident. Rather, what happened to Maurice is the direct result of stovepiped, deeply entrenched, and increasingly arcane university structures and procedures conflicting with the needs and expectations of today's university students. Raised in an era of user-friendly access to information through their electronic devices, Generation Z students justifiably expect clear communication and efficient problem-solving that, much to their frustration, universities often fail to deliver.

Today's eighteen- to twenty-four-year-old college students bring a different set of expectations to the university experience than their predecessors. They expect seamless service via smartphone and simultaneously face an unprecedented multitude of complex, inherited, yet rapidly evolving societal problems, many of which threaten their safety and even their existence. University leaders alone cannot solve climate change or structural racism for their students, but they *can* improve the student experience at their institutions. Residential four-year nonprofit colleges and universities can and must adapt to the new needs of today's students. If they do not, they risk losing their students to other competitive educational and experiential options, potentially compromising their position as the educational destination of choice.

The COVID-19 pandemic is a moment of reckoning for university administrators, forcing many of them to balance the safety of the university community with declining enrollments and revenue, and increased expenses. For most, it is a uniquely stressful time, where meeting the public health crisis and fiscal challenge are front and center. It is difficult in this situation to look downstream, well after the pandemic, toward the market position of one's college or university. The pandemic will impact the psyche of an entire generation and will be remembered not only by those who are applying to or are in college now, but by the children whose lives have been disrupted and will be applying to college in a decade. This is therefore a moment to reexamine long-standing operations in the name of improving the academic product and confronting its increasing cost. It is a chance to dismantle outmoded structures and craft a holistic educational experience that meets the needs of current students as well as those yet to come.

The Crucibles of 2020–2021

In early 2020, when the novel coronavirus first began to ravage the world, over ten million undergraduate students were enrolled in America's public and private nonprofit four-year colleges and universities.[1] The vast majority were in their late teens and early twenties, with only two out of every ten over the age of twenty-five.[2] Many of the schools they attended have their origins in the late nineteenth century, when the modern American university took shape, and retain the organizational structures and traditions that characterized their founding.[3] These schools survived world wars, economic hardship and depressions, dramatic enrollment shifts, natural disasters, and previous pandemics. The pandemic that began in 2020, however, has proved more disruptive to more residential academic settings than any other event in the last century.

Even before the pandemic, the American residential college and university system was facing strong headwinds. Demographic trends, rising college costs, a volatile economy, and increasingly restrictive immigration policies were already reducing the number of potential college students. The popular press and families of current and prospective students had begun to question the value of a college degree and the return on the substantial investment. Universities had become mired in controversies involving college admissions bribery scandals, polarized political rhetoric on and off campus, racial tensions, and even questions of institutional mission. As they have done since early in the history of the modern American university, critics questioned the value of a liberal arts education, arguing that colleges should instead emphasize career training and the kinds of technical skill-building that lead to employment. Investigative reports revealed shocking instances of faculty, staff, and coaches using their power to abuse and exploit students. On campus, students themselves had been demanding a more pluralistic curriculum, greater inclusion, and stronger protections from harassment.

The residential four-year nonprofit university has fallen out of step with today's students. While venerable, the established structures and traditions of colleges and universities have hampered their ability to adapt to the needs of twenty-first-century students. More diverse in their personal backgrounds and life experiences, the students of Generation Z bring different expectations and higher levels of stress and anxiety to the college experience than previous generations. A seemingly minor but extraordinarily significant difference is that they are the first generation to have grown up with the smartphone. It's not just that today's students spend great amounts of time peering at their screens. It's that the smartphone, the services it provides, and the information that flows on its cascade of pixels defines this generation's expectations about how the world, including the world of the university campus, should work. Most colleges and universities are not meeting those expectations.

The crises of 2020–2021 have revealed important realities about the nature of the university. At the onset of the pandemic, American residential campuses swiftly closed and, for the most part, shifted courses online – an option not available during pandemics of the past. Faculty and staff remained in their homes and communicated electronically. Most students did the same. By highlighting the absence of in-person contact, the abrupt transition made clear that residential colleges provide more than an academic education. The residential college experience is a pivotal social exchange, where what students learn outside the classroom is often as important as what they learn inside it. As psychologist Mary Alvord quipped, "People go to college not only for an education but to seek social connections, become independent and explore their identity – all of which are rather difficult to do over Zoom."[4] For people in their late teens or early twenties, the college experience serves as a bridge to adulthood, a place to explore ideas, to challenge and shape individual perspectives of the world. Beyond classroom content, this experience involves interacting daily with people from different backgrounds, unexpected in-depth conversations with faculty and peers, developing lifelong friendships, exposing oneself to new intellectual challenges, joining in special events, and engaging with stimulating outside speakers. Living on a campus away from home can be a transformative experience that exposes students to a broader community dedicated to discovery, dissemination of knowledge, and a collective spirit enriching the life of the mind.

As campuses shifted to online instruction in the spring of 2020, the sense of loss around these missing interpersonal interactions was palpable. Students eager for traditional pomp and circumstance, large-scale campus events, new friends, parties, and quality time with peers were wary of the value of the online instruction that many campuses were offering during the pandemic. Some educators, meanwhile, saw online teaching as a cost-effective prescription for the university's future. But students made clear their lack of enthusiasm for that approach and their hopes to return to the face-to-face interaction and socialization of the residential college. In one large survey of public university students, 81 percent of respondents said they would choose to return to campus rather than study online; nearly 87 percent reported that they learn more effectively on campus.[5] Justin Reich, director of the MIT Teaching Systems Lab, predicted that "when vaccines arrive, most students will return to campus and most teaching will return to classrooms."[6] Some students who had paid full tuition for the Spring 2020 semester sued, demanding partial refunds for what they described as a rushed online experience. Parents, many of whom were hit hard in the economic downturn, were understandably concerned about cost as well as the safety of their children. But this was more than a financial loss. The lack of ceremonies, rites of passage, and recognition among peers and colleagues saddened everyone in the university community.

As soon as the enormity of the novel coronavirus's threat to public health became apparent, a second crucible appeared, this one economic. A combination of stay-at-home orders and consumer caution shuttered businesses all over the country. Millions of workers were thrown on unemployment. Many of the kinds of jobs students depended on to help pay for their education, for spending money, and in some cases, for survival, disappeared. Some students' parents, meanwhile, suddenly found themselves in economic circumstances ranging from frightening to desperate. The value of the stock market dropped precipitously in March 2020 before beginning a remarkable rebound, quite different from what happened during the Great Depression. As a result, most investors and university endowments retained a significant portion of their invested funds and accumulated wealth while the virus levied the greatest economic toll among the most vulnerable. In fact, more than a year after the onset of the pandemic, the New York Stock Exchange reached record highs. According to *Forbes*, the annual ranking of billionaires leapt by nearly 30 percent, further highlighting the wealth inequality between the wealthy and the poor.[7] People of color, whose death rates from COVID-19 well outpaced their share of the population, took a particularly hard economic hit. While the rich prospered, others of lesser means were left hungry and faced the threat of eviction or foreclosure from their homes. The implications are evident for lower-income families or those who have become downwardly mobile – the resources available to earn a college degree have become that much more precarious.

The Memorial Day 2020 killing of George Floyd under a Minneapolis policeman's knee, captured of course on a smartphone, fired the year's third crucible: a sense of injustice over centuries of discriminatory treatment against Black Americans. The cumulative resentment of historic indignities, of unequal justice and incarceration, of generations of Black men, women, and children harassed or killed by police, could no longer be contained. Frustration and outrage touched the soul of the nation. Despite the silent and lethal virus, thousands of protestors of all races, many of them traditionally college-aged, poured into the streets in cities and towns throughout America and around the world. Many of them continued to participate in peaceful protests throughout the summer, even as threats of violence increased around them, reflecting the nation's ever-deepening ideological divisions.

These ideological divisions were driven by disinformation, extremism, and increased polarization, the fourth crucible of 2020–2021, which have lasting implications for students, colleges, and universities. Throughout the Trump presidency, the voices of conspiracy theorists, QAnon supporters, far-right extremists, White supremacists and nationalists, anti-vaxxers, anti-immigrationists, coronavirus deniers, illegal militia groups, and neo-Nazis all found in President Trump's rhetoric both vindication and fuel for their anger about the direction of America. This anger reached its terrifying apex on January 6, 2021, when avid Trump supporters violently attacked the US Capitol. Having been told repeatedly, and without evidence, by the president himself that the integrity of the election vote count had been violated and Donald Trump was the real victor, the armed mob attempted to break up the joint session of Congress that was meeting to count and certify the electoral votes for then President-elect Joe Biden. Five people died and many more were injured in the insurrection, including 138 police officers.

High school or college students, often sheltered due to the pandemic, witnessed parents, aunts and uncles, brothers and sisters, or acquaintances trying to overturn a democratic election; some saw them as seditionists and others saw them as patriots. Enticed by their own emerging identification with the ideas of the far-right, some of these observers became social media targets for recruiters harboring disinformation and extremist perspectives. These recruits include students who are entering or returning to college as campuses manage their way through the pandemic. The anger that might have once found an outlet in etching a swastika in a bathroom stall may now find young allies emboldened to voice their hate in a more open and violent forum.

During the Trump presidency, the president's supporters and the president himself decried democratic institutions, dismissed the establishment press as fake news, and disregarded public health measures and scientific evidence. In this sphere of thinking, expertise derived from years of education and professional experience was no longer a valued qualification; indeed, it was sneered at as a trick of the liberal elite. Many in the far-right vilify and criticize the university itself as a bastion of leftist propaganda, full of pompous faculty who denigrate America's past accomplishments and indoctrinate students with ideas associated with critical race theory and White privilege. Sometimes it is the students themselves who make these criticisms; according to a study by Foundation for Individual Rights in Education, incidents of students reporting on faculty discourse in the classroom increased more than fivefold between 2015 and 2020.[8] The most frequent topics that triggered a student complaint were how faculty dealt with issues of race, political partisanship, or gender.

Some faculty called out for their teaching have become targets of harassment. For example, student reports of perceived faculty liberal biases or restrictions associated with free speech, along with the names of these faculty, have been published on a conservative website, *Campus Reform*. 40 percent of the faculty members identified on the website reported receiving messages of hate, threats of violence, or death threats.[9] The climate in the classroom has changed as students have found outlets that reflect the country's underlying polarization.

Added to this overall context, some elected state officials have raised concerns about the content taught in college classrooms, particularly when it comes to matters of race, raising new concerns over faculty academic freedom in the classroom. The Florida State Board of Education, for example, now requires public universities to assess and report on the "viewpoint diversity" of all of their courses.[10] In this age of disinformation, issues that reflect the nation's divisions, from adherence to public health recommendations to the content of classroom instruction, unfortunately, are framed as sides to be taken, as matters of equally valid opinions rather than matters of objective facts and objective falsehoods.

These multiple crucibles of 2020–2021 will be etched into the memory of a generation, affecting their sense of themselves and how they perceive the world, much as the Great Depression affected the perspectives of those who lived through it. For students returning to their college or university campus, the influences will be immediate. Having experienced the power of protest, many students of color will no longer be willing to tolerate instances of racism on their campuses. Many White students who joined in the protests or witnessed videos of police brutality on unarmed Black individuals, for their part, may now be more willing to confront the forms of systemic racism that their predecessors might have ignored or denied, but that were always familiar to their Black peers. Across the board, students and faculty have made it clear that they expect their own colleges and universities to pay greater attention to aspects of systemic racism. And, along with this movement, we have a growing counter-movement of White supremacists and neo-Nazis in America impelled and emboldened by disinformation campaigns. These potential conflicts pose new challenges for academic administrators at residential campuses.

The nation's campuses are being reforged by the crucibles of 2020–2021. Over the spring and summer of 2020, different campuses considered as many as fifteen variations of in-person and online education, as well as changes to the academic calendar.[11] Some financially vulnerable institutions were forced to close their doors, merge with other campuses, or suspend operations. Few were able to weather the pandemic without reductions in personnel expenses and operational costs. Even as they lost revenue, campuses incurred additional expenses from adjusting their methods of delivering education. Those included support for additional course design, technical assistance, and infrastructure for distance learning; thinning residential, classroom, and meeting locations; sanitizing; testing for and tracking infections; screening visitors; purchasing protective clothing and equipment; identifying quarantine rooms; and creating safe socially distanced spaces. Some campuses cut back their array of academic programs, amended their support services, reduced contributions to pensions, made across-the-board cutbacks, froze hiring and eliminated pay increases, shrank the number of staff in positions for which the campus simply had less demand, and furloughed others.

Quality academic programs, dependent on talented faculty, take years to build. Yet in a tone-deaf moment, Purdue University proposed that 10 of the 16 directorships focused on race, gender, and ethnicity be slated for elimination. In the wake of the swift outrage that followed, Purdue rolled back the reductions. The incident reflects the challenges universities face in balancing budgets and meeting academic priorities.[12] In another painful cutback, the University of Akron announced that it would eliminate 6 of its 11 academic colleges and eliminate 178 positions, including 96 members of its tenured faculty.[13] Reports of campus cutbacks and program terminations were all too common. Cocurricular programs and activities placed in hibernation during the pandemic will take time to reemerge and revamp once the danger passes – if they are to return at all.

As colleges and universities reopen and as students return, administrators will need to face these multifaceted issues. They will also need to face an underlying issue: a dated structural configuration out of sync with student expectations and a limited capacity to bring the fragmented curricular and cocurricular pieces into a coherent whole for the benefit of students. This can bedevil too many students and challenge capable professionals to effectively manage in such an environment.

The question of how to make the university experience better and more valuable for students in a post-pandemic world demands attention as universities compete with each other and with alternative educational institutions for shrinking numbers of traditional-age students. The very scope of the present crises presents an opportunity to finally embrace long-discussed and sorely needed changes. In its annual survey taken during the pandemic, *Inside Higher Ed* found 47 percent of university senior business officers agreed with the statement, "My institution should use this period to make difficult but transformative changes in its core structure and operations to better position itself for long-term sustainability."[14] A subsequent survey of college and university presidents echoed this sentiment.[15] The task before academic leaders is not simply to restore what once was, but to recognize these tragic moments as a unique space to assess multiple institutional weaknesses, even failures, and reemerge stronger and better prepared to educate a changed student body for the uncertain world they will inherit.

Three Central Arguments

Administratively Adrift presents original data about modern student encounters with traditional four-year degree residential colleges and universities, fresh perspectives on the inner workings of the university, and fact-based insights gleaned from a four-year, university-wide innovation initiative I led as provost of American University. The student experience is the sum of all encounters, whether in or outside of the classroom. As a result, this book pays as much attention to student services and administrative operations as it does to academics, if not more. I show how the hundred-plus-year history of the American university has led to its current structure; distill the voices of students, faculty, and staff; and explore how successful organizations outside of higher education deliver services. I use these insights to produce recommendations for reorganizing and revitalizing residential universities, with the goal of providing today's diverse students with a holistic learning experience. The book rests on three central arguments.

Argument One: Generation Z and Structural Lag

First introduced as a theoretical concept by sociologist Matilda White Riley, the term structural lag refers to the phenomenon of society and its institutions failing to keep up with the changing needs of population cohorts or distinct population constituencies.[16] This lag creates challenges for the most vulnerable or those less visible, as their needs can be underserved. I use the concept to examine the emerging gap between the evolving needs of contemporary students and the institutional structures of four-year nonprofit residential colleges and universities.

Today's students, frequently referred to as Generation Z, are a unique and distinctive generation that began arriving on college campuses a few years before the pandemic.[17] Born on the cusp of the new millennium (1997–2015), they have lived through school shooting drills (and sometimes school shootings) and the 2008 recession. They have participated in the struggles of the LGBTQIA, #MeToo, and Black Lives Matter movements. They are living through a worsening climate of national polarization, rampant online disinformation and its consequences, the environmental crisis of global warming, and the threat, for some of them, of deportation. An unprecedentedly racially and ethnically diverse cohort confronted with widening socioeconomic inequality, Generation Z arrives on campus with levels of anxiety, stress, and depression not previously observed among college students, concerns only exacerbated by the pandemic and social unrest (a topic I discuss at length in Chapter 2).[18]

It is highly significant that, in Gen Z's experience, information has always been ubiquitous and available at a moment's notice on a smartphone. They are experienced digital natives who have grown up in a connected world where personalized access to goods and services is only a click or a swipe away, where bureaucratic structures have been mediated by the technology available in an app or through artificial intelligence. Their expectations for how organizations provide goods and services are in marked contrast to the often bureaucratic, impersonal, and sluggish operations of the university.

The disconnect between Gen Z's expectations and the residential university's current operations and organizational structure – one of semi-independent units loosely stitched together, each with its own distinct professional identity and operations – can at times inadvertently add to student burdens and as a consequence impede their academic success and well-being. The fragmented structure of the university too often results in different administrative units delivering services in isolation from one another, producing omissions, delays, contradictions, limited authority to resolve problems, and poor coordination across relevant service offices. This, in turn, limits universities' ability to effectively support students in the classroom. The frustrations of coping with an unresponsive bureaucracy increase costs, stress, extend the time to earn a degree, and disproportionately impact those who are most vulnerable. In some cases, they can push students to abandon the campus. All this dilutes the effectiveness of a college education and increases society's skepticism about whether college is worth the cost and accumulated debt. The pattern of operational functions of the university lagging behind the needs and expectations of its students adds to their frustrations and in some cases impedes their success – hence a structural lag has emerged between setting and constituency.

A significant portion of the residential student experience happens outside the classroom, in encounters involving personnel from dozens of offices. From the student's perspective, each of these encounters contributes to their total experience at college, but the university customarily views student issues from the perspective of separately functioning academic departments and administrative units, often described as stovepipes or silos (see Chapter 7 on the flow of information). Even the university's preferred mode of communication highlights the stark differences between student and university cultures: in a survey of 1,143 Gen Z college students, university reliance on email was described as equivalent to "what hand-written or typed office memos and snail mail were to previous generations."[19] Yet, the university's communication with students relies on email, which at times students do not read. The crises of 2020–2021 are an opportunity to reconsider the fragmentation that characterizes universities' operations, an issue of some urgency, given their impact on students' well-being and eventual success.

When organizations' administrative and organizational operations fall out of harmony with the people they serve, they are experiencing structural lag. This book chronicles such a gap between residential colleges and universities and their students. While Riley introduced the term in the context of an aging society, the theoretical framework can be applied to any institution or societal circumstance lacking congruence between people's lives and the social structures they encounter. Historic examples of efforts to mitigate structural lag include the physical accommodations sparked by the disability rights movement or the replacement of institution-based psychiatric wards with community-based care.

In the for-profit sector, market demands force businesses to either remain in step with customers' changing expectations and needs or quickly go out of business. In the nonprofit or governmental world, such direct accountability is less immediate and often only appears after repeated and forceful pressure to change. One example is the shift in drivers' licensing procedures in many states. Instead of forcing drivers to wait in line for hours to renew their licenses in person, many states have shifted to easy-to-use email-in renewals (thank goodness).

While American nonprofit residential colleges and universities offer students many different choices in location, size, cost, academic emphasis, and cocurricular/extracurricular opportunities, they are bound by strikingly similar underlying bureaucratic structures, procedures, and operations. Too often, once Gen Z students become immersed in their academic setting of choice, they find that the total educational encounter bears little resemblance to their prior lived experience. For those most at-risk or vulnerable, the lack of alignment between their needs and the *modus operandi* of the university can create obstacles to their success. In contrast, those students whose parents or siblings are college savvy are more likely to have access to the tools that allow them to adjust to the more baffling, fragmented aspects of university bureaucracy. Some students will muddle through; others will fail. Universities typically view such failures as the student's fault for not fitting in and not performing well academically, if they even attempt to assess the student's departure at all. What is striking is that across the nation, and before the entrance of Gen Z students, less than half of students who started a four-year college degree graduated in four years; after six years, graduation rates barely exceeded the 60 percent threshold at the institution where they first enrolled.[20] Yet, the academic community rarely acknowledges its responsibility to meet students where they are.

This book incorporates students' descriptions of their encounters, often in their own voices, as they navigate the university. Drawn from student journals and feedback at focus groups and meetings, these accounts show how students can easily run afoul of university processes. All it takes is a chronic health condition, or forgetting to file a required form, or a misunderstanding regarding a mandatory procedure, or an interruption in the flow of relevant information about them to their counselors or faculty advisers. Take Maurice, whose encounter is summarized at the opening of this chapter. In his case, the campus offers an early warning system on student progress, but no one bothered to notify the advisor of Maurice's failing academic performance. Of his five different faculty members (of whom all but one professor taught classes of twenty students or less), not one bothered to send an early warning to Maurice's advisor that might have changed his trajectory.

In the chapters that follow, I present evidence of the consequences of an archaic bureaucratic system. In addition to diagnosing the problem, I point to specific efforts to foster a more holistic approach to student support, including original strategies that wrestle with the organizational problems.

Argument Two: Shaped by History

My second claim is that we must understand the history of the university's structure and governance if we are to transform its operations. Many of the obstacles to change are rooted in century-old patterns that strengthen faculty independence and encourage staff expertise, but also foster something like a guild structure for each group, with its own culture, subcultures, norms, and national alliances. In his classic history of the American university, Laurence Veysey wrote, "By 1910 the structure of the American university has assumed its stable twentieth-century form," including the familiar hierarchy of presidents, vice presidents, deans, departments, faculty, and core disciplinary divisions (see Chapter 3).[21] Given their heavy schedule of teaching, research, and service, most faculty see the overall student experience at the university as someone else's responsibility. They are guardians of the cognitive domain; others can assist with psychosocial and administrative experiences (much more on the subject in Chapters 4 and 6).

As the university expanded, so did the number of professional staff hired to administer a myriad of programs and services in response to an expanding array of regulations, expectations, constituencies, and obligations. Over time, these activities have become institutionalized, a routine part of campus operations, their personnel allied with national associations that advance standards for their specialization. The pattern of replication, viewed as best practices and promulgated by peers affiliated with the respective national association, is seen in nearly every one of the professional services offered at colleges and universities, ranging from academic advising to financial aid, from the university registrar to admissions officers, from disability services to student judicial affairs.

In Chapter 6, I identify thirty-six different national professional organizations in which those who provide student services (directly or indirectly) can exchange ideas, explore best practices, and connect with peers at other campuses. The result of this professionalization, while important for professional development, also has its consequences: first, a level of uniformity within the professional specialization is institutionalized nationwide, and second, with so many different specializations that are available on campus too often they become disparate, poorly connected, and even, at times, operate in conflict with one another. Furthermore, the faculty and staff serving students have become bifurcated – the faculty engaged with academic life and other professionals with campus life and administrative functions. Even at mid-sized universities few, if any, faculty would discuss their students with residential housing personnel, even though these staff members have nearly daily contact with the students who appear in the classroom. Instead of coalescing around the needs of students, university personnel in different domains have been moving in centrifugal directions away from each other. But if a student has economic problems, is not eating or sleeping well, feels unwelcome, alone, or homesick, or is stressed about problems back home, that is likely interfering with their ability to learn. In the end, it should matter to everyone.

In recognition of and out of concern for the increasing specialization etched into the fabric of the academy, in 1937 the American Council on Education explicitly demanded that colleges and universities "consider the student as a whole person" in every respect – not just their academic development, but "the development of the student as a person rather than upon his [or her] intellectual training alone."[22] It speaks explicitly to the expectation of a holistic learning experience, an idea central to this book. Unfortunately, this remains an aspiration rather than an achievement. The question today is whether we have reached a point where the structure and the culture of the university directly conflict with its purpose – the preparation of students for life.

Throughout the book, I draw upon this concept of holistic education, deeply admired by academic leaders but too often lost in implementation, that can powerfully influence all sectors of the academy that touch student life, including the curriculum.

Argument Three: Integrated Student Pathways, Holistic Education, and Alignment

The third theme of the book is a broad reflection on how the learning experience can be made more holistic to better prepare students to assume roles in an increasingly polarized and divided society. Yes, the overall university structure is dated; yes, our students expect more clarity across university operations; and yes, we are hampered by a deeply engrained history and alliances that make change very difficult. However, as other effective organizations outside the academy have evolved to be more end-user focused, so can the university become more student-centered by coalescing appropriate academic, administrative, and service components.

The university is labor-intensive, dependent on learned faculty and skilled professionals. Expanded numbers of faculty and staff over the decades have been added to an existing infrastructure designed decades ago. It is time to question if the bureaucratic structure and the expansion of specialization are working in the best interest of students.

Transforming the academy will take the same sort of assessment and analysis that have proven successful for other organizations. Aspects of that methodology (discussed in Chapters 8 and 9) provide insights into the everyday problems students encounter in the university. What we have learned from other industries is to reassess the alignment of services from the perspective of the end-user. The end-user, in this case the student, needs to know where authority rests, who has the power to resolve problems that are beyond the domain of any single individual or office, and who is eventually accountable. At the moment, answers to these questions are highly diffuse in the academy. Once they are determined, administrators can map the flow of information and the alignment and sequence of actions. This is a large and complex undertaking, not just intellectually, but politically, as it potentially reshapes positions and responsibilities ingrained in the different specializations and offices.

Given the scale and complexity of student psychosocial and academic life, academic leaders will need to design and provide new pathways for student data and information and designate those with the responsibility and authority to act. In Chapter 10, I present ideas that amend aspects of the current structure to be more responsive to students.

The early twenty-first century is a time of two contradictory trends. On one hand, there is evidence of unprecedented social and political polarization. On the other hand, outside the sociopolitical realm, it is a time of unprecedented convergence, as the amalgamation, integration, and alignment of what used to be disparate functions become more and more the norm. The evidence of convergence is not limited to electronic devices, smartphones, or cars, but includes organizational functions and even ideas in emerging academic fields. Organizations that provide services have reorganized with the end-user in mind, with an emphasis on providing smart, efficient, personalized, and accessible services. Students are quite comfortable with this form of organization and the thoughtful integration of information – particularly when it is delivered via a smartphone. Additional incorporation of the smartphone into university functions can potentially aid the integration and alignment of administrative and support functions that are currently segregated, providing a designated university official and the student with immediate information and directed access to support services.

Beyond just combining the data kept in separate repositories or speeding access to this data, designers must carefully work out new sequences and pathways that make it easier and faster to support the end-user. Central to this alignment of multiple specialties is the rethinking of the pathways from the perspective of the student, and identifying a central point of contact with the authority to promptly leverage support for the student.

The same integrative thinking can be applied to the academic sphere where a foundation of liberal arts coursework and subject specialization are aligned with skill sets relevant to the intertwined and complex global, scientific, and social problems students will eventually encounter.[23] A capstone component helps ensure the convergence of the learning experience. Issues of truth, justice, ethics, morality, civic responsibility, civility, and character development are part of a holistic learning experience and maybe a modest antidote to the destructive nature of the aforementioned societal polarization.[24]

Many of the specialized databases that currently exist for students were designed to meet the needs of professional office personnel. Too often, digital documents travel the same routes through different offices that paper documents once did. The university has lagged in planning and reconceptualizing the flow of information for students, allowing units to retain their autonomy and control of information, leaving the student end-user with balkanized functions – digitized, yes, but not smart (see Chapters 7 and 10).

To illustrate the problem of multiple actors and diffuse lines of authority in the university, let me highlight just four of the numerous direct contacts students have: (1) the faculty member teaching a course, (2) the academic advisor counseling on an academic plan, (3) the financial aid officer, and (4) the resident director overseeing student behavior in the residence hall. Should something go wrong for the student, each of the four has a different path to follow to intervene and access student data. The people in these roles may occasionally share information, but most often they work within their existing lines of communication.

The instructor has the option, but not the requirement, to provide additional tutoring to a student outside of the class during office hours or at a mutually agreed-upon time. The instructor can notify the academic advisor or encourage the student to seek additional support if there are problems with academic performance or evidence of excessive stress. (On some campuses, the instructor also carries an advising load.) Beyond the course roster, email address, ID number, and a grade sheet, a typical faculty member has little other data about the student other than what the student chooses to share.

If the academic advisor is informed that the student is having difficulty in any of their classes, they discuss the situation with the student and afterward can recommend academic support services, recommend seeing a counselor, or work with the student on a change of major. Customarily, advisors maintain a file on each of their advisees and have access to course registration and the student transcript. On certain problems they might engage their immediate supervisor, involve an assistant dean, associate dean, or dean. The dean, if necessary, can reach out to the vice provost to resolve a problem involving several administrative units.

Financial aid officers encountering a problem involving the ability to pay or not meeting Satisfactory Academic Progress (SAP) will be in touch with the student. They maintain an array of records on the family's financial circumstances, the federal financial aid request, the determination of need, and the loans, scholarships, and financial aid received, including any changes or adjustments over time. They also have access to the transcript and course registration. The officer may consult with a supervisor and, on occasion, the advisor, registrar, or bursar, while maintaining confidentiality regarding the financial records.

If there is an incident in the residence hall where the student, for example, fights with another student, the residence hall director is likely to reach out to their supervisor and the dean of students. They might recommend a meeting with the student, counseling, or disciplinary action. The residence hall personnel and dean of students maintain their own confidential records on student behavior.

Note that these four individuals in direct contact with students only occasionally interconnect or share information and often do not know that they may be dealing with the same student. Only when there is a serious problem and issues have escalated do officials meet and discuss the situation. However, it is less likely that the faculty member will be involved.

From the student perspective, issues of social and psychological adjustment with peers, financial capacity to make tuition payments over four or more years, success in courses, and overall academic progress and area of focus are but one interwoven topic. In the university, academic progress is separated into one domain, social development in another, economic and financial circumstances are managed in yet a different one, and physical and mental health in a fourth domain – all of which are independent of one another (and at times further fragmented within these domains). Yet no one has taken on the systemic challenge of thinking through how the necessary information flows can be appropriately connected to provide timely advice and support to maximize student academic success and personal well-being.

The integrative task becomes even more complex when we consider the array of interactions beyond this highly simplified description of four university functionaries to include career planners, counselors, Title IX officers, coaches, officers of clubs and fraternity/sorority life, spiritual leader, staff for orientation, and health care providers, to name a few. In the final chapter of the book, I explore ways to connect the disparate intellectual components along with the administrative and service components.

University leadership has paid too little attention to the organization of the administrative and service functions vital to student success, either because problems in those areas are at a level deemed acceptable, or they are not fully understood, or leadership has simply not prioritized the issue. Some defenders of arcane university procedures argue that forcing students to navigate such systems provides them with a valuable life skill. But surely a liberal arts education should be designed to prepare students for the future, not to cope with a legacy of the past. Cumbersome institutions in the private sector have already been disrupted by more nimble innovators that are increasingly responsive to their customers/stakeholders. The university needs to adapt to this changing environment, both for the sake of its students and for its own sake. If it doesn't, it will face the same sort of disruption as other industries – something that has already begun. For-profit colleges are already grabbing a share of the student market, not because they provide a better education (they do not, as graduation rates demonstrate),[25] but because they are customer-focused in pursuit of the singular goal of making a profit. The stakes for students are high, too. The quality of education in the classroom is affected by the quality of their life outside it.

The Certainty of Uncertainty

Historians remind us that universities have faced crises before. At the turn of the twentieth century, college administrators and faculty confronted student rebellion, unpopular wars, and physical conflict. Issues of race and class have been woven through the history of American higher education. Then, as now, the cost of college was an issue, leading to searches for less expensive options. Long before there was an internet, correspondence schools provided low-cost courses through the mail.

Not even the current pandemic is unique. The influenza pandemic of 1918–1919 is estimated to have caused 50 million deaths worldwide and 675,000 in the United States alone; the heaviest losses were among healthy young men aged 25–40.[26] Despite this tragedy, many colleges and universities remained open, with closures limited to weeks. With no vaccine, most campuses relied on nonpharmacological interventions – wearing masks, eliminating large-scale events, instituting hygienic procedures, and segregating the sick. College and university archives are replete with photos of auditoria or gymnasia filled with cots for the infirm along with tributes to students who had died.[27] Yet, despite the turmoil and suffering, college enrollments continued to grow. *The Harvard Crimson* wrote in 1919 that the enrollment surge was

> larger by 42 per cent than in 1918 and larger by 21 per cent than in 1916, the record-breaking year of pre-war prosperity. So immense and insistent has been the flow of men, that for many colleges the old-time problem of how to attract more students has given way to the problem of how to take care of the students who want to enter.[28]

Even if not unprecedented, the contemporary crises facing residential educational settings are exacerbated by demographics. The United States is entering a trough of declining numbers of traditional-age college students because of multiple factors, including a decline in birth rates beginning nearly two decades ago. Other factors include student loan debt, price sensitivity, and the financial strain facing middle-class families, all of which have created a smaller pool of graduating high school seniors seeking residential college options. Some high school graduates are deciding to forego college altogether. Competition among residential colleges and universities for qualified students to meet enrollment targets has already led to tuition-discounting in private colleges, which now has reached over 50 percent of the advertised price.[29] Can the residential undergraduate experience demonstrate its cost-benefit value to families in an increasingly competitive marketplace and a challenging economy?

Still, placing the current plight in an historical perspective reminds us that educators overcame the challenges of the past. In 1939, at the beginning of World War II, Abraham Flexner wrote in *Harper's Magazine*:

> It is not a curious fact that in a world steeped in irrational hatreds which threaten civilization itself, men and women – old and young – detached themselves wholly or partly from the angry current of daily life to devote themselves to the cultivation of beauty, to the extension of knowledge, to the cure of disease, to the amelioration of suffering, just as though fanatics were not simultaneously engaged in spreading pain, ugliness, and suffering. The world has always been a sorry and confused sort of place – yet poets and artists and scientists have ignored the factors that would, if attended to, paralyze them.[30]

Certainly, there is turmoil and a tremendous loss of life worldwide today – life-threatening disease, environmental degradation, unequal justice and discrimination, disinformation and political polarization, human suffering, famine, poverty, economic struggle, war, and despotism. But just as in 1939, faculties continue to create, imagine, teach, and discover at the remarkable institution of the university while serving millions of students every day. Whatever the crisis and whatever its duration, colleges and universities will remain central to American society. Our task, as campuses fully reopen is to make the experience more efficient, enriched, and responsive to the post-pandemic generation of students. Our challenge is to embrace a model of residential education that is holistic and student-centered.

This book urges universities to become more student-focused and sensitive to the overall student experience, both in and beyond the class-room. It recognizes that all university experiences, from coursework to social life, from library support to quality food, from efficient course registration to thoughtful career planning, and from the clarity of financial aid rules to students' relationships with their roommates, influence whether a student thrives, struggles through, or possibly exits college without a degree.

The seeds for a more holistic and student-centered university have already been planted. While provost at American University from 2008 to 2018, I worked with colleagues on a four-year effort to better understand the entire student experience and take steps to improve it. This book draws on information and insights from that experiment (described in detail in Chapters 8 and 9), including material from student journals; interviews with faculty, staff, and students; data gleaned from campus surveys; and exploration of service models outside higher education. It could not have been written without these multiple perspectives.

The following chapters are building blocks toward a better understanding of the rewards and constraints that influence faculty, staff, and academic administration in priority-setting and decision-making. These rewards and constraints are common and deeply embedded across many colleges and universities. The final chapter offers suggestions that can move a college or university toward a more integrated, holistic, and cost-effective residential learning experience better matched to incoming students. It suggests adjustments to both faculty roles and staff responsibilities and explores student-centered approaches that can strengthen the relationships so critical for student well-being and success. I trust other scholars and administrators will both critique and build upon them.

Information about the students whose stories I tell in the book has been edited to ensure they remain anonymous. Also, many of the situations and complications regarding administrative operations at American University have been revised, updated, and changed since I chronicled them here and are part of a process of continuous improvement. They are intended as examples; over time, other issues will undoubtedly replace them.

Notes

1 "Total Undergraduate Fall Enrollment in Degree-Granting Postsecondary Institutions, by Attendance Status, Sex of Student, and Control and Level of Institution: Selected Years, 1970 through 2028," table 303.70, National Center for Education Statistics, accessed January 21, 2020, https://nces.ed .gov/programs/digest/d18/tables/dt18_303.70.asp.

2 "School Enrollment in the United States: October 2017 – Detailed Tables," table 5, United States Census Bureau, December 11, 2018, accessed August 16, 2019, www.census.gov/data/tables/2017/demo/school-enrollment/2017-cps.html.

3 Throughout the book, I use the words "college," "university," and "academy" interchangeably. Certainly, there are differences in scale and complexity between small colleges and large public research universities. However, the

underlying academic structure of traditional four-year residential institutions is common to all.

4 Suzanne Hirt, "'Shame and Blame': Are College COVID-19 Cases the Fault of Campuses Full of Reckless Partiers? Experts, Students Say No," *Augusta Chronicle*, August 31, 2020, 10:12 a.m. EDT, accessed September 4, 2020, www.augustachronicle.com/news/20200831/shame-and-blame-are-college -covid-19-cases-fault-of-campuses-full-of-reckless-partiers-experts-students- say-no.

5 Purdue Student Government, *PSG COVID-19 Student Survey Report*, July 1, 2020, 1, accessed September 4, 2020, https://static1.squarespace.com/static /5980ddo5d482e9f36b9d9160/t/5efdb3140227f53a11f1f01c/1593684758580/ PSG+COVID-19+Student+Survey+Report.pdf.

6 Justin Reich, "Ed-Tech Mania Is Back," *Chronicle of Higher Education*, September 14, 2020, www.chronicle.com/article/ed-tech-mania-is-back.

7 Kerry A. Dolan, "Forbes' 35th Annual World's Billionaires List: Facts and Figures 2021," *Forbes*, April 6, 2021, 6:00 a.m. EDT, accessed April 8, 2021, www.forbes.com/sites/kerryadolan/2021/04/06/forbes-35th-annual-worlds-bil lionaires-list-facts-and-figures-2021/?sh=6cdc6bad5e58.

8 Colleen Flaherty, "Tracking Attacks on Scholars' Speech," *Inside Higher Ed*, August 31, 2021, accessed September 24, 2021, www.insidehighered.com /news/2021/08/31/fire-launches-new-database-tracking-attacks-speech.

9 Hans-Joerg Tiede et al., "Data Snapshot: Whom Does Campus Reform Target and What Are the Effects?," American Association of University Professors, Spring 2021, accessed September 24, 2021, www.aaup.org/arti cle/data-snapshot-whom-does-campus-reform-target-and-what-are-effects# .YWm9SxDMLuo.

10 Florida enacted the law on July 1, 2021, and Indiana has since introduced a similar bill.

11 Edward J. Maloney and Joshua Kim, "15 Fall Scenarios," *Inside Higher Ed*, April 22, 2020, accessed May 29, 2020, www.insidehighered.com/digital -learning/blogs/learning-innovation/15-fall-scenarios.

12 Dave Bangert, "Purdue Reverses Cuts to African American, Women's Studies, among Others, on Eve of Creating Diversity Task Force," *Lafayette Journal & Courier*, last modified August 6, 2020, 3:22 p.m. EDT, accessed October 19, 2020, www.jconline.com/story/news/2020/08/06/purdue-reverses-cuts-african -american-womens-studies-among-others-eve-creating-diversity-task-force/330723 1001/.

13 Lilah Burke, "University of Akron to Cut 6 Colleges," *Inside Higher Ed*, May 6, 2020, accessed September 15, 2020, www.insidehighered.com/quicktakes /2020/05/06/university-akron-cut-6-colleges; Jennifer Pignolet, "University of Akron Trustees Vote to Eliminate 178 Positions; Faculty Yell 'Protect Our Students!,'" *Akron Beacon Journal*, July 15, 2020, 2:44 p.m. EDT, accessed October 30, 2020, www.beaconjournal.com/story/news/local/2020/07/15/u niversity-of-akron-trustees-vote-to-eliminate-178-positions-faculty-yell-ldqu oprotect-our-studentsr/113365458/.

14 Doug Lederman, "COVID-19's Forceful Financial Hit: A Survey of Business Officers," *Inside Higher Ed*, July 10, 2020, accessed September 4, 2020, www.insidehighered.com/news/survey/covid-19s-forceful-financial-hit -survey-business-officers.

15 Doug Lederman, "Pandemic-Fueled Confidence for College Presidents," *Inside Higher Ed*, March 22, 2021, accessed April 8, 2021, www .insidehighered.com/news/survey/survey-shows-college-presidents-emerging-covid-19-more-confident-their-institutions-can.

16 See Matilda White Riley, Robert L. Kahn, and Anne Foner, eds., *Age and Structural Lag: Society's Failure to Provide Meaningful Opportunities in Work, Family, and Leisure* (New York: John H. Wiley & Sons, 1994).

17 See Corey Seemiller and Meghan Grace, *Generation Z Goes to College* (San Francisco: Jossey-Bass, 2016).

18 American College Health Association, *American College Health Association – National College Health Assessment II: Reference Group Executive Summary-Fall 2018* (Silver Spring, MD: American College Health Association, 2018), 13–14, accessed August 20, 2019, www.acha.org/documents/ncha/NCHA -II_Fall_2018_Reference_Group_Executive_Summary.pdf.

19 Seemiller and Grace, *Generation Z*, 60.

20 "Graduation Rate from First Institution Attended for First-Time, Full-Time Bachelor's Degree-Seeking Students at 4-Year Postsecondary Institutions, by Race/Ethnicity, Time to Completion, Sex, Control of Institution, and Acceptance Rate: Selected Cohort Entry Years, 1996 through 2011," table 326.10, National Center for Education Statistics, accessed January 21, 2020, https://nces.ed.gov/programs/digest/d18/tables/dt18_326.10.asp.

21 Laurence R. Veysey, *The Emergence of the American University* (Chicago: University of Chicago Press, 1965), 338.

22 American Council on Education, *The Student Personnel Point of View* (Washington, DC: American Council on Education, 1937), 1.

23 See Chris W. Gallagher, *College Made Whole: Integrative Learning for a Divided World* (Baltimore: Johns Hopkins University Press, 2019).

24 See Derek Bok, *Higher Expectations: Can Colleges Teach Students What They Need to Know in the 21st Century?* (Princeton, NJ: Princeton University Press, 2020).

25 National Center for Education Statistics, "Graduation Rate," table 326.10.

26 "1918 Pandemic (H1N1 Virus)," Centers for Disease Control and Prevention, last modified March 20, 2019, accessed May 11, 2020, www .cdc.gov/flu/pandemic-resources/1918-pandemic-h1n1.html.

27 Laura Stephenson Carter, "Cold Comfort," *Dartmouth Medicine*, Winter 2006, accessed May 11, 2020, https://dartmed.dartmouth.edu/winter06 /html/cold_comfort.php.

28 "1919 Record-Breaking Year for American Colleges," *Harvard Crimson*, December 6, 1919, accessed May 11, 2020, www.thecrimson.com/article /1919/12/6/1919-record-breaking-year-for-american-colleges/.

29 "Private Colleges Now Use Nearly Half of Tuition Revenue for Financial Aid," press release, National Association of College and University Business Officers, May 9, 2019, accessed March 22, 2020, www.nacubo.org/Press-Releases/2019/Private-Colleges-Now-Use-Nearly-Half-of-Tuition-Revenue-For-Financial-Aid.

30 Abraham Flexner, "The Usefulness of Useless Knowledge," *Harper's Magazine*, June/November 1939, 544.

CHAPTER 2

Generation Z and the Traditional University

Academic leaders often regard public and private nonprofit four-year colleges and universities, the bedrock of higher education in the United States, as among the best in the world. These institutions are formative research engines that disseminate knowledge worldwide, advance human progress, and provide a proven pathway to economic mobility.[1] Countless families have made great personal sacrifices to see their children graduate from college.[2]

But despite their reputations and the resources and hopes invested in them, American residential nonprofit colleges and universities have been less successful in educating and graduating their students than one might imagine. United States government statistics reveal that for a significant percentage of students, a four-year college doesn't mean four years until graduation. At the top-tier selective institutions, students are likely to graduate in four years, but nationally we see a different picture.

Table 2.1 shows that just 40.7 percent of students enrolled in public and, a bit over half, 56.4 percent in private nonprofit four-year institutions graduated after four years at the institution where they had initially enrolled in 2013.[3] By gender, the rates are lower for men (35.0 percent at public and 50.9 percent at private nonprofits) than for women (45.5 percent and 60.8 percent, respectively). They are appreciably lower among all Black students (22.7 percent at public institutions and 33.8 percent at private nonprofits) and for all Hispanic/Latinx students (30.7 percent at public and 51.1 percent at nonprofit institutions).[4] The more years enrolled, the more graduation rates improve, but overall, after six years of study, just 62.4 percent graduate from public institutions. Private nonprofits do slightly better, with two out of three students (67.9 percent) graduating from the institution where they had initially enrolled in 2013.[5]

This is not a new phenomenon. These rates have been the pattern for years. The resulting loss is palpable, both psychologically and financially.[6] In 2010, the aggregate lost earnings and income taxes for one year for all

Table 2.1 *Graduation rates after four years from first institution attended for first-time bachelor's degree–seeking students entering in 2013 at four-year public and nonprofit colleges and universities, by gender and race/ethnicity as defined by White, Black, and Hispanic*

Graduation Rates at Public Four-Year Institution in Percentages

Students after Four Years of Study

All Students		
40.7		

Male	Female	
35.0	45.5	

White		Black		Hispanic	
45.1		22.7		30.7	
Male	Female	Male	Female	Male	Female
38.7	50.7	16.8	26.7	25.1	35.0

Graduation Rates at Nonprofit Four-Year Institution in Percentages

Students after Four Years of Study

All Students		
56.4		

Male	Female	
50.9	60.8	

White		Black		Hispanic	
60.3		33.8		51.1	
Male	Female	Male	Female	Male	Female
55.0	64.6	26.1	40.1	46.2	54.6

Source: United States Department of Education, Institute of Education Sciences, National Center for Education Statistics, "Graduation Rate from First Institution Attended for First-Time, Full-Time Bachelor's Degree-Seeking Students at 4-Year Postsecondary Institutions, by Race/Ethnicity, Time to Completion, Sex, Control of Institution, and Acceptance Rate: Selected Cohort Entry Years, 1996 through 2013," Table 326.10.

students who dropped out of college were estimated at $4.5 billion.[7] And even for many of those who do graduate, the experience can be a painful struggle.

While American nonprofit residential colleges and universities have evolved and adapted over the past century, they face a new challenge in preparing a diverse and technologically adept generation – Generation Z – for a dynamic and changing world. From the current student perspective, the structure and culture of these universities have become anachronistic and, at times, obstacles to their success. Too many students are unable to navigate the gap between the decentralized structure and culture and their own life experiences, producing stress and confusion in young adults who are still learning to live on their own.

A Generation under Stress

The transition to college has always been a complex moment in students' lives. Many students arrive at college straight from high school; others take a more circuitous route. Some are the first in their families to attend college. At residential campuses, these young adults encounter a setting where almost all daily activities – food and lodging, social life, health care, intellectual engagement, recreation, athletics, spiritual life, entertainment, and even judicial processes – take place primarily in and around a single institutional venue. Particularly for students enrolling immediately after high school, this is an eventful transition.

Only three months before arriving on campus, the then-high school student would need a hall pass to go to the bathroom. Try to imagine the anticipation and thrill of the first-year student heading to a college campus. Students move from a fairly programmed structure of high school, extracurricular activities, possibly part-time work, and home life to a college setting with considerably more freedom. The transition can be dramatic. It takes place at a pivotal time in both cognitive and affective development – the transition from late adolescence to early adulthood.[8]

Some students arrive well prepared for the decentralized administrative structure of college, but others struggle to navigate the university operations, traditions, and culture, and the university itself. Students encounter a thicket of new terms, like syllabus, prerequisite, convocation, and mentor.[9] This "hidden curriculum" is yet another thing students need to learn.[10] Imagine what it's like to be a student who is the first in their family to ever attend college.[11] Or a student from rural America who arrives at an urban campus only to realize that the undergraduate population is larger than their entire hometown. Or a student whose parents navigated everything for them and now, for the first time, has to learn – among other things – how to do their own laundry! Or a student from a high school where they and almost all the other students were of color, now arriving at a predominantly White liberal arts college. The transition and adjustment for these and many other students can be difficult, even under the best of circumstances.

But today's students, born at the dawn of the new millennium, face new, unique, and fundamental challenges beyond the struggles common to previous generations. Compared with their predecessors, today's students come from a wider and strikingly more diverse array of backgrounds. There are greater numbers and percentages of Black, Hispanic/Latinx, Asian American, and multiracial students.[12] Today's students also come from more varied economic strata,[13] geographical regions, religions, political perspectives, cultures, and sexual and gender identities. Some of them suffer from disabilities both hidden and visible. Since we know approximately eighteen years in advance what the profile of potential college students will be, we can anticipate that in the near future they will come from an even wider array of backgrounds. It is incumbent on the university to welcome the current and future communities of America – as well as other nations – to an inclusive and supportive environment.

Even before the onset of the COVID-19 pandemic, the students of Generation Z demonstrated significantly greater incidence of serious psychological distress than previous generations, frequently reporting experiences with depression – even despair.[14] Thoughts of suicide exceeded those reported by past student generations.[15] In fact, the number of students reporting previous diagnosis or treatment of depression more than doubled in 2019, compared to a decade earlier.[16] Today's students worry about the cost of college, the debt they have accumulated, their ability to secure a job that will lead to a middle-class life, and the environment they will inherit. Tensions and conflicts in the larger society, including political fragmentation, amplify their concerns about personal safety. This generation, Generation Z, faces a broader, faster-moving, more complex set of problems that often intersect – including intensifying economic and racial inequality, alternative facts and conspiracy theories, cybercrime, screen addiction, public shaming, doxxing (the perils of life lived mostly online), opioid abuse, the rise of neofascism, war, terrorism, school shootings, disinformation, job outsourcing, and climate change, to name a few – than perhaps any generation before. These stresses at times can impede their ability to function, let alone study.

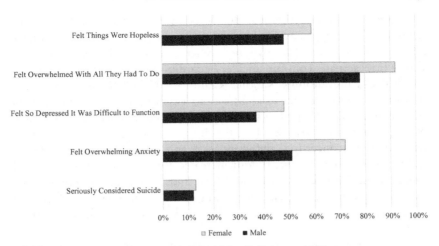

Source: American College Health Association and the National College Health Assessment, 2019

Figure 2.1   National Annual Mental Health Assessment 2019: college student responses about the previous twelve months

Source: American College Health Association and the National College Health Assessment, 2019

The pandemic has only increased levels of anxiety and depression. The Substance Abuse and Mental Health Services Administration, for instance, reported for all age groups a dramatic increase in requests for crisis counseling support to its Disaster Distress Helpline in April 2020 – 20,000 text requests compared to 1,790 the same month the year before.[17] The daily stress of increasing death counts from COVID-19; fears about the proximity of strangers and the potential consequences of touching things; and concerns about money, isolation, and dependence on the Internet are but a few of the residual stressful experiences of those living through the disruption of 2020–2021. Today's and tomorrow's students have become a generation marked by a pandemic and the events that surrounded it.

The American College Health Association (ACHA) and the National College Health Assessment have conducted an annual national survey of students since 1998. Some responses from the Spring 2019 survey of 67,972 students, summarized in Figure 2.1, point to real areas for concern regarding Generation Z's mental health and coping mechanisms.[18]

Stress, anxiety, and feelings of being overburdened have never been unusual for college students. But when students feel hopeless, find it difficult to function, and consider suicide, we have crossed into very dangerous territory.

There is a significant gender difference in the statistics regarding students who say they have considered suicide compared to those who have taken their own lives. More young women report the thought, but more young men actually commit suicide. According to the Centers for Disease Control and Prevention's National Center for Health Statistics, 20.5 per hundred thousand males aged fifteen to twenty-four years old died by suicide in 2016, compared to 5.4 females.[19] This difference has held steady over the past two decades, but the increase among young women is particularly disconcerting. Between 2000 and 2016, the suicide rate for females aged fifteen to twenty-four increased from 3.0 to 5.4 per hundred thousand individuals – nearly doubling, and is now at the highest rate recorded in forty years. Rates for young men fifteen to twenty-four also increased, from 17.1 to 20.5 per hundred thousand individuals from 2000 to 2016.[20]

Another study on seventy-one campuses found that gender minority students – defined as transgender, genderqueer, and gender-nonconforming individuals, as well as those who have another self-identified gender – are far more likely to experience a mental health problem than the general student population, which already has high levels of stress. In fact, in the 2015–2017 Healthy Minds Study of 65,213 students, the 1,237 gender minority students who participated revealed that their odds of having at least one mental health problem was 4.3 times greater than the general student population.[21]

These figures raise serious concerns about the declining state of mental health among young Americans in general, and college students in particular. The pandemic serves as a further accelerant. Too many within the Generation Z cohort are struggling to cope with daily life. On campuses, students have demanded additional counseling support. A study of ninety-three different counseling and mental health centers on college campuses revealed a 30 percent increase in caseloads over the six academic years from 2009 to 2015.[22] Whether it is delivered virtually or face-to-face, the need for such support is only likely to increase in the future.

There is some debate as to why college students are experiencing such high levels of stress and mental health struggles. Perhaps since more students are receiving treatment for mental health issues at an earlier age, more of them are staying on track to attend college. Other commentators have pointed out that young people may be more open than previous generations to discussing and seeking professional mental health support.[23] But even if either of these factors contributes to higher reported rates, it's abundantly clear that today's college students worry about meeting family expectations, may lack experience communicating about and acting on specific stressors, including the pandemic, face challenges in sustaining healthy relationships, may have anxiety about college costs and debt, perhaps worry about their loved ones at home, feel insecure about their academic preparation and performance, are anxious about their future and jobs, and acknowledge their dependency on social media and the Internet.[24]

Other stressors that can heighten student anxiety include racism, sexual harassment, bullying, hate crimes, greater political and cultural polarization in American society, and concern over the future of the environment (to name only a few). Many faculty, meanwhile, have limited experience in bridging polarized divisions in the learning environment, whether online or face-to-face, or in managing external threats. Students can often sense their instructors' uncertainty. Clearly, new dynamics are at play in teaching a diverse student body seeking a more inclusive and supportive experience in an increasingly polarized world.

The academic program itself can pose challenges for students' mental health. For students who are used to succeeding effortlessly in their high school classes, the possibility of academic failure can come as a shock. Not all will make the grades needed to become doctors, lawyers, or engineers, despite their long-held aspirations. Poor grades in an advanced physics or organic chemistry course have been the bane of many a student. Given the other uncertainties in their lives, many contemporary students experience academic failure as crushing blows, not only to their future but to their sense of self-worth.

Hiring more clinical counselors is not the only answer to student despair. A more supportive and coordinated community of advisors, faculty, and support personnel can help students adjust to new realities, just as an uncoordinated patchwork of professionals can complicate life. Accomplishing this, however, will take a concerted effort by university leaders to recognize and address the fragmented structure of the contemporary university.

Born Digital

The students of Generation Z are the most technologically savvy and technology dependent to ever arrive on campus. Their experience with the world has been mediated via their handheld devices since the first iPhone appeared in 2007. The smartphone has been a salient part of their developmental years, and its presence and impact continue to evolve in their lives. It has influenced how they interact with others and how they spend their time, as well as how they access information, goods, and services. It was the go-to medium throughout the pandemic, with young people reporting long hours on their electronic devices.[25] By 2021, just fourteen years after the introduction of the smartphone, ownership had reached 85 percent of the United States population; among those aged eighteen to twenty-nine, ownership reached 96 percent.[26] According to technology company Asurion, Americans check their smartphones on average every ten minutes, which comes to ninety-six times a day.[27] Use may be even more frequent for those aged eighteen to thirty-four, 60 percent of whom acknowledge concern about overuse.[28]

No other generation has been so tethered to this powerful technology. Costly long-distance calls, driving to the video store ("be sure to rewind"), the screech of modems, multiple volumes of encyclopedias, library card catalogs, the distinctive scent of a hand-cranked mimeograph machine, the glare of overhead transparencies, and the once indispensable slide rule are all the stuff of historical legend for Generation Z. For those born after the year 2000, the changes have taken place so swiftly that most are largely unaware of how dramatically the information revolution has disrupted the organizations and institutions on which we all rely.

The students of Generation Z livestream films and podcasts, customize music collections, play games, and read weather reports and breaking news instantly, all with a few taps. They record, view, and disseminate significant moments on their smartphones with near-immediate social impact. Many shop online instead of at a store. If they need transportation, they find and rent a bike or motor scooter through a phone app, or hail an Uber or a Lyft. Directions are right on their phones, and Google can attempt to answer almost any question. Students can customize their phones to access almost anything. Individuals have become accustomed to a level of personalized attention, customized communication, frequent feedback, timely service, and instant information unprecedented in human history.

Students born in the twenty-first century have absolutely no idea what life used to be like; because of the revolutionary new information tools available to them, today's college students interact with the world differently than any generation before them.[29] Students who did not learn cursive writing in elementary school create a unique scrawl to serve as a signature. Paper checks are a thing of the past; an app can transfer money. They infrequently go to a bank, since they rarely use cash and can deposit a grandparent's check with an image on their phones. They consider paper handouts wasteful. The expectation that someone would get a faculty signature on a printed form and walk it across campus to another office is, to them, akin to asking someone to order blocks of ice for the icebox.

A couple of years ago, I met with a group of students and faculty in Geneva, Switzerland. When most of the students left for another venue, one stayed with the faculty group for additional discussion. Afterward, she was unsure how to join her classmates since she was unfamiliar with the area. When a faculty member offered a map, she admitted she did not know how to read it. She usually followed directions from Google Maps.

Every generation shares a unique set of social and lived experiences. This generation, both before and after the pandemic, assumes that their inter-actions with public and private organizations, institutions, and people are best mediated through smartphones. Their most common shared experi-ence involves accessing personalized goods and services via technology and near-constant immersion in social media. This combination, at times, makes the traditional structure, culture, and administrative operations of the university feel like an anachronism.

Academic Life Is only Part of It

When looking at colleges, students and their families tend to focus on a school's ability to provide a quality education in the form of a baccalau-reate degree. For high schoolers choosing a residential four-year college or university, the top four factors are the institution's reputation/academic quality, the availability of a desired program of study, job placement experience, and cost.[30] These factors loom large over other concerns, such as social adjustment with peers or a sense of belonging and engagement. Academic excellence is what drives an institution's reputation.

But once students enroll and settle in at the university, their perspective shifts. Then, *all* of their experiences affect their ability to thrive and succeed. They suddenly find themselves deeply affected by the delivery of student services and the coordination of academic, student support, and administrative operations. Conflict with a roommate, feelings of loneliness or homesickness, problems managing time, a relationship gone awry and highlighted on social media, wrestling with sexual identity, finding one's passion, worry about money, frustration about getting into required courses, anxiety about making the team or joining a social club, concerns about family members back home, conditions in the dormitory – suddenly all of this is just as important, if not more so, than what's happening in the classroom. In fact, recent survey research on the most frequent reasons students leave college points to concerns over "family, work, physical and mental health, and burn out" rather than "lack of focus or academic challenges."[31]

How has the university dealt with these complex and intertwined situations? Do its existing procedures limit its capacity to respond effectively to the expectations of a changed undergraduate student population? Do they hamper the development of a well-rounded and educated person – a central element of the university's mission?

Structure and Culture

In 1963, when Clark Kerr was president of the University of California, he quipped, "central heating was about the only unifying element in a contemporary multipurpose campus."[32] The traditional hierarchy of the university clusters faculty and staff by their area of specialization, overseen by a scaffolding of supervisors and administrators with relevant experience and expertise. Each unit has an administrative leader who reports to a supervisor with ever-wider responsibilities, eventually reaching the university or college president. This, the classic model embraced by many large organizations at the beginning of the twentieth century, has generally served the nation and global community of educators well. Within it, for the most part, units operate independently in their areas of specialization and expertise, and their performance and accomplishments are assessed based on metrics exclusive to them. Their functions are separate and insulated, as if in silos. While units often share goodwill and a cooperative spirit, individual accomplishments within their area of expertise matter most for their annual review. What one unit views as a success may prove to be a problem for another. The highly fragmented nature of the university Kerr identified in 1963 remains the case today.

Outside higher education, this functional organizational structure has recently come under criticism for its slowness, its resistance to change, poor cross-unit communication, and a sense of territoriality that hampers cooperation. In the university setting, almost all units outside of faculty academic affairs maintain this traditional functional organization, with its attendant limitations.

Of course, in a multifaceted organization such as the university, not all the hierarchical functional units operate in the same way. While the academic center of the university has the basic bones of a traditional bureaucracy, its operations are complex and nuanced. Three historic elements differentiate faculty organizational units from the rest of the university: the tradition of academic freedom, the status of tenure, and its accompanying concept of shared governance.[33] These powerful elements, deeply rooted in faculty culture, have fostered maximum individual independence for faculty members, a minimum of day-to-day bureaucratic responsibilities and intrusions on their time, and extensive use of committee governance structures to safeguard academic standards. Time away from campus and teleworking as a result of the pandemic has further diminished faculty interactions with the campus. The result for faculty is what I call a multimodal functional operational structure: a conventional hierarchal organization, segmented into departments or schools, with reporting lines amended to intentionally limit top-down decision-making and, consequently, enhanced faculty academic prerogatives, autonomy, and authority. Chapter 6 provides a more detailed discussion of university structure, culture, and operations.

Besides faculty, the traditional residential university includes professional staff employed in a host of offices such as finance and treasury, procurement, facilities and real estate, student affairs, development and alumni relations, communications and marketing, enrollment management, legal affairs, financial aid, public safety, information technology, human resources, and athletics, as well as other offices that report to the vice presidents, provost, and university president. These administrative and support units operate within a traditional functional organizational structure but with a culture, norms, and processes different from that of the faculty. Staff experience less autonomy than faculty. Personnel in the administrative and service units within a multiunit division are customarily separate and independent from each other and are uniformly separate across divisions. This stovepiped, or siloed, structure limits engagement with others in the academy outside of their limited professional spheres. In a roundtable discussion, which I joined at a national conference with IT professionals, one individual spoke up and said he had tried to help provide greater connectivity across student service areas, but "I was told by my supervisor to stay in my lane"; others quickly chimed in agreement.

The university's capacity to shift from face-to-face instruction to online delivery within days of pandemic-induced campus closures revealed its potential to adapt when necessary. But this is not typical. The university's basic organizational structure has evolved and endured for more than a century. It is an open system, so it will adapt, albeit slowly, to the changing milieu and larger political and environmental forces. Geoffrey Cox refers to this process of adjustment as "accretive change."[34] He points to changes over the past century that have led to the development of community colleges, for-profit educational institutions, and, more recently, the establishment of several creative experimental colleges. Futurists point to further changes in the university after the pandemic recedes, including more flexible course scheduling and digital instruction. To give only one example: the construction of new campus facilities will likely give far more consideration to public health concerns around contagious diseases, germs, and potential infection.

Incremental changes introduced by colleges and universities rarely deal with the fundamental operations that influential internal stakeholders oversee and protect. A university might introduce new online graduate programs, an online transcript that provides descriptive information for employers, partnerships with companies, satellite programs for returning adult students, a statement about free expression on campus, a new core curriculum, or model Title IX procedures – but all of these changes and adjustments do little to address the fragmentation at the heart of the university's structure.[35] At most colleges and universities, fundamental issues surrounding university structure and culture too often remain relatively untouched, as they have for previous generations of faculty, staff, and students.

A residential university aspires to transform its undergraduates into fully educated people prepared for a career or further study, and who have a sense of moral and ethical judgment and a greater understanding of humanity and their role as stewards of society. With today's specialized and fragmented academic and support operations, it is increasingly difficult to achieve this aspiration.[36] A student's university experience is the sum of all interactions, whether haphazard or more thoughtful. To the extent that the university can better integrate these experiences into a holistic educational experience – a transformation it can enrich through the strategic use of design, planning, and technology – it can enhance the academic success of its students and simultaneously better meet societal needs.

College and university administrators recognize that their low graduation rates need improvement. At higher education conferences and in the scholarly literature, university leaders focus on improving student success and retention. Entrepreneurs have gotten into the game, creating predictive analyses to help universities understand the individual academic choices students make. Universities use the tools of big data and campus surveys to diagnose, assess, and intervene as necessary to help students be more successful. Many of these interventions have yielded improvements in retention at some of the most challenging institutions.[37]

Nevertheless, students continue to encounter a bewildering variety of professional and administrative services outside the academic core: athletics and recreation, career planning and internships, counseling, entertainment, financial aid, food services, study abroad, health care, housing, information technology, safety, residential life, spiritual life, community service, and transportation, among others. Student services are among the fastest-growing expenditures on campuses across the nation, having more than doubled at private institutions between 1987 and 2013 – the largest sector increase of all spending per student – and increasing by 54 percent at public institutions.[38] Any of these support services may touch a student at different times and have a significant positive or negative impact on their college experience.

Caught between Silos

In the opening chapter, I shared Maurice's story, a classic example of how fragmented administrative services amplify the consequences of the most mundane student errors. His experience, unfortunately, is not rare. Consider the case of Shanice, a strong high school student with high SAT scores. She is also an accomplished pianist. Shanice could go to a conservatory for further study but, with her family's support, decides that she wants to go to a liberal arts college that also has a music program. All the colleges to which she applied have offered her scholarships. Her school of choice has offered her the Claudette and George Gruene Family Scholarship Award – funds set aside specifically to support rising musicians. (As with all student names in this book, the name of the scholarship has been changed.) While the award itself does not cover all of Shanice's costs, it tops off her federal financial aid to cover the remainder of her tuition – all four years of tuition would be fully funded.

Shanice accepts the offer and eagerly enrolls. Once on campus, a member of the Gruene family, along with the university president, meets briefly with Shanice and wishes her well with her studies. The Gruene family member says that she would like to keep in touch with Shanice and, when possible, attend one of her recitals.

Shanice is excited to be on campus and easily makes friends. In addition to her courses, she continues her regular piano practice, volunteers as a reading tutor at a nearby elementary school, becomes involved in two campus clubs, and joins a sorority. While busy, she does well in all of her courses, save one – calculus. Shanice struggles in calculus, and as a result, her first-term GPA is lower than she had hoped. She decides not to take any more mathematics classes. Looking ahead to the Spring Term, she registers for an introductory chemistry course to fulfill one of her natural science requirements. Unhappy with the large lecture format and the subject matter, Shanice drops the course just before the close of the add/drop period. With the term already underway, and with a busy schedule, she opts not to enroll in a replacement course, leaving her with twelve credits for the term. She is very happy with her schedule, her friends, and her life at the university. She tells her parents that she is certain she made the right choice for college. Her parents suggest that she send a thank you note to the Gruene family member, and Shanice does just that.

As the Spring Term winds down, Shanice is fully engaged in writing a paper about the history of piano design and construction. Professor M., who is teaching the course, thinks the paper is excellent. Given Shanice's interest in the subject matter and the paper's possible contribution to Shanice's professional music portfolio, Professor M. offers to assign an Incomplete with the unusual default grade of A to allow her more time and support (beyond the submission deadline) to produce an important paper for her portfolio. Shanice takes Professor M. up on the offer and is looking forward to polishing the paper over the summer.

This turns out to be a critical error. Federal regulations classify failure to complete coursework within the allotted time frame as evidence that a student is not making Satisfactory Academic Progress (SAP). Per Federal Title IV regulations, Shanice's combination of an Incomplete, her cumulative GPA, and her number of completed credit hours means that she is not making Satisfactory Academic Progress. Routine reporting by the Financial Aid Office to the Department of Education on student progress, including Shanice's records, triggers a notice back from the Department of Education that Shanice is no longer eligible for federal financial aid. In theory, both Shanice and her family might have known of this risk. The Financial Aid Office sends regular reminders and communications regarding aid eligibility and renewal requirements, as does the Department of Education. Unfortunately, Shanice's family did not connect the dots. Nor did anyone in the Financial Aid Office attempt to notify the dean, the provost, or the president's office that the recipient of an award from a prominent donor was at risk of losing her eligibility. Based on the Department of Education's decision, the Financial Aid Office sends a letter to Shanice's home informing her of her loss of federal financial aid, along with the opportunity to appeal the decision.

As one might imagine, the letter causes consternation for Shanice and her family, and for the president's office when Shanice's upset parents call.

Her family informs the Financial Aid Office that they cannot make up the tuition shortfall. Shanice is embarrassed and disheartened. Unless her appeal is approved, Shanice will have to withdraw from the university.

Shanice now enters yet another bureaucratic morass: the federal financial aid appeals process. She has to offer both an acceptable explanation of the cause of the problem and lay out a credible plan to rectify it. Shanice prepares an appeal indicating that she will complete the paper for the course, adds supporting documentation strengthening her case, and shows that she has registered for a full course load in the upcoming semester. However, summer schedules complicate matters. While the financial aid officer can reach the department chair and brief her on the matter, Professor M. is doing research abroad and is unavailable to comment on the quality of Shanice's work and the rationale behind the grade of Incomplete. The appeal is submitted to the Department of Education without a letter from the professor.

Fortunately, the Department of Education accepts the appeal, and Shanice is awarded federal financial aid for the Fall Term. But the approval is conditional, good for only one semester, and dependent on further academic performance. At the end of the Fall Term, Shanice must demonstrate that she has met the conditions of the appeal to receive funding through the remainder of the academic year.

Eventually, all the pieces come together. Shanice does an excellent job on her final paper, which her professor praises and assigns a letter grade of "A." A change of grade form is sent to the registrar, who amends the transcript. Based on the federal regulations, Shanice is placed on probation and can conditionally regain aid eligibility. In the end, it all works out, but only after two months of conversations with Shanice and her family, high stress levels for Shanice and her family, a delicate conversation with the donors of the music scholarship assuring them of Shanice's ability, and substantial staff time and aggravation.

The case reveals how the routine nature of university procedures can unintentionally cause unnecessary student and family stress. Shanice was unaware of the financial implications of dropping her chemistry course and agreeing to take an Incomplete. But so was the professor who suggested the idea in the first place, as was the Registrar's Office that entered the grade. There are many times when an Incomplete is an appropriate grade for a course, but this was not one of them. Nor was there an electronic fail-safe mechanism in the registrar's office to catch and address the problem of assigning an Incomplete for a talented student on federal financial aid. Once the damage was done, the Financial Aid Office proceeded on autopilot, issuing notices without investigating the circumstances involved. The various offices implemented their customary procedures without adequate communication across divisions. Shanice and her family suffered uncertainty and stress as a result.

Siloed university operations affect the student experience even when individual students aren't involved. In one case, a procurement officer negotiated a new contract with the university's food service vendor. The vendor wanted a substantial increase in fees to cover higher labor costs. To hold costs down, the procurement officer suggested reducing the workers' hours by thirty minutes a day, while still ensuring that dining operations would continue one hour past the end of the last late afternoon class time slot. This brought the cost of the proposed contract down to almost the level of the previous contract. The deal was struck, the contract signed, and the procurement officer subsequently received praise from his supervisor, recognition that was rewarded in his annual review.

The new contract hours, however, changed the student dining experience. The students who showed up for dinner after late classes now found staff cleaning up and preparing to leave, rather than making hot meals. They were left with whatever cold food had not been consumed or cleaned up. The procurement office had successfully kept costs in check, but there was no communication with other divisions of the university, nor with students, about the potential consequences. One administrator's narrow success produced negative consequences for many students.

Even before new students arrive on campus, the lack of coordination and communication across separate operations is evident in notifications to their homes from different university offices. One private university with a total yearly cost of over $60,000 learned, to administrators' surprise, that students and their families had been sent over 130 different communications by email, telephone, text, and postal mail between the acceptance date and the start of classes. The messages, from various university administrative units, were uncoordinated, different in format and style, and evidenced no sense of the appropriate timing of the information. Each office administrator was unaware of the other communications being sent during the same period. Can you imagine any other industry sending such a barrage of uncoordinated information to customers it is billing almost a quarter-million dollars over four years? As one administrator told me, "Our students have stopped reading our emails. So what do we do? We send them another email telling them to read their emails!"

Students and their families pinballing from one administrative office to another; policies that are dated or no longer enforced; practices that remain uncodified; electronic links that lead to dead ends; uncoordinated messages from different authorities; lack of clarity about who is in charge; essential information to which access is limited; and an uncoordinated and inefficient administrative culture: could this be the modern university of the twenty-first century?

The Age of Convergence in a Sea of Specialization

One year before the creation of Amazon.com, Michael Hammer and James Champy argued in *Reengineering the Corporation* that organizations built on the late-nineteenth- and early-twentieth-century model of specialized structures and fragmented processes cannot adapt to major changes in the contemporary marketplace. They wrote, "Inflexibility, unresponsiveness, the absence of customer focus, an obsession with activity rather than the result, bureaucratic paralysis, lack of innovation, high overhead – these are the legacies of past business practices."[39] Sadly, this description applies to too many American residential colleges and universities outside of, perhaps, the enrollment management and recruitment team.

The opening chapter introduced the idea that we live in a time of two simultaneous trends: (1) increased specialization, so abundant in the university (along with social polarization), and (2) large-scale convergence, that is, the integration and alignment of previously fragmented services, devices, and information. While specialization and fragmented internal processes are commonplace in older organizations and government, Hammer and Champy point out that whole industries have been disrupted by the availability of simpler, easier, and faster services made possible by the integration of artificial intelligence and data analytics on mobile devices. Convergence depends on a wholesale rethinking of how underlying business processes are sequenced to better meet customer needs. Once this hard work of detailed design thinking and planning is done, technologists can leverage new tools to operationalize the identified sequences and multiple pathways. Across the globe, the pandemic has forced institutions to rethink how they do business. This moment presents a unique opportunity for the residential college or university to become more nimble and responsive to its student population.

Artificial intelligence and algorithms that map a pattern of individual choices have significantly improved the customer experience in selected industries and services. Amazon, Zappos, Warby Parker, Stitch Fix, Wayfair – the list of profitable businesses that prioritize a tech-mediated service experience is long and growing. Nor is this phenomenon unique to online retailers; organizations that prioritize customer service and individual attention include local independent bookstores, L.L. Bean, Wegmans' supermarkets, Nordstrom's, Apple, and the Cleveland Clinic. In most cases, the customer, client, or patient comes first. These companies meet their customers' needs with less stress and a minimum of aggravation. They ensure their customers' satisfaction by providing them with goods or services in a responsive and personalized manner reflective of quality and value. The consumer has confidence that the transaction was fair and the assurance that there is recourse, should there be a problem later.

In each case and for each organization, someone has carefully thought through how to make transactions easier, more efficient, and even rewarding for the consumer – and the search for ways to improve the experience continues. Consider the number of transactions that have been seamlessly integrated when you use your credit card to purchase gas for your car. The moment you swipe your card at the pump, the credit card is reviewed for authorization and security. Once approved, you are asked if you would like to add a car wash to your bill. If you have points accrued at your local supermarket accepted by the gasoline brand, you are automatically asked if you would like to allocate them to lower the per-gallon price of the gasoline at the pump on the grade of gas you prefer. After pumping the gas, you are asked if you would like a receipt, printed at the pump, that summarizes the entire transaction. Your account is debited the amount and the service station is paid. All these steps, previously conducted as separate actions, have been seamlessly integrated nearly instantaneously. Attention to detail can make all the difference. For example, Sam's Club has announced it will pilot stores without checkout lanes and cashiers. Instead, shoppers will complete their entire transaction by relying on a smartphone app and "all available technologies – including computer vision, augmented reality, machine learning, artificial intelligence, robotics, just to name a few – to redefine the retail experience."[40]

Operating at this level of performance in industries that rely on human services and social interactions adds to the complexity of the transaction. It requires considerable attention to detail, an organizational culture in which everyone plays a role in the success of the organization, an openness to feedback from frontline workers to improve the experience, an administrative structure that enhances dialogue and interaction among staff and emboldens employees with a sense of authority to solve problems, and a culture of systematic planning of sequences of interaction and follow-up. All this requires that managers, as well as frontline workers, constantly put themselves in the shoes of the end-user to better understand their experience and how to make it better, simpler, more responsive, and easier to navigate.

Let me distinguish a few terms to clarify what convergence might mean in historic organizations in constant direct contact with people, like colleges and universities. For them, convergence and the integration of functions involve more than "coordinating" across different service and administrative domains. Coordination implies that each of the disparate parts will retain their specialized control of information, with the relevant parties deciding to interact to assist an individual case. Such a model leads to the inefficiency cited above and the inability to resolve cases in a timely fashion. Further, it diffuses responsibility and accountability for outcomes. Convergence in human service settings means something less than the total amalgamation and collapsing of the disparate parts, wherein existing operations are then fed to a central source. In human services, such an approach would likely overwhelm the capacity of a professional to manage the volume and flow of information and serve the end-user (student) well. Convergence, in this case, involves aligning timely information or functions in such a way that a central source can manage and allocate the necessary resources to resolve or mitigate the matter. The central source maintains accountability for the transaction along with the follow-through of the case. In an institution like academia, which is human interaction-intensive and involves different kinds of experts and expertise, convergence looks more like what might be observed in a case management approach.

In the modern economy, we have seen technology transform the delivery of goods and services. To integrate what were previously compartmentalized services, experts in the core industry examine actual functions and procedures from the perspective of the service recipient. The task of the leadership of the core industry, then, is to reconfigure and align existing administrative functions to provide a smoother and more efficient flow of information. If done well, the interaction between the service recipient and the provider becomes easier, more intuitive, and likely faster. This is the promise of technological convergence.

Ironically, the university, an intellectual fountain and incubator for the modern technological revolution, has as yet to embrace the organizational and operational transformation other industries have undergone or are undergoing. The university's mission of providing a quality learning experience resulting in an educated graduate remains front and center, but the university structure has not embraced the service-focused mindset. In a world of limited resources, the current student service structure and its culture remain inefficiently segmented, unnecessarily draining precious human time and talent, frustrating too many stakeholders, and at times hampering the very mission of the academy. Universities routinely fail at meeting the customer-service standards and expectations increasingly common in any number of organizations outside of higher education and to which students (as well as an increasing number of faculty and staff) are accustomed. Felton et al. reinforce this point, writing, "Thriving institutions transform silos into systems by supporting cross-unit coordination and by paying more attention to the student experience than to how the organizational chart divides up the campus."[41] Universities seeking national recognition, product distinctiveness, and enhanced student outcomes have an opportunity to fill this niche.

Universities are not Luddite institutions. They create online courses and programs, support advanced technological research, digitize their libraries, manage sophisticated software packages, create new apps, draw upon robust data analytics, support expanded bandwidth, and offer students and faculty increased computing power. But when it comes to altering structures, functions, and autonomy within and across university units, the reluctance to change existing practices runs deep. Too often, the university merely introduces a digitized student services tool that rehashes the same sequence of processes, albeit more rapidly. Simply taking a process online doesn't force administrative units to question the processes, sequences involved, or eventual relationship to the other functional units.

The contrast between university functions and what is available to students in their interactions with other industries has produced a structural lag between the academic setting and its students. The challenges of the pandemic and the necessity to consider changes that were previously unthinkable present colleges and universities with an opportunity to redesign their services to match the quality of that of the private sector. All will benefit – not just students, but the entire academic community.

Structural Lag in the Residential College and University

Structural lag occurs when institutional operations fall out of sync with the people and populations they serve and cannot respond adequately to changing expectations. As indicated in Chapter 1, the concept was introduced in 1994 by Matilda White Riley and elaborated by Riley, Kahn, and Foner.[42] Institutions do not change quickly, Riley argued, and some struggle to adjust to larger societal forces – changing demographics, untapped human capacity and potential inequitable treatment, political shifts, or technological revolutions. A lag develops between the historic practices of the institution and the evolving needs of those it serves.

The university is a prime example. Colleges and universities need to catch up to the students they so eagerly recruit. As sweeping changes continue to shape American life, traditional four-year colleges and universities would do well to ask students what the university mission ought to include. In what ways does the current collegiate structure and culture, developed over the past century, meet – or fail to meet – the hopes and expectations of a generation of students who have grown up in a world radically changed by the unprecedented challenges of the twenty-first century?

Students have a long history of making their expectations regarding university operations known. More recently, some complain about a professor's course because they "paid for it," an attitude understandably offensive to faculty members who distinguish between a customer and a student. In turn, some faculty express concern that the students in their classes enter with a sense of entitlement. Students attend college to learn, to grow, and to be challenged, faculty point out. Being a student means, at times, receiving painful reviews of one's work. Failure is part of the learning experience, and professors have an obligation to provide honest and fair feedback. Just as a patient doesn't tell the surgeon how to operate, so the student shouldn't tell the faculty member how to teach or assess academic achievement.

This visceral faculty response to customer entitlement about academic learning has merit. But what about the student experiences outside the classroom? Here the student truly is both consumer and customer, having paid for support services with hard-earned (or hard-borrowed) tuition and fees. Students pay for services in housing, food, entertainment, personal safety, scheduling, advising, general health care, and social services. They should receive a high quality of service in exchange for their money. Few of us would support a university that allows students to live in residence halls filled with mold, for example. That would fall below a reasonable standard of expected care and service, yet it has occurred – with tragic consequences.[43]

How a student encounters the campus community outside the classroom, including interactions with the administrative system, can directly affect their academic performance. Faculty might not be aware of these encounters, but they witness the unhappy results when those services fail to give students the timely support they need.

At American University (AU), starting in 2015, an internal research team asked students to share their campus stories through focus groups, journaling projects, and retreats. Building on what they told us, we identified over sixty areas that caused tension for students and warranted improvement at the university. (I discuss these findings in greater detail in Chapter 8.) As an administrator, I had no idea about the scale of the problems these students were experiencing until we asked them directly about it. My colleagues shared my surprise. How had we put our students in such untenable positions?

Years ago (thankfully not anymore), AU students referred to the offices of Financial Aid, the Registrar, and Student Accounts as the "Bermuda Triangle" – once caught, you never emerged. Faculty and staff attempted to assist students through unanticipated landmines and to correct unexpected errors, but they too reported encountering problems when dealing with the "Bermuda Triangle." The time spent responding to uncoordinated rules or inefficient systems is costly. Sometimes the irritants and inefficiencies are minor, such as a delay in obtaining a transcript from the registrar, but over time they can add up – and shape enduring perceptions of the institution, including by alumni. In the end, inefficient and poor services leave students, faculty, and staff feeling undervalued and disrespected.

Because few people have a bird's-eye view of the entire university operation, the aggregate human cost of these shortcomings is masked. But these shortcomings have pushed some students away, never to return. For others, they shape an experience that students must simply endure to earn a degree.

To understand why this gap between the life experiences of the incoming college student and the structure and culture of the traditional residential university persists, we need to understand the history of the academy, its complicated culture, its power dynamics, and the long-standing tension between centralization and decentralization across the institution. Though aware of the difficulties, I remain optimistic about our capacity to shrink the structural lag. Several universities, including my own, have already taken steps toward that end.

Theories of Student Success, Persistence, and Departure

Over sixty years or more, scholars have studied and theorized about why college students persist, pause, or leave a residential college education.[44] Theories have emanated from, and reflect the perspectives of disciplines including sociology, psychology, anthropology, economics, organizational development, history, and political science.

Vincent Tinto's initial paper in 1975 and his 1993 book *Leaving College: Rethinking the Causes and Cures of Student Attrition*, among his other works, are perhaps the most widely cited collection of writings in the literature on student attrition.[45] Tinto developed the theory of interactionalism, which points to a young adult's capacity to progress from their previous home and family life (separation) to the structure and culture of the residential academic environment they have selected (transition). The necessary adjustment involves both academic and social integration with the setting, resulting in building binding ties (incorporation), helping the student stick with the college and leverage these internal relationships to overcome different barriers they might encounter. The theory draws upon the sociological imagination from a developmental perspective of late adolescence and early adulthood. Tinto, in extending his theory on interactionalism and student departure, points to "the important notion that colleges are systemic enterprises comprised of a variety of linking interactive, reciprocal parts, formal and informal, academic and social. Events in one segment of the college necessarily and unavoidably influence events in other parts of the institution."[46] Tinto's contributions have led to a host of elaborations and commentaries among other scholars inspiring other theoretical perspectives and relevant research studies that support or refute his original premises.

Tinto's 2012 work, *Completing College: Rethinking Institutional Action*, links the extensive undergraduate student persistence, retention, and graduation research to initiatives designed to promote student success. In this book and other articles during this period, he emphasizes the importance of what takes place in the classroom between faculty and student and the influential ways faculty can provide early intervention and support to students who may be struggling. The book provides specific recommendations for building a culture of student success. Many of Tinto's recommendations, as well as the best practices identified in a review of the literature by Kuh et al. commissioned by the National Postsecondary Education Cooperative, reflect elements that are integrated throughout this book, and in particular, in Chapter 10.[47] Tinto writes that efforts at promoting student success are "the result of intentional, structured, and proactive actions and policies directed toward the success of all students." He goes on to say that these actions "are proactive: they take action to control events, shaping student success rather than merely responding to events."[48]

Alan Seidman pushes Tinto's concepts further by emphasizing the university's obligation to provide the necessary funds to support students once the university decides to admit them and the student accepts the offer. Early identification and intervention, such as summer bridge programs and academic support centers, that are intensive, continuous, and timely serve critical roles in fostering retention. His "Seidman Formula and Success Model" explicitly prescribes a thorough professional assessment of student skills and provision of the necessary academic support throughout the educational experience.[49]

Bean and Eaton draw upon psychodynamic perspectives in conceptualizing an attitude-behavior theory for college success.[50] The theory points to psychological and personality traits congruent with expectations in college, arguing that the psychological styles that are most harmonious with collegiate expectations are prone to lead to success. These traits include self-efficacy, coping strategies, personal motivation, preparation of relevant skills and abilities, previous behavior, and locus of control. Students who arrive with these favorable characteristics are more likely to be successful in mediating the college academic and social environment. Rewards and reinforcing messages of institutional fit can result in a student's determination to persist despite challenges in college.[51]

To assess the determinants of student success, Astin and Oseguera examined data involving the progression of 56,818 undergraduate students from 262 colleges and universities. They found that a variety of personal factors, such as strong high school grades, stable family circumstances, higher socioeconomic status, and high parental educational attainment, favorably influence persistence. Living on campus, involvement in collegiate activities, limited off-campus employment, and modest need for financial aid are also positively associated with timely graduation. The more selective the university, the better the chance that a student completes their degree within four years. Those rates are lower at public compared to private universities.[52] The findings can provide predictive data on student success. Once again, the study affirms that there are underlying social inequities that prevent students from less favored backgrounds or circumstances from achieving the preconceived definitions of student success. A contemporary view of these findings indicates the need for colleges and universities to recognize the uneven playing field for less privileged students and the need to commit the necessary resources to provide support to all students.

Economists raise the issue of cost-benefit when exploring theoretical frameworks for examining student success.[53] Even if a student can afford the cost of a residential college, there is an individual choice to assess the value and time of the expenditure. Students who have other options, like a good job, the opportunity to work in a family business, an offer to play professional sports, a calling for the trades, a choice to leave school to raise a family earlier in life, or the desire to travel or have other life experiences outside of a formal setting may find the opportunity cost of college to be dispensable. And, of course, some simply cannot afford college. There are too many tragic cases of students who begin college facing a future of heavy student loan debt. As circumstances unfold and financial pressures rise, they find themselves unable to meet their expenses. The unfortunate result is exiting college with debt and no degree.

In a qualitative study of the first-year student experience, Godwin and Markham found that the range of student service offices on campus left students uncertain as to what office was responsible for what task. Students bounced from one office to another. Lost paperwork and delays in financial aid processes left students with unanticipated problems in need of resolution.[54] What makes Godwin and Markham's study so interesting is that it was done in 1996, on students born in the late 1970s. While most students in the study reported accepting this as business as usual and tolerating the inefficiencies they encountered, others found this initial college experience frustrating and disquieting. A decade before the introduction of the smartphone, perhaps students were more accepting of runarounds and inefficiencies in organizations. In their comprehensive review of the literature mentioned previously, Kuh et al. reveal that "how new students perceive and interact with the bureaucratic elements of the institution may well affect student success."[55]

The aforementioned theoretical work appeared before the college enrollment of Generation Z – a generation of students with vulnerabilities and strengths that cut across all the different theoretical perspectives presented above and who have life experiences distinct from prior cohorts. They may be less amenable to the traditional collegiate formula for success, but they are nonetheless academically capable with timely support. Their transition from home to a residential campus setting has been influenced by living through a pandemic. Their psychological outlook, which already evidences stress, will be further influenced in ways yet unseen. Finally, the cost of four years of college will likely exclude more students whose family's income has been decimated by the pandemic from attending, with implications of more students seeking financial aid.

A different and more complex student body has arrived. A theoretical framework for student success that is holistic and that explicitly addresses the structural and cultural lag between college and student and the subsequent impact on students' lives is needed. Such a theory would question the capacity of semi-independent student services and programs to effectively meet student needs. The source of the problem is not the faculty and professionals themselves, but the inherited bureaucratic structure that fosters inefficient and fragmented responses.

Any theoretical framework addressing the needs of contemporary students must include the insights of critical race theory to student success. Emerging from legal writings and discourse by Derrick Bell and others in the late 1980s, critical race theory has been applied to organizational settings whose policies and practices emerge from underlying racist practices and assumptions. Critical race theory argues that racism is normative and pervasive in all of our institutions and reward structures. It advantages those with power over others and seeks to maintain such inequities. The theory further argues that race is a social construct, not a scientific one, and that systemic change is required to address long-standing societal injustices.[56]

The clamor for racial justice in America forces colleges and universities to uncover and confront the underlying suppositions that institutionalize traditions, rituals, symbols, and rewards that are exclusionary or marginalize people of color but that are often invisible to the White community. The documented experiences of Black and Latinx students in colleges and universities serve as evidence of the subtle and at times overt racial insensitivities and prejudices transmitted in the curriculum, selected readings, assignments, historic and intellectual figures studied, and revealed in the dialogue and preferences of some faculty, administrators, and staff. Students of color encounter power differentials that are reinforced by illusions of color blindness and meritocracy.[57] University administrators and scholars concerned with student success and well-being must consider such a powerful theoretical perspective as critical race theory by drawing insights from Black and Latinx students themselves.

Of the theoretical frameworks on student success and well-being detailed in this very brief summary, those that lead to institutional and organizational changes – changes that move the setting to be more congruent with the students they serve – resonate the most with me. Such changes will result not just from altering the operations of the specialized areas of the faculty and staff professionals, but from aligning and integrating these functions to be more responsive to students. In an article reflecting on the many studies on why students do not persist in college, Tinto writes, "we have not yet fully explored what institutions can do to help more students stay and succeed. More importantly, we have yet to develop an effective model of institutional action that provides institutions guidelines for the development of policies, programs, and practices to enhance student success."[58]

The Student-Centered University

Several universities, among them Tufts, Georgetown, Syracuse, Northeastern, University of Virginia, Arizona State University, and American University, have prepared mission statements on the importance of being a student-centered or a student-focused research university. Many other universities use the term "student-centered" in their marketing materials. But what does this mean in practice? What might the ideal student-centered university look like? Much of what we know about this comes from the perspective of university professionals: their standards, staffing expectations, budget needs, service utilization levels, and data requirements. But we know far less about the students' perspective of their total experience and how it can be improved.

For Kenneth Shaw, the chancellor of Syracuse University for thirteen years until 2004, designing a student-focused university meant aligning the faculty's traditional emphasis on intensive, graduate-level research with programs designed to enhance the undergraduate experience. He writes in *The Intentional Leader*, "we created a new vision: to become the nation's leading student-centered research university."[59] This initiative took place at a time of deep budget cuts in the late 1990s. But rather than cutting across the board, Shaw and his team reduced selected areas to free up additional funds for both academic and service areas specially selected to improve the undergraduate experience. "What we learned," Shaw later wrote, "was the need to focus on our 'customer.' This means we needed to ask ourselves who our customer was, and then ask what their needs were and how best to meet them."[60] Indeed, a controversial statement for many faculty.

Richard Freeland, president of Northeastern University from 1996 to 2006, credits Shaw with inspiring his own commitment to student success at Northeastern. In his book, *Transforming the Urban University*, Freeland devotes an entire chapter to this effort.[61] Early in his presidency, Freeland focused the entire campus on improving graduation rates, with every administrative unit developing goals along these lines. The recommendations included reducing the dependence on part-time instructors and increasing the number of full-time faculty, improving collaboration and communication across student service units for more personal student attention, and then following up with student surveys about the quality of services – all to improve the student experience. Northeastern also committed to enhancing first-year advising and creating an early warning system to identify at-risk students. Because students had complained about the available technology services, this too was improved. According to Freeland, the most important efforts focused on increasing student financial aid and improving the quality of student housing.

Georgetown University provost Robert Groves wrote in 2017 about the obligations that being a student-centered research university triggers. Of particular note is his discussion of the changing student population and the influence of world events and the extensive exposure to the Internet on the needs of the entering students. He states, "With these cohorts of students having been socialized to acquire information in very different ways than earlier cohorts, aspiring to be a 'student-centered' university must also be different from what it was."[62]

The University of Maryland, Baltimore County (UMBC), and others have created specific programs to nurture the curricular and cocurricular components of the student experience. UMBC's Meyerhoff Program, which is a selective science and engineering undergraduate cohort approach, is a national model for promoting high academic standards and cultivating the whole person as an educated citizen. The results have been impressive. With significant contributions from graduates of the Meyerhoff Program, the Black alumni of this midsized university have gone on to earn more combined MD/PhD degrees than Black graduates from any other university, independent of size, in the United States.[63] Much of the credit for this achievement rests with the vision of Freeman Hrabowski III, president since 1992. Hrabowski has taken a personal interest in the development of students at UMBC and hired outstanding faculty and staff who have dedicated themselves to providing an immersive and personalized education for UMBC's students, and in particular to those in the Meyerhoff Program.

Other colleges and universities have deep commitments to a more student-centered and holistic learning experience. Leading Historically Black Colleges and Universities (HBCUs) provide particularly supportive and nurturing educational opportunities that could serve as models for other campuses. The same is true of many women's colleges. Many community colleges, too, have identified specific steps to retain students facing severe life challenges. The Achieving the Dream network represents nearly three hundred community colleges working together "breaking down (physical) silos and streamlining communication . . . systematically changing the way . . . staff and faculty work. This means changing roles and responsibilities, and sometimes bringing in new positions to create a more student-centered experience."[64]

Toward a More Holistic Student Experience

In *The Innovative University*, Christensen and Eyring write, "The student-centered university is the exception today. In the future, no other kind is likely to succeed."[65] Let's examine a bit of the history of Tufts University to see how it evolved into a student-centered university.

After the Great Depression, only a handful of universities, including Ivy League leaders like Princeton, Yale, and Harvard, and selected public research universities within the Association of American Universities could afford to offer an outstanding undergraduate program while remaining preeminent research universities. Over the next twenty years, however, as many universities recovered financially, they sought to increase their academic heft in a search for national recognition, reputation, and prestige. In 1953, Tufts College, a liberal arts college seeking to improve its national standing and expand into the graduate and research arena, renamed itself Tufts University. With deep roots in the small college liberal arts tradition, but with limited resources, the leadership of Tufts understood that it would not be able to compete on the same playing field with the other two major powerhouses in the Boston region – Harvard and MIT. It would need to become something else.

To reconcile budgetary constraints and institutional ambition, Tufts' leadership decided to enhance its undergraduate studies by expanding the number of research-active faculty in its graduate school and affiliate them with the undergraduate program. These new faculty would teach both undergraduate courses and graduate courses. By 1960, Tufts had become known as a "college-centered university" dedicated to small undergraduate classes taught by distinguished scholars and research faculty.[66] It filled a niche that proved highly successful. Today, Tufts University is known for the quality of its programs, its research, and its attention to the undergraduate experience. It has embraced the idea of being a "student-centered research university."[67]

The student-centered university is both a relatively new concept and, as yet, somewhat undefined. Nevertheless, the term sends a clear message as to the kind of university to which the leadership and community aspire – one where faculty educational services and staff administrative operations are integrated to meet individual students where they are, where the academic, career, and human development aspects of the student's personal growth are closely linked. A student-centered university provides students with customized attention from administrative, business, academic, psychosocial, and communal services to give them a sense of being welcomed and included. It demonstrates through its actions, every day and for every student, that it cares deeply about their personal growth and development.

It is not enough for a university to simply reorganize its existing organizational chart. Achieving genuine student-centeredness requires a wholesale rethinking of the curricular program and the activities that engage faculty and staff. Universities must examine their functions from the perspective of changing student populations who are, after all, the ultimate users of the university's services. Universities need both structural and cultural changes to foster more integrated professional roles, functions, and accountability.

Individual universities can identify their own paths to integrating student services – there is no single prescription. It is, however, important that universities begin by assessing the current student experience and identifying areas that chafe students and their families. Administrators should focus on ways to amend current processes, procedures, and subsequently job descriptions to make operations work more seamlessly from the student perspective. I present several strategies to better align structure and culture to serve institutional missions in this book's final chapter.

The disruptions of 2020–2021 are an opportunity for universities to implement a broader, more holistic student-centered vision, one informed by the management strategies university leaders have devised in response to past financial challenges. Like Chancellor Shaw amid cutbacks at Syracuse, administrators facing the challenge of pandemic-induced increased expenses and decreased revenue should consider which areas of the university are most vital to the student experience and reallocate their funds accordingly. Georgetown University has already moved in this direction, making deep strategic budget reductions in response to the deficits caused by the 2020–2021 pandemic. Hopefully, these changes will allow it and other schools to emerge stronger and more focused on the student experience.

Such changes require strong leadership sensitive to the unique culture of residential higher education. Larger issues about the way the institution operates and interacts with the changing student body equally merit our attention, and I will address them in greater detail throughout this volume.

Notes

1 "Total Undergraduate Fall Enrollment in Degree-Granting Postsecondary Institutions, by Attendance Status, Sex of Student, and Control and Level of Institution: Selected Years, 1970 through 2028," table 303.70, National

Center for Education Statistics, accessed January 21, 2020, http://nces.ed .gov/programs/digest/d18/tables/dt18_303.70.asp. This book focuses on the largest enrolled segment of higher education, public and private nonprofit four-year colleges and universities. Across all sectors of higher education in 2017, six million students were enrolled in nonprofit and for-profit two-year colleges, as well as another 655,471 in four-year for-profit colleges and universities.

2 For further information, see Caitlin Zaloom, *Indebted: How Families Make College Work at Any Cost* (Princeton, NJ: Princeton University Press, 2019).

3 "Graduation Rate from First Institution Attended for First-Time, Full-Time Bachelor's Degree-Seeking Students at 4-Year Postsecondary Institutions, by Race/Ethnicity, Time to Completion, Sex, Control of Institution, and Percentage of Applications Accepted: Selected Cohort Entry Years, 1996 through 2013," table 326.10, National Center for Education Statistics, accessed April 11, 2021, https://nces.ed.gov/programs/digest/d20/tables /dt20_326.10.asp. Note that the graduation rate for students after four years of study at for-profit, four-year institutions is 19.4 percent.

4 National Center for Education Statistics, "Graduation Rate," table 326.10.

5 National Center for Education Statistics, "Graduation Rate," table 326.10. Note that the graduation rate for students after six years of study at for-profit, four-year institutions is 26.3 percent.

6 For further information, see David Kirp, *The College Dropout Scandal* (New York: Oxford University Press, 2019).

7 Mark Schneider and Lu Michelle Yin, *The High Cost of Low Graduation Rates: How Much Does Dropping Out of College Really Cost?* (Washington, DC: American Institutes for Research, 2011), 4, accessed October 30, 2019, https://files.eric.ed.gov/fulltext/ED523102.pdf. For more information, see Kirp's *College Dropout Scandal*.

8 Alexander W. Astin, *Four Critical Years: Effects of College on Beliefs, Attitudes, and Knowledge* (San Francisco: Jossey-Bass, 1977), 6.

9 Anthony Abraham Jack, *The Privileged Poor: How Elite Colleges Are Failing Disadvantaged Students* (Cambridge, MA: Harvard University Press, 2019), 190.

10 John R. Thelin, *A History of American Higher Education*, 2nd ed. (Baltimore: Johns Hopkins University Press, 2011), 328.

11 See Rachel Gable, *The Hidden Curriculum: First Generation Students at Legacy Universities* (Princeton, NJ: Princeton University Press, 2021).

12 "List of 2018 Digest Tables," tables 301.20, 302.10, 302.20, and 302.60, National Center for Education Statistics, accessed August 20, 2019, https:// nces.ed.gov/programs/digest/2018menu_tables.asp. The findings summarized by the National Center for Education Statistics show that the numbers of students who earned the bachelor's degree grew from 1,237,875 in 2000 to 1,956,032 in 2017. They also show a sustained trend from 2000 through 2017 of increases in overall enrollments for both men and women. However, women make up a larger percentage of enrollments and graduation rates based

on their percentage of the population. The percentage of college enrollments among Black eighteen- to twenty-four-year-olds increased by 6 percent between 2000 and 2017. During this same period, the percentage of Hispanic eighteen- to twenty-four-year-olds who were enrolled in college grew by 4.5 percent, and the percentage of Asian eighteen- to twenty-four-year-olds who were enrolled in college increased by 8.8 percent. Data prepared by the US Census Current Population Survey also provide a historical overview of the percentage of high school graduates who have enrolled or graduated within six years from four-year colleges and universities.

13 Thomas D. Snyder, Cristobal de Brey, and Sally A. Dillow, *Digest of Education Statistics 2017* (Washington, DC: National Center for Education Statistics, 2019), 395, table 302.30. According to the Current Population Survey conducted by the US Census, in a time of increasing college enrollments from 2000 to 2016, the percentage of low-income students enrolled in college increased by 15.7 percent. Over the same period, middle-income students increased by 5.5 percent and high-income students increased by 6.8 percent. Note that this number includes community colleges.

14 Jean M. Twenge et al., "Age, Period, and Cohort Trends in Mood Disorder Indicators and Suicide-Related Outcomes in a Nationally Representative Dataset, 2005–2017," *Journal of Abnormal Psychology* 128, no. 3 (2019): 185–199, accessed June 5, 2020, doi.org/10.1037/abn0000410.

15 American College Health Association, *American College Health Association – National College Health Assessment II: Reference Group Data Report – Fall 2018* (Silver Spring, MD: American College Health Association, 2018), 32, accessed August 20, 2019, www.acha.org/documents/ncha/NCHA-II_Fall _2018_Reference_Group_Data_Report.pdf.

16 Ted Mitchell and Suzanne Ortega, "Mental Health Challenges Require Urgent Response," *Inside Higher Ed*, October 29, 2019, accessed October 30, 2019, www.insidehighered.com/views/2019/10/29/students-mental -health-shouldnt-be-responsibility-campus-counseling-centers-alone.

17 William Wan, "The Coronavirus Pandemic Is Pushing America into a Mental Health Crisis," *Washington Post*, May 4, 2020, 12:57 p.m. EDT, accessed June 5, 2020, www.washingtonpost.com/health/2020/05/04/mental-health -coronavirus/.

18 American College Health Association, *American College Health Association – National College Health Assessment II: Reference Group Data Report – Spring 2019* (Silver Spring, MD: American College Health Association, 2019), 30–32, accessed December 16, 2020, www.acha.org/documents/ncha /NCHA-II_SPRING_2019_US_REFERENCE_GROUP_DATA_REPORT .pdf.

19 Holly Hedegaard, Sally Curtin, and Margaret Warner, *Suicide Rates in the United States Continue to Increase*, NCHS Data Brief no. 309 (Hyattsville, MD: National Center for Health Statistics, 2018), 2, accessed July 31, 2019, www.cdc.gov/nchs/products/databriefs/db309.htm.

20 Hedegaard, Curtin, and Wagner, *Suicide Rates*, 3.

21 Sarah Ketchen Lipson et al., "Gender Minority Mental Health in the US: Results of a National Survey of College Campuses," *American Journal of Preventive Medicine* 57, no. 3 (September 2019): 293.

22 Center for Collegiate Mental Health, *2015 Annual Report*, January 2016, accessed April 24, 2019, http://sites.psu.edu/ccmh/files/2017/10/2015_2, CCMH_Report_1–18-2015-yq3vik.pdf.

23 Carolyn Crist, "Mental Health Diagnoses Rising among US College Students," *Reuters*, November 1, 2018, 2:33 p.m., accessed October 21, 2020, www.reuters.com/article/us-health-mental-college/mental-health-diag noses-rising-among-u-s-college-students-idUSKCN1N65U8.

24 Jean M. Twenge et al., "Increases in Depressive Symptoms, Suicide-Related Outcomes, and Suicide Rates among US Adolescents after 2010 and Links to Increased New Media Screen Time," *Clinical Psychological Science* 6, no. 1 (2018): 3–17. Also see Jean M. Twenge et al., "Decreases in Psychological Well-Being among American Adolescents after 2012 and Links to Screen Time during the Rise of Smartphone Technology," *Emotion* 18, no. 6 (2018): 765–780, accessed November 5, 2019, doi.org/10.1037/emo0000403.

25 Jenny Radesky and Randy Kulman, "My Kids Are on Screens All Day: Is That Okay?," *ADDitude Magazine*, last updated January 21, 2022, accessed June 5, 2020, www.additudemag.com/screen-time-limits-during-pandemic/.

26 "Mobile Fact Sheet," Pew Research Center, April 7, 2021, accessed June 2, 2021, www.pewresearch.org/internet/fact-sheet/mobile/.

27 Asurion, "Americans Check Their Phones 96 Times a Day," press release, November 21, 2019, accessed June 5, 2020, www.asurion.com/about/press -releases/americans-check-their-phones-96-times-a-day/.

28 Deloitte, *Global Mobile Consumer Survey: US Edition*, 2018, accessed October 30, 2019, www2.deloitte.com/content/dam/Deloitte/us/Documents/tech nology-media-telecommunications/us-tmt-global-mobile-consumer-survey-extended-deck-2018.pdf.

29 Robert Groves, "Student-Centered," *The Provost's Blog*, March 15, 2017, accessed April 23, 2019, https://blog.provost.georgetown.edu/student-cen tered/.

30 National Center for Education Statistics, *Factors That Influence Student College Choice*, November 2018, figure 1, accessed May 16, 2019, https:// nces.ed.gov/pubs2019/2019119.pdf.

31 Civitas Learning, "One Quarter of Current College Students Believe It Will Be Difficult to Graduate; Cite Anxiety, Non-Academic Responsibilities as Top Barriers to Completion," press release, July 12, 2018, accessed April 23, 2019, www.civitaslearning.com/press/one-quarter-of-current-college-student s-believe-it-will-be-difficult-to-graduate-cite-anxiety-non-academic-responsibi lities-as-top-barriers-to-completion/.

32 Thelin, *Higher Education*, 314.

33 See William G. Bowen and Eugene M. Tobin, *Locus of Authority: The Evolution of Faculty Roles in the Governance of Higher Education* (Princeton, NJ: Princeton University Press, 2015).

34 Geoffrey M. Cox, *Theorizing the Resilience of American Higher Education: How Colleges and Universities Adapt to Changing Social and Economic Conditions* (New York: Routledge, 2019), 28.

35 See David J. Staley, *Alternative Universities: Speculative Design for Innovation in Higher Education* (Baltimore: Johns Hopkins University Press, 2019) for creative ideas for larger-scale change.

36 See Chris W. Gallagher, *College Made Whole: Integrative Learning for a Divided World* (Baltimore: Johns Hopkins University Press, 2019).

37 For examples, see Michelle Burke et al., *Predictive Analysis of Student Data: A Focus on Engagement and Behavior* (Washington, DC: NASPA: Student Affairs Administrators in Higher Education, 2017), www.naspa.org/images /uploads/main/PREDICTIVE_FULL_4-7-17_DOWNLOAD.pdf; Timothy M. Renick, "How to Best Harness Student-Success Technology," *Chronicle of Higher Education*, July 1, 2018, www.chronicle.com/article/how-to-best -harness-student-success-technology/; Jeffrey R. Young, "What Clicks from 70,000 Courses Reveal about Student Learning," *Chronicle of Higher Education*, September 7, 2016, www.chronicle.com/article/what-clicks-from -70-000-courses-reveal-about-student-learning/; Jennifer Patterson Lorenzetti, "The Power of Predictive Analytics for Student Retention," *Academic Briefing*, June 14, 2017, www.academicbriefing.com/marketing/retention/analytics-stu dent-retention/; Civitas Learning, "Measuring Supplemental Instruction Direct Impact on Persistence," accessed December 2, 2019, https://media .civitaslearning.com/wp-content/uploads/sites/3/2020/02/Civitas_Learning_ University_Missouri_Kansas_City_CASE_STUDY_Impact.pdf?_ga=2.2489 17319.1528597137.1586787617-1303241950.1580755375; Chrissy Coley, Tim Coley, and Katie Lynch-Holmes, *Retention and Student Success: Implementing Strategies That Make a Difference* (Fairfax, VA: Ellucian, 2016), www.ellucian.com/assets/en/white-paper/whitepaper-retention-and -student-success.pdf; and Andrew W. Gumbel, *Won't Lose this Dream: How an Upstart Urban University Rewrote the Rule of a Broken System* (New York: The New Press, 2020).

38 Peter L. Hinrichs, "Trends in Expenditures by US Colleges and Universities, 1987–2013," *Economic Commentary, Federal Reserve Bank of Cleveland*, September 14, 2016, accessed April 23, 2019, www.clevelandfed.org/en/news room-and-events/publications/economic-commentary/2016-economic-commen taries/ec-201610-trends-in-expenditures-by-us-colleges-and-universities.aspx.

39 Michael Hammer and James Champy, *Reengineering the Corporation: A Manifesto for Business Revolution* (New York: HarperBusiness, 1993), 33.

40 Maria Halkias, "A One-of-A-Kind, No Checkout Sam's Club Is about to Open on Lower Greenville in Dallas," *Dallas Morning News*, October 28, 2018, 11:00 p.m. CDT, accessed April 23, 2019, www.dallasnews.com/busi ness/retail/2018/10/29/a-one-of-a-kind-no-checkout-sam-s-club-is-about-to-open- on-lower-greenville-in-dallas/.

41 Peter Felten et al., *The Undergraduate Experience: Focusing Institutions on What Matters Most* (San Francisco: Jossey-Bass, 2016), 7.

42 For additional information, see Matilda White Riley, Robert L. Kahn, and Anne Foner, eds., *Age and Structural Lag: Society's Failure to Provide Meaningful Opportunities in Work, Family, and Leisure* (New York: John H. Wiley & Sons, 1994).

43 Amanda Woods, "Students Fear Dorm Mold Led to Freshman's Adenovirus Death," *New York Post*, November 23, 2018, 2:37 p.m. EST, accessed August 22, 2019, https://nypost.com/2018/11/23/students-fear-dorm-mold-prob lem-led-to-freshmans-adenovirus-death/.

44 For an extensive review of the literature, see George D. Kuh et al., *What Matters to Student Success: A Review of the Literature; Commissioned Report for the National Symposium on Postsecondary Student Success: Spearheading a Dialog on Student Success* (Washington, DC: National Postsecondary Education Cooperative, 2006), https://nces.ed.gov/npec/pdf/Kuh_Team _Report.pdf.

45 Vincent Tinto, "Dropout from Higher Education: A Theoretical Synthesis of Recent Research," *Review of Educational Research* 45, no. 1 (March 1975): 89–125; Vincent Tinto, *Leaving College: Rethinking the Causes and Cures of Student Attrition*, 2nd ed. (Chicago: University of Chicago Press, 1993), 84–137.

46 Tinto, *Leaving College*, 118.

47 See Kuh et al., *What Matters*.

48 Vincent Tinto, *Completing College: Rethinking Institutional Action* (Chicago: University of Chicago Press, 2012), 116–117.

49 Alan Seidman, "Taking Action: A Retention Formula and Model for Student Success," in *College Student Retention: Formula for Student Success*, 2nd ed., ed. Alan Seidman (Lanham, MD: Rowman & Littlefield Publishers, 2012), 267–284.

50 See John P. Bean and Shevawn Bogdan Eaton, "A Psychological Model of College Student Retention," in *Reworking the Student Departure Puzzle*, ed. John M. Braxton (Nashville, TN: Vanderbilt University Press, 2000), 48–61.

51 Bean and Eaton, "Psychological Model," 57.

52 Alexander W. Astin and Leticia Oseguera, "Pre-College and Institutional Influences on Degree Attainment," in *College Student Retention: Formula for Student Success*, 2nd ed., ed. Alan Seidman (Lanham, MD: Rowman & Littlefield Publishers, 2012), 134–135.

53 Edward P. St. John et al., "Economic Influences on Persistence Reconsidered: How Can Finance Research Inform the Reconceptualization of Persistence Models?," in *Reworking the Student Departure Puzzle*, ed. John M. Braxton (Nashville, TN: Vanderbilt University Press, 2000), 29–47.

54 Glen J. Godwin and William T. Markham, "First Encounters of the Bureaucratic Kind: Early Freshman Experiences with a Campus Bureaucracy," *Journal of Higher Education* 67, no. 6 (November–December 1996): 675–676, accessed October 7, 2020, doi.org/10.2307/2943816.

55 Kuh et al., *What Matters*, 55.

56 Richard Delgado and Jean Stefancic, *Critical Race Theory: An Introduction* (New York: New York University Press, 2001), 6–9, accessed October 12,

2020, http://uniteyouthdublin.files.wordpress.com/2015/01/richard_delgad o_jean_stefancic_critical_race_thbookfi-org-1.pdf.

57 For more detail on critical race theory, see Dorian L. McCoy and Dirk J. Rodricks, "Critical Race Theory in Higher Education: 20 Years of Theoretical and Research Innovations," *ASHE Higher Education Report* 41, no. 3 (April 2015): 1–117.

58 Vincent Tinto, "Moving from Theory to Action: A Model of Institutional Action for Student Success," *College Student Retention: Formula for Student Success*, 2nd ed., ed. Alan Seidman (Lanham, MD: Rowman & Littlefield Publishers, 2012), 263.

59 Kenneth A. Shaw, *The Intentional Leader* (Syracuse, NY: Syracuse University Press, 2005), 149.

60 Shaw, *Intentional Leader*, 150.

61 Richard M. Freeland, *Transforming the Urban University: Northeastern, 1996–2006* (Philadelphia: University of Pennsylvania Press, 2019), 71–92.

62 Groves, "Student-Centered."

63 Megan Hanks, "UMBC Leads Nation in Producing African-American Undergraduates Who Pursue MD-PhDs," *UMBC News*, January 2, 2018, accessed August 22, 2019, https://news.umbc.edu/umbc-leads-nation-in-pro ducing-african-american-undergraduates-who-pursue-m-d-ph-d-s/. Note that this data was prepared by the Association of American Medical Colleges.

64 Cammille Powell, "Bridging the Gaps: Connecting Student Services to Promote Student Success," *EdSurge*, April 4, 2018, accessed August 22, 2019, www.edsurge.com/news/2018-04-04-bridging-the-gaps-connecting-stu dent-services-to-promote-student-success.

65 Clayton M. Christensen and Henry J. Eyring, *The Innovative University: Changing the DNA of Higher Education from the Inside Out* (San Francisco: Jossey-Bass, 2011), 351–352.

66 Richard M. Freeland, *Academia's Golden Age: Universities in Massachusetts, 1945–1970* (New York: Oxford University Press, 1992), 180.

67 "Academics at Tufts," Tufts University, accessed September 8, 2020, https:// admissions.tufts.edu/discover-tufts/academics/.

CHAPTER 3

University Tradition and Conformity: Insights and Persistence

Many leaders have attempted large-scale change in the university, only to find themselves facing no-confidence votes from their faculty or a lack of support from their board. Yet even in the face of such deep-seated traditions and beliefs, the university has adapted over time. Those who have made an art of institutional change know that it requires a deep understanding of the history of the institution in question along with an appreciation of the values and traditions that its community holds to be nearly sacred.[1]

The form of the American residential college and university has evolved over nearly four hundred years. Over a long gestation that started with Harvard University and drew on traditions from the great European academies, the American university has grown in numbers and approaches. Many of the traditions and the underlying organizational structure we observe today crystallized around one hundred years ago. These traditions reflect deeply held beliefs that have been handed down from one generation of academics to the next. They are enshrined by normative standards that are attached to accreditation standards and reinforced by peer expectations.

What follows is a brief historical survey of the development of the modern American residential college or university, offered to help guide those seeking to influence its path forward. The powerful influences of tradition and conformity remain ever-present today – even in the wake of a global pandemic and calls for greater racial justice. Anyone hoping to effect systemic change with the intent of better aligning campuses with students' needs would do well to heed these signposts.

Despite the many challenges the modern university faces, it has, for the most part, persisted across a century of social transformation. Its resilience and determination to weather the darkest of times have cloaked the university with a sense of destiny and permanence as a pivotal American institution. These are salient factors in imagining how the university might emerge stronger and better after the disruptive events of 2020 and 2021.

Many historians point to the years between 1890 and 1910 as the formative era of the American university. A key moment came a few decades earlier when Charles Eliot was appointed president of Harvard University in 1869. Over the course of his influential forty-year presidency, much of the structure and organization of the contemporary university came into being. This dynamic period also generated many of the traditions to which we adhere today, and that we missed in times of social distancing.

Up until the late 1800s, the administration of the American university or college was often led, or more accurately, directed, by a president. The faculty of that era were laborers in a setting that was rather uninspiring and intellectually laborious by today's standards. The primary instructional method involved "daily recitations and a punitive system of grading" with a curriculum composed of "classical study of languages, science and mathematics with the aim of building character and promoting distinctive habits of thought."[2] The academic traditions of the early American colleges were distinct from what was about to emerge in the wake of the rapid technological and societal advances of the late nineteenth century.

Eventually, however, the university was touched by the large-scale technological, organizational, and economic forces that gripped the nation in the late nineteenth century. Virtually every aspect of society was influenced as the nation rose to become a powerhouse based on technology, economic growth, and innovation. The first automobile appeared in 1886, just a year after the first skyscraper appeared on the streets of Chicago. The Wright brothers took flight in 1903. Electrification spread quickly to cities between 1896 and 1910. In 1885 there were fewer than 350,000 telephones in use throughout the United States, but just 15 years later nearly 8 million telephones connected American homes and businesses.[3] A national ethos of professionalism and the scientific principles of organization, hierarchy, and management emerged in business and industry, while the techniques of measurement, statistics, and financial planning grew in sophistication. These organizational approaches, business techniques, and administrative operations were essential to effectively manage the scale and scope of thriving new American industries and businesses. For many of these organizations, it meant shifting from autocratic empires where employees' labor, tasks, and hours were at the discretion of the employer, to more professional-managerial arrangements.

American entrepreneurs developed systems of efficiency that, accompanied by a level of risk-taking, built highly profitable industries and companies. For example, thirty-five years after Andrew Carnegie started an iron-producing corporation in 1865, the United States was producing more steel than all the other leading world producers combined.[4] In the meatpacking industry, Gustavus Swift devised a replicable system known as the vertical integration of production, whereby all stages of production from the raw material to finished products were controlled by one company, leading to greater efficiencies and profitability. John D. Rockefeller developed the related concept of horizontal integration, squeezing out competitors and leaving them little option but to become part of his large conglomerate. As a result, Rockefeller gained control of most of the nation's oil manufacturing capacity. Similar strategic consolidations took place in other industries. With little regulation, the new barons of industry created both lower-paid heavy labor jobs in coal mines, oil production, and steel mills, as well as jobs that demanded the know-how and management skills associated with being a college graduate.[5]

This was also a time when the United States set its sights on becoming a leading world power. The War of 1898 with Spain brought the Philippines, Guam, Puerto Rico, and Cuba into the possession of the United States. In 1901, following the assassination of President McKinley, Theodore Roosevelt became president of the United States. A savvy student of world affairs, Roosevelt believed that the USA had a role in the "proper policing of the world."[6] Roosevelt brought forth an era of imperialism and US expansionism that reverberated through many aspects of American life, including the development of the university.

Contributions emerging from applied research by inventors and innovators, including those in government-sponsored organizations, enhanced all of this ambition. General Electric established an applied research laboratory in 1900; other industries soon followed suit with their own laboratories. The federal government supported research through the Bureau of Fisheries, the Bureau of Standards, and the Department of Agriculture. In 1887 Congress passed the Hatch Act, establishing a nationwide network of agricultural experimental stations linked to the land grant colleges that were established by the Morrill Act of 1862.[7] With the founding of Johns Hopkins University in 1876, the American vision for the research university came into being and was molded by a prescient board of trustees, a transformative president, and a talented faculty. Its doctoral graduates swiftly outnumbered those of Ivy League campuses and with their hiring at other leading universities became the forebearers of the modern American research university.[8] Other universities, following that path, expanded their research capabilities.[9]

This broader cauldron of national ambition, organizational management, and intellectual ferment created space for the university to thrive. Early twentieth-century ideas about corporate form shaped the organizational structure the expanding university would take. Many corporations have since undergone dramatic changes in management style and structure, but the university – as we shall see – remains tightly bound to its roots.

The Organizational Origins of the Modern University

At the beginning of the twentieth century, the emerging development of universities intertwined with the needs of the nation. The scale and scope of postsecondary education demanded a more robust infrastructure to accommodate the growing numbers of students who sought to prepare for the expanding opportunities in business and industry. From 1890 to 1910 US enrollments in colleges and universities more than doubled, growing from 156,756 to 355,430.[10] Such growth required much more complex management than what existed in the small colleges of the 1800s. Increasingly, the universities hired faculty who held appropriate doctoral degrees. Business leaders who served on college and university boards of overseers sought a more professional and business-like organization to replace the prevailing structure, or lack thereof, at the time. Their oversight and direction of the university encouraged presidents to develop managerial plans reflecting best practices from the private sector.

During this period, reformers in both the private corporate and public sectors trumpeted the merits of professionalism. They sought to reform many questionable business practices, including the patronage system in hiring, no-bid contracts, and exploitative employee oversight. One example of reform initiatives includes the 1883 Civil Service Reform Act, which required some categories of federal government jobs to be filled based on merit rather than as political spoils. The national mood expected increased management, oversight, and professionalism in private and public institutions, and the academy was no exception.

Among the earliest leaders in the development of university management and administration were the aforementioned president of Harvard University, Charles Eliot, and the president of the University of Michigan, James Angell. Each managed their institution with a central administrative staff as early as the 1870s and 1880s.[11] Soon other university presidents, supported by their boards, adopted administrative structures and the accompanying personnel. Over time, and to accommodate growth, college and university presidents hired and developed professional teams and an organizational structure that still exists today. From 1890 to 1910, the professional staff working in the sector of higher education more than doubled from 15,809 to 36,480 – and this during a period when the number of colleges and universities actually declined slightly (from 977 to 951).[12]

By the early 1900s, faculty members, who previously were treated as laborers and were primarily "responsible for maintaining discipline, building character, and passing on wisdom to their students,"[13] became increasingly professionalized. They allied themselves with academic departments organized around their academic disciplines and created national associations linking colleagues across the United States. These departments became the very bones of the university, as they remain today. Deans and department chairs became responsible for the oversight of the academic unit. Universities retained a new generation of faculty, one with curricular expertise and preparation in their respective academic disciplines. This professionalization backed by advanced degrees, including the PhD, prompted "faculty members to demand greater autonomy and academic freedom in order to carry out their expanded responsibilities as teachers and researchers."[14]

As with laborers in other industries, it was not uncommon for faculty to demand a greater say in university operations. Faculty members argued that their expertise merited a voice in determining faculty qualifications for hiring. Presidents, many of whom served long terms, began gradually relinquishing responsibilities to the faculty, but not necessarily to the professional administrative staff. This transition was not without some tension, however, since the business leaders who dominated the college or university boardroom were less enamored with faculty acquisition of authority. As historian Larry G. Gerber notes, "In the end, however, by recruiting strong faculty members committed to an ideal of professionalism, the powerful presidents of the late nineteenth century planted the seeds for the reduction of unilateral administrative authority."[15]

It was here, in the formative years of the century, where organizational models were needed to better manage the increasing complexity and size of business, industry, government, and university operations. Perhaps the most influential intellectual work on bureaucratic structures was being produced in Germany by Max Weber. His ideas began to filter across the Atlantic, and Weber accepted an invitation from Harvard professor Hugo

Munsterberg to attend a meeting of world-renowned scholars in St. Louis, Missouri in 1904.[16] Most of Weber's work was not translated into English until the 1920s, yet his ideas were influential in shaping American organizational structures.

Weber idealized a hierarchy-based organizational structure, with formal lines of communication and authority linking different levels of authority. His model deviated from previous organizational structures in which individual laborers reported to the central executive or owner, replacing it with one in which organized offices or group units reported to the executive. Different divisions within the organization would house specialists trained to carry out their duties; they would report through a chain of command that eventually led to an executive in charge. Weber argued that this structure would foster objective, rational, legal, and fact-based decisions. A worker's obligations would be clearly defined and focused on expertise related to the work itself. The structure marked a major change from systems in which individuals who lacked specialized expertise performed tasks assigned by the person in charge, with little clarity as to working hours or duties.

Weber argues, "The decisive reason for the advance of bureaucratic organization has always been its purely technical superiority over any other form of organization."[17] He described his vision of bureaucracy as an improvement over prior organizational models: "Precision, speed, unambiguity, knowledge of the files, continuity, discretion unity, strict subordination, reduction of friction and of material and personnel costs – these are raised to the optimum point in the strictly bureaucratic administration."[18] This form of bureaucratic structure also has some elasticity, having the ability to grow and expand with additional reporting units as needed to better fulfill a changing organization's mission and functions. Over time, this form of bureaucracy became the prevalent structure in larger organizations with multiple administrative units. And, beginning with the most influential academic universities, colleges and universities also adopted it – but with special privileges enjoyed only by the faculty.

"In 1897," Veysey notes, "one could observe two countertendencies at work in American higher education: fragmentation and centralization."[19] On one hand, university and college leadership sought to impose greater uniformity in campus administrative operations via centralized authority. On the other, faculty demanded greater independence and autonomy in decision-making. In the midst of this, universities continued to add layers of bureaucracy and hired ever-increasing numbers of skilled personnel to manage their increasingly complex operations.

In 1920 the concept of faculty-shared governance became codified as a principle in colleges and universities. At that time, the American Association of University Professors Committee on College and University Governance issued a statement that emphasized the faculty role in key decisions regarding operations and management, including the selection of leadership; the ability to hire and review other faculty; the responsibility to make decisions about curricula and academic programs; and, finally, the development of the campus budget.[20] Faculty engagement remains a salient factor in the modern university; anyone who does not recognize this does so at their own peril.

Led by university presidents with dreams as big as those of the industrialists and aided by their philanthropic spirit, the modern university took root. While these leaders had traditionally modeled their institutions on the image of the great European universities, the moment had arrived for a new, vibrant, American form. The faculty and the leaders of some of the most influential American colleges and universities shared a belief that excellence rested upon a broad exposure to the liberal arts ingrained with a foundation in the arts, humanities, social sciences, life sciences, and physical sciences.

In 1900, fourteen universities established the prestigious and influential American Association of Universities (AAU) to distinguish themselves from other rising universities. They also hoped to develop shared standards in the area of graduate education, which had only recently arrived on American shores. Of the fourteen, three were the public universities of California, Wisconsin, and Michigan. The remaining eleven, all private, were, in alphabetical order: Catholic, Chicago, Clark, Columbia, Cornell, Harvard, Johns Hopkins, Leland Stanford, Jr. (soon to be Stanford), Princeton, Pennsylvania, and Yale. In 1909, the distinguished group expanded to include eight additional public universities – balancing the membership of the AAU halfway between public and private academies. The additions included the flagship campuses of Indiana, Illinois, Iowa, Kansas, Minnesota, Missouri, Nebraska, and Virginia.

Today, Catholic University, Clark University, and the University of Nebraska-Lincoln are no longer members of the AAU. Mostly, however, this has been a story of expansion rather than contraction. Over the years, the AAU has grown to include sixty-five research universities, institutions endowed with strong financial backing and recognized as world-class research centers. Each university in this original elite 1900 club sought academic excellence in what was and still is a highly competitive marketplace. One way of fostering greater exclusivity was by banding together and forming the AAU community to share ideas, ensure high academic standards, and serve as models for aspiring schools. One must note that the historical development of these selective universities implicitly or explicitly excluded certain kinds of institutions, and by extension, certain kinds of people. Absent were exclusively women's colleges and historically Black colleges and universities, even if they had graduate programs. Almost all of the original AAU universities remain preeminent institutions today. Their leadership and faculty remain concerned, even preoccupied, with stature, prestige, and academic excellence. Other universities, seeking similar prestige, have emulated many of the attributes and aspects of the AAU members.[21]

One of the defining qualities of the turn-of-the-century American university was a focus on research. University leaders were eager to gain the respect of national and international intellectuals, particularly those associated with great European universities. Philanthropists associated with the business empires founded during the American Industrial Revolution gave generously to these emerging influential American universities. Individuals such as Rockefeller, Duke, Vanderbilt, Hearst, Stanford, Hopkins, Field, Tulane, Cornell, Mellon, and Carnegie all provided large financial gifts to universities before and during this expansionist period in higher education. Their wealth provided the decisive resources that allowed university leaders to build endowments and a margin of excellence. Their philanthropy, while a symbol of generosity, was also a way to enshrine their names for posterity in institutions whose influence – they hoped – would be measured over centuries.

Even the seeds of university rankings and comparative academic strength were evident by 1910 when journalist and science writer Edwin E. Slosson published *Great American Universities*. Slosson earned his PhD in chemistry in 1902 and in 1904 became editor of *The Independent*.[22] As part of his assignment, he visited and wrote about universities across the United States. These articles eventually became a book in which he identified fourteen universities as the "great" American universities.[23] Perhaps *The Independent*, a bygone relic, was a precursor of the much more extensive *US News & World Report Best Colleges* annual ranking.

Referring to the development of the university at a considerably later time, American studies scholar and former university president Richard Freeland wrote that the emergence of the research university "created a compelling vision of excellence and stature at the top of the nation's academic pecking order."[24] Aspiring university leaders pursued that vision, emulating the success of leading universities, fostering a process that had become evident by 1910 and remains so today.

The basic administrative structure of president, dean, department chair, and faculty was institutionalized throughout higher education by the early 1900s. The same can be said for the administrative structure for the emerging professional staff. As a result, campuses began to produce certain administrative procedures that will be familiar to contemporary students of the university. In 1896, Harvard produced variants of what we know as punch cards for course registration.[25] In 1902, Columbia University created the administrative structure to manage the increasing complexity of billing and course registration.[26] Universities hired administrators for these areas, and they, in turn, created opportunities for future administrators. Universities began establishing standard course credit hours, and students selected courses from expanded catalogs. Other universities followed their lead and added administrators to manage their expanding functions.

The Emergence of Institutional Isomorphism

Most of the functions of higher education associated with student services – career services, financial aid, registration, advising, enrollment management, counseling, spiritual life, student accounts, student affairs, recreation programs, clubs, Greek life, academic support, and health services, along with the people to manage them – all grew out of the early 1900s. Over the decades, each professional area developed its own identity and performance standards that would eventually become common across colleges and universities. It is to these services, which directly impact students, that we will direct our attention in the following chapters.

Organizational theorists contend that once an organizational field – in this case, academic and professional service areas in universities – has been established, "powerful forces emerge that lead them to become more similar to one another."[27] These forces include the search for enhanced reputation, a response to regulatory oversight, mobility among professionals in specialized sectors that, over time, establish a pattern of conformity. In addition these forces influence professional guilds and membership societies, impact sources of funding and their predispositions, reinforces bureaucratic inertia, and contributes to priority setting among influential external constituencies. In higher education, the prevailing culture of competition for prestige and stature fostered a process in which leaders of universities large and small, public and private, replicated the administrative structures of those institutions deemed successful. These are only some of the forces that prompt higher education institutions to mimic one another and foster what Frumkin and Galaskiewicz call "institutional isomorphism."[28]

While the structure of universities follows a common pattern, implementation varies, resulting in differences across campuses in the reporting lines of authority and chain of accountability. The director of athletics, for example, might report to a president or an executive supervising student affairs, to the provost, or someone else – this is part of campus distinctiveness, masking what actually is likely a level of sameness. This variability of reporting lines can be seen in other units, as well, such as the executive leadership in marketing and communications, student affairs, information technology, housing, registration, or enrollment management. The functions exist, but the specific reporting lines may vary across settings. Still, universities pride themselves on their uniqueness and distinctiveness such as size, number of students, private or public setting, location, cultural norms, facilities, historic academic accomplishments, distinctive programs, graduate or doctoral programs, and traditions. The significance of competitive athletics, social life, internships, study abroad, research focus, national rankings, religiosity, endowed wealth, academic emphases and specializations, multidisciplinarity, unique cultural identity, work environment, collegiality, and political expression, for example, all can vary in intensity across campuses. It is here where campuses express their differences. But these differences belie their essential uniformity – a uniformity that arose around the turn of the twentieth century and endures today.

University Expansionism

On the business side of the university, the simultaneous growth of revenue, budgets, endowments, and funded research required administrators to hire professionals with expertise in investment and money management. Following World War II, the federal government vastly expanded its support for academic research. In response, the university established compliance units to manage grants and contracts. Eventually, their duties would include overseeing researchers' adherence to regulations around human subjects, animal care, safety protocols, and technology transfer.

Richard Freeland points to 1945–1970 as the "golden age of the university." Freeland identifies three forces that shaped the golden age: (1) institutional ambition wherein academic distinction, pride, and reputation were at the forefront of institution-building; (2) intellectualism and the power of influential ideas generated by scholarship and pathbreaking research; and (3) "organizational dynamics" that involved the "political characteristics and administrative capabilities of universities."[29] One of the reasons these forces were so impactful in the golden age is that they were deeply rooted in the formative age of the American research university. While the structure, culture, and operations remained basically the same, what was different was the scale, scope, intensity, complexity, and subsequent impact.

Concomitant with these broad forces for research expansion were the dynamics of the Cold War competition, with substantial funds linked to the emerging needs of the defense establishment. On October 4, 1957, the Soviet Union launched Sputnik, the first artificial satellite to orbit Earth. American leadership became preoccupied with a perceived gap in scientific leadership between the United States and the Soviet Union, accelerating the forces associated with university research growth. As a result, additional federal dollars flowed to America's emerging research universities, further fueling the golden age. In addition to research funding, in 1958 Congress passed the National Defense Education Act, which provided funds for college student loans and support for college programs in the sciences and mathematics. The act included funding for foreign languages along with support for college libraries. The infusion of these resources, particularly low-cost educational loans, further accelerated college and university enrollments.[30] The competitive race among American universities, coupled with the international race to lead the world in research and development, was fully engaged.

During this expansionist golden age following 1945, universities went on a facilities-building spree that complemented the architectural prowess of the previous century. Some of the architectural gems from the earlier round of expansion included Memorial Church at Stanford; the grounds at Harvard, Yale, Vanderbilt, Princeton, Amherst, and Williams; the libraries at the University of Virginia and Columbia; the arch at the dormitory quadrangle at the University of Pennsylvania; and the Main Hall at the University of Wisconsin. The facilities built in the more recent golden age added additional elements of art and beauty to the college campus, but also took the specialized needs of students and especially researchers into account. Universities engineered highly specialized buildings for acoustical precision and constructed advanced laboratories that could regulate temperature, humidity, vibration, lighting, and air quality within precise increments. Elaborate equipment and experimental designs required precise specifications and brought with them high acquisition and construction costs.

But not all of these investments were driven by the demands of faculty research. Alumni enthusiasm and pride drove universities to invest in new arenas, museums, libraries, and training facilities for popular athletic programs. As students demanded better accommodations, dormitory halls evolved from barracks-style structures to residence hall suites with nearby kitchenettes and exercise rooms. Campuses came to resemble manicured grounds, with gardens, bikeways, and arboreta. The building boom on campus and the almost insatiable desire for more space have not yet abated.

In the late twentieth century, the administrative complexity of the university snowballed with professional staff in a traditional hierarchical structure, often operating semi-autonomously from other administrative divisions of the academy. As colleges and universities grew and matured, they needed to preserve archival records, provide food services on a large scale, and move students, faculty, staff, and guests with expanded transportation services. With students seeking a wider array of food choices, campuses invited restaurants, coffee shops, and brand-name commercial food vendors to campus. Universities needed teams to manage, repair, clean, and maintain their facilities. The campus bookstore became a revenue center, selling not only books and merchandise but branded university memorabilia. Marketing teams furthered the branding and identity of the institution. Competitive athletics – especially football and basketball – became enterprises with their own reputations, media contracts, and passionate alumni support. To manage the exponential growth in communication and technology, universities employed experts in systems design and augmented their services with contracts to private vendors, including major vendors of complex enterprise software systems. A help desk with round-the-clock support for technology became indispensable. Human relations and university personnel managed employee records, disputes, payroll, and worker benefits. Parking, traffic management, mail services, printing, publications, and public safety became core services. With philanthropy serving as such a key source of investment in the university and a differentiator in areas of excellence, universities required a large staff of development officers focused on alumni relations and gift management. Some universities run precollege programs, others run noncredit programs and courses, and many offer distance courses and degree programs. Some universities operate radio or television stations, hotels, and conference centers, incubate for-profit companies, manage real estate, and oversee hospitals. The oversight of all the contracting, compliance, regulatory, and legal issues requires a core team of lawyers with contracted legal specialists on call. The list goes on and on.

With the end of World War II and the advent of the GI Bill in 1944, enrollments surged; universities needed these new and expanded facilities to meet the needs of their growing student populations.[31] In 1940, overall college enrollments were 1,494,203. Ten years later, enrollments were 2,444,900; more than a million more students were enrolled in the following decade (3,639,847). By 1964, the first baby boomers had reached college age, and by 1970 they dramatically swelled the enrollment ranks to more than eight million students. Today, nearly seventeen million students are enrolled in undergraduate institutions, of which ten million are in public or private four-year colleges.[32] A college degree has become a commodity available to the broader public, as access expanded from relatively few to the many.

With resources available and enrollments strong in the late twentieth century, states significantly expanded enrollments at their flagship public campuses. At the same time, they expanded the number of regional university campuses, providing greater access to state residents. Some of these new campuses were research universities offering the doctoral degree. Others were state colleges, and still others were two-year junior colleges (community colleges). With the injection of federal research funding, state-of-the-art laboratories and research centers expanded and flourished. Meanwhile, the underlying traditions, culture, and structure of university administration remained in place.

The university has become a small city unto itself, enveloped in a culture torn between centralization and unit autonomy. This tension, inherited from the university's formative years, provides a unique institutional duality.

An Era of Turbulence

The expansion of the American university in the second half of the twentieth century took place against the backdrop of a powerful movement for civil rights. Black Americans had long demanded the rights denied by discriminatory laws and institutions, but the movement gained traction in 1951 when Oliver Brown filed a class-action suit against the Topeka, Kansas, Board of Education for refusing the admittance of his daughter, Linda, to an all-White elementary school. In 1954, the US Supreme Court ruled in *Brown* v. *Board of Education* that racial segregation in schools was unconstitutional. As written, the decision allowed Linda and others to attend the local previously White-only school.

On March 2, 1955, a year after the Brown decision, Claudette Colvin, a fifteen-year-old Black high school student in Montgomery, Alabama, refused to relinquish her bus seat and move to the back of the bus. The driver had her arrested. In December of that same year, Rosa Parks, too, was arrested for refusing to relinquish her bus seat to a White man and move to the back of the bus. Confrontations and struggles for equal treatment, access to public facilities, and the dismantling of Jim Crow laws brought racial activism to the forefront. A high point came on August 28, 1963, when two hundred thousand people from different races and backgrounds peaceably assembled in Washington, DC, to march for racial justice, demand equal employment laws, and federal civil rights legislation. At this historic moment, Rev. Dr. Martin Luther King, Jr., told his determined audience, "I have a dream."

At the same time that the nation was struggling with internal issues of equity and racial justice, the United States was engaged in an escalating war in Vietnam with roots dating back to the administration of Harry S. Truman. Under President Lyndon B. Johnson, the armed engagement in Vietnam deepened, troop deployments expanded, and American soldiers began returning in body bags. By 1966, the United States had more than four hundred thousand troops in Vietnam; the numbers did not stop there. Johnson was overseeing an unpopular war at a moment of intense domestic discontent – discontent that was expressed through large-scale anti-war protests and demonstrations in 1967 and beyond.

The combination of the war, civil unrest, and the emerging cultural revolution created a level of discord and distrust across races, institutions, and generations. The national political turmoil ignited the passions of students on numerous college campuses. The large cohort of the baby boom generation, many enrolled in colleges and universities, were subject to the Selective Service draft. Dissatisfaction with US involvement in the Vietnam War led students to become active protesters. As widely chronicled, student culture, style, and attention radically changed throughout the volatile late 1960s. Students became outspoken about the lack of diversity on campus, the relationship between the military-industrial complex and research on campus, their opposition to the war, and their support for civil rights, the women's movement, and free speech. Casual dress, use of drugs, and sexual expression spread – it was heralded as a time of "sex, drugs, and rock and roll." As students occupied campus buildings and made demands of campus administrators, national and world events swirled around them. Student protesters and their allies were vocal in demonstrating for change on a local, national, and international level.

Not all protests were peaceful during this period. In the mid-to-late 1960s, confrontations between police and Black protestors spilled over into the streets of major American cities with beatings and loss of life. At the height of the movement, cities such as Philadelphia (1964), Los Angeles (1965), Newark and Detroit (1967), Chicago, Washington, DC, and Baltimore (1968) were engulfed in conflicts between police and citizens. Each eruption was triggered by an incident of extreme force inflicted by police officers against Black citizens and the steady drumbeat of racism experienced in the Black community. In the urban unrests of 1967 alone, 83 people across US cities were killed – 43 of them in Detroit – and 1,800 people injured.[33]

Concerns for racial justice ricocheted among college campuses. Within thirty miles of Detroit is the University of Michigan. Beginning in 1969, following the insurrection in Detroit, student activists began a dialogue with the university administration about the need for greater inclusion of minority students and faculty at the university. The dialogue eventually escalated to a campus protest, known as the Black Action Movement, where students boycotted classes and effectively closed the campus for twelve days in 1970. Eventually, President Robben Fleming agreed to the students' demands and set a goal of 10 percent minority enrollment.[34] I participated in these protests as a student, and the chant was "Open it up or shut it down." Over time, other student groups and faculty found the university sluggish in meeting its goals; they renewed a push for inclusion in 1975 and again in 1987. As a result of student pressures, the University of Michigan has become a more welcoming and inclusive community for both faculty and students of color. Other campuses listened as well and welcomed a more diverse academic community.

Protests against the Vietnam War and activism for civil rights continued to swell on college campuses. On May 2, 1970, Mayor Leroy Satrom requested that Governor James A. Rhodes send in National Guard Troops to quell student protests against the war at Kent State University in Ohio. Despite protests being banned and classes being in session, two thousand people arrived on campus to protest the war on May 4. The National Guard appeared in full weaponry, with bayonets on their rifles. They deployed tear gas and ordered the crowd to leave. Some did, but others continued to shout and throw objects at the troops. The Guardsmen ultimately fired more than sixty rounds of bullets into the crowd, killing four unarmed students and wounding nine others.[35]

Ten days later, at Jackson State College, a predominantly Black college in Mississippi, a confrontation took place between police and students and other youths. Late in the evening, confronting rocks and bricks, police advanced on a women's residence hall targeting protesters stationed there. In all, police officers fired more than "400 bullets or pieces of buckshot" at the crowd, killing two unarmed young Black men and wounding twelve others. The holes in the wall from the police weapons' bullets remain today as reminders of the tragedy.[36] These and other horrific incidents were permanently etched into nearly every student's mind of that era and exposed the university's failure to keep its students safe.

These shocks, among other student disruptions, left campuses reeling. Questions arose among the broader public and elected officials as to the university's management and even its governability. The fact that so many of these incidents took place on the campuses of public universities caught the attention of state legislators, on whose financial support the universities depended. Federal legislators, too, wanted more stability. Higher education, in general, entered an era of greater government regulation and oversight.

In 1971, the Department of Health, Education, and Welfare (HEW) issued the highly critical *Report on Higher Education*. Historian John Thelin quotes from it:

> It is not enough to improve and expand the present system. The needs of society and the diversity of students now entering college require a fresh look at what "going to college" means. The panel of authors elaborated: "As we have examined the growth of higher education in the postwar period, we have seen disturbing trends toward uniformity in our institutions, growing bureaucracy, overemphasis of academic credentials, isolation of students and faculty from the world – a growing rigidity and uniformity of structure that makes higher education reflect less and less interest in society."[37]

These were strong words about the state of higher education more than fifty years ago. The Weberian model of bureaucratic structure had given colleges and universities the framework to grow and expand, evolving from an authoritarian model of governance where faculty served at the behest of the president or board. It professionalized the hiring of faculty and staff and created the organizational structure we know today. It gave rights to all employees and allowed faculty to have a unique voice in management. Alongside this dynamic growth, however, remained the tensions of centralized and decentralized authority. The university's embrace of hierarchical bureaucracy fostered the development of specialized expertise among administrative service divisions and across institutions; administrators' desire to follow the leader produced isomorphic congruity across academic settings. It institutionalized formal divisions between academics and service, creating a situation in which different branches of the university acted in semi-independence from one another.

To what extent does this 1971 HEW statement reflect today's colleges and universities? Today's residential colleges and universities are home to a different student population than the students who filled the campuses of the twentieth-century university. Today's students are more diverse than any previous cohort and they are also more stressed, pandemic-worn, and more technologically savvy than any previous cohort. They routinely interact with settings that have integrated discrete functions to make services easier to access and navigate. Yet, the university has remained steadfastly loyal to its highly professional segmented service units that seem impervious to the needs expressed by students who seek individualized and integrated support.

In examining the 1971 HEW statement, we might ask: Does an over-emphasis on credentialing remain? Has the university become an inclusive setting that supports its greater student diversity? To what extent are students and faculty engaged in the world around them? Are we in a time of institutional rigidity with uniformity of structure that dates back to the early 1900s? Should we not, from time to time, look at the intertwined needs of students entering college and ask ourselves whether our underlying institutional structure and operations meet their needs? Is this what we want the university of the future to be?

Notes

1 I have drawn considerable insight into the historical developments of higher education from Laurence R. Veysey's classic volume, *The Emergence of the American University*, as well as John R. Thelin's book, *A History of American Higher Education*, which I cite throughout. This chapter is a summary of an extensive and detailed literature. As a summary, it misses many of the complexities and intricacies of the era, particularly in the critical years on either side of the turn of the twentieth century. Further, the brevity of the section will limit some of the more detailed analysis available in the sources. I encourage readers interested in further insight into the development of the American university and its historical context to explore the volumes cited. One particular treasure is a collection of original articles prepared by educational leaders from 1890 to 1910. The volume, *Portraits of the American University, 1890–1910*, was compiled by James C. Stone and Donald P. DeNevi and published in 1971 by Jossey-Bass.

2 John R. Thelin, *A History of American Higher Education*, 2nd ed. (Baltimore: Johns Hopkins University Press, 2011), 64.

3 Merle Curti et al., *An American History* (New York: Harper & Brothers, 1950), 183.

4 James A. Henretta et al., *America: A Concise History, Vol. 2: Since 1865*, 6th ed. (Boston: Bedford/St. Martin's, 2015), 498.

5 Henretta et al., *Concise History*, 554.

6 Frank D. Pavey, William Nelson Cromwell, and Philippe Bunau-Varilla, *The Story of Panama: Hearings on the Rainey Resolution before the Committee on Foreign Affairs of the House of Representatives* (Washington, DC: United States Government Printing Office, 1913), 573, accessed August 26, 2019, https://books.google.com/books?id=1IY-AAAAYAAJ.

7 "The Hatch Act of 1887 (Multistate Research Fund)," United States Department of Agriculture, National Institute of Food and Agriculture, accessed February 17, 2021, https://nifa.usda.gov/program/hatch-act-1887-multistate-research-fund.

8 Roger L. Geiger, *To Advance Knowledge: The Growth of American Research Universities, 1900–1940* (New York: Routledge, 2017), 7–9, accessed April 14, 2021, https://books.google.com/books?id=0803DwAAQBAJ&source=gbs_book_other_versions.

9 Curti et al., *American History*, 236–264.

10 Thomas D. Snyder, ed., *120 Years of American Education: A Statistical Portrait* (Washington, DC: National Center for Educational Statistics, 1993), 75, table 23, accessed May 6, 2021, https://nces.ed.gov/pubs93/93442.pdf.

11 Laurence R. Veysey, *The Emergence of the American University* (Chicago: University of Chicago Press, 1965), 305–306.

12 Snyder, *120 Years*, 75.

13 Larry G. Gerber, *The Rise and Decline of Faculty Governance: Professionalization and the Modern American University* (Baltimore: Johns Hopkins University Press, 2014), 25.

14 Gerber, *Rise and Decline*, 28.

15 Gerber, *Rise and Decline*, 32.

16 Wolfgang J. Mommsen, "Max Weber in America," *American Scholar* 69, no. 3 (Summer 2000): 103, accessed April 24, 2021, www.jstor.org/stable/41213044.

17 Max Weber, *From Max Weber: Essays in Sociology*, ed. H. H. Gerth and C. Wright Mills (London: Routledge, 2009), 214.

18 Weber, *From Max Weber*, 214.

19 Veysey, *Emergence*, 311.

20 "Shared Governance," American Association of University Professors, accessed March 4, 2021, www.aaup.org/our-programs/shared-governance.

21 Clayton M. Christensen and Henry J. Eyring, *The Innovative University: Changing the DNA of Higher Education from the Inside Out* (San Francisco: Jossey-Bass, 2011), 20.

22 Dorothy Barton, "Edwin Emery Slosson: A Chemist of the West," *Journal of Chemical Education* 19, no. 1 (January 1942): 19, accessed July 12, 2019, doi.org/10.1021/ed019p17.

23 Thelin, *Higher Education*, 111.

24 Richard M. Freeland, *Transforming the Urban University: Northeastern, 1996–2006* (Philadelphia: University of Pennsylvania Press, 2019), 24.

25 Veysey, *Emergence*, 307.

26 Veysey, *Emergence*, 312.

27 Paul J. DiMaggio and Walter W. Powell, "The Iron Cage Revisited: Institutional Isomorphism and Collective Rationality in Organizational Fields," *American Sociological Review* 48, no. 2 (April 1983): 148.

28 Peter Frumkin and Joseph Galaskiewicz, "Institutional Isomorphism and Public Sector Organizations," *Journal of Public Administration Research and Theory* 14, no. 3 (July 2004): 283.

29 Richard M. Freeland, *Academia's Golden Age: Universities in Massachusetts, 1945–1970* (New York: Oxford University Press, 1992), 11.

30 "Sputnik Spurs Passage of the National Defense Education Act," United States Senate, accessed February 17, 2021, www.senate.gov/artandhistory /history/minute/Sputnik_Spurs_Passage_of_National_Defense_Education _Act.htm.

31 Thelin, *Higher Education*, 260.

32 Snyder, *120 Years*, 75.

33 History.com Editors, "Kerner Commission Report Released," *History.com*, accessed June 2, 2020, www.history.com/this-day-in-history/kerner-commis sion-report-released.

34 MLK Day Committee, "Diversity in Student Life," in *Michigan's Story: The History of Race at U-M* (Ann Arbor, MI: University of Michigan Library, 2018), digitized library exhibit, accessed June 12, 2020, www.lib.umich.edu /online-exhibits/exhibits/show/history-of-race-at-um/diversity-in-student-life /activism.

35 For further information, see Carole A. Barbato, Laura L. Davis, and Mark F. Seeman's *This We Know: A Chronology of the Shootings at Kent State, May 1970* (Kent, OH: Kent State University Press, 2012).

36 Whitney Blair Wyckoff, "Jackson State: A Tragedy Widely Forgotten," *National Public Radio*, May 3, 2010, 12:00 a.m. EDT, accessed February 17, 2021, www.npr.org/templates/story/story.php?storyId=126426361.

37 Thelin, *Higher Education*, 320.

student experience. The current organization of the faculty within the university, with its simultaneous possibilities for rigidity and messiness, orients faculty toward academic priorities and traditions. The overall student experience beyond the classroom is less visible to faculty members and less central to their reward structure than it should be. Strategies for greater faculty engagement with the overall student experience will be discussed in the final chapter.

Notes

1 Andrew Abbott, *Chaos of Disciplines* (Chicago: University of Chicago Press, 2001), 122.
2 For further discussion on this subject, see Hugh Davis Graham and Nancy Diamond, *The Rise of American Research Universities: Elites and Challengers in the Postwar Era* (Baltimore: Johns Hopkins University Press, 1997).
3 Abbott, *Chaos*, 121–153.
4 Jerry A. Jacobs, *In Defense of Disciplines: Interdisciplinarity and Specialization in the Research University* (Chicago: University of Chicago Press, 2013), 16.
5 John V. Lombardi, *How Universities Work* (Baltimore: Johns Hopkins University Press, 2013), 124.
6 Bill Hussar et al., "Characteristics of Postsecondary Faculty," in *The Condition of Education 2020* (Washington, DC: National Center for Education Statistics, 2020), 150, accessed June 2, 2021, https://nces.ed.gov/pubs2020/2020144.pdf.
7 "Data Snapshot: Contingent Faculty in US Higher Ed," American Association of University Professors, October 11, 2018, accessed August 13, 2019, www.aaup.org/news/data-snapshot-contingent-faculty-us-higher-ed#.YLhJWn1Kjb9.
8 Clayton M. Christensen and Henry J. Eyring, *The Innovative University: Changing the DNA of Higher Education from the Inside Out* (San Francisco: Jossey-Bass, 2011), 20.
9 "At a Glance," ABET, accessed on February 19, 2021, www.abet.org/about-abet/at-a-glance/.
10 See William G. Bowen and Eugene M. Tobin, *Locus of Authority: The Evolution of Faculty Roles in the Governance of Higher Education* (Princeton, NJ: Princeton University Press, 2015).
11 Mitchell L. Stevens, Cynthia Miller-Idriss, and Seteney Shami, *Seeing the World: How US Universities Make Knowledge in a Global Era* (Princeton, NJ: Princeton University Press, 2018), 39–60.
12 Gale, *Research Centers Directory*, 50th ed. (Farmington Hills, Michigan: Gale Research, 2021), accessed April 29, 2021, www.cengage.com/search/productOverview.do?N=197+4294904996&Ntk=P_EPI&Ntt=100905912519879224222018110920455375 8&Ntx=mode%2Bmatchallpartial.

CHAPTER 4

Faculty Influence and Influences on Faculty

An essential element of the transformation of American universities between 1890 and 1910 was the increased hiring of academically well-prepared faculty. These credentialed experts enhanced the reputation and stature of their institutions while simultaneously disseminating knowledge to their students. In the previous chapter, I noted how faculty members came to play a unique role in shaping and governing aspects of the university. This chapter explores how, in the years since, outlook on university priorities, functions, norms, expectations, rewards, and traditions have been transmitted from one generation of faculty to the next. Anyone seeking change in an institution, even after a cataclysmic disruption like a pandemic, must understand how these norms, priorities, and expectations have been implicitly and explicitly conveyed over many decades and across generations to key stakeholders – in this case, to the faculty.

In American residential colleges and universities, faculty members' priorities are influenced by two important organizational forces: the university's departmental structure and scholars' professional associations. Like the steel girders that braced the towering skyscrapers of the early twentieth century, departments support and assist the university's academic functions. According to sociologist Andrew Abbott, "The departmental structure of the American university has remained largely unchanged since its creation between 1890 and 1910."[1] This stability over generations gives the collective voice of the department or school substantial influence over the priorities of current and future faculty members. Beyond their own individual campuses, faculty members share expectations and standards with their colleagues across the country as a result of their graduate training, almost exclusively dominated by research university departments, and the academic associations to which they affiliate. These organizations – the department and the national associations – play a significant role in influencing the faculty.

We see the faculty department imprint in many aspects of the university: a sense of shared intellectual interests, rewards for faculty performance, sensitivity to departmental rankings and assessment by accreditation bodies, expectations for hiring decisions, benchmarks for tenure decisions, peer review of art or publications and the establishment of academic standards, priorities assigned to the placement of academic work, quality of doctoral training (where appropriate), assessment of faculty productivity, teaching expectations, control of the curriculum, establishment of academic benchmarks, and a desire for excellence in the field or discipline. The roadmap and pathways for individual faculty success have been passed down through successive generations of scholars. A high value is placed on publication in the best journals or academic publishers, the leading juried panels, and the most prestigious awards. Unfortunately, in terms of national prestige, rankings, and eventual personal financial remuneration, devoting time to nurturing and guiding undergraduates outside of the classroom does not top the reward structure for many faculty (this may vary for those who have earned tenure or those at teaching-intensive liberal arts colleges). A colleague once quipped to me, half-seriously, that the university would be a wonderful place for faculty "if we just didn't have any students."

National Academic Associations

Even before most colleges and universities established a departmental structure, scholars with similar research interests created national academic associations where they could affiliate, meet, exchange and explore ideas, and set academic standards. One of the first national academic associations in the country was the American Association for the Advancement of Science, founded in 1848. By 1915, almost all the core academic disciplines in the United States had formed national associations: the American Chemical Society (1876); Modern Language Association (1883); American Historical Association (1884); American Economic Association (1885); American Psychological Association (1892); American Anthropology Association (1899); American Physical Association (1899); American Philosophical Society (1900); American Political Science Association (1903); American Association of Geographers (1904); and the Mathematical Association of America (1915).

As the disciplines matured and association membership grew, some of these associations created regional affiliations to allow more convenient meeting locations for members. Disciplines that established their associations early became models for others to follow. One way that disciplinary associations retained an affiliation with emerging subfields was through developing a series of related but specialized scholarly journals. In the field of biology, for example, journals expanded over time in areas including anatomy, biochemistry, biophysics, biotechnology, botany, cell biology, ecology, genetics, immunology, microbiology, molecular biology, physiology, virology, and zoology. Conflicts sometimes developed between emerging subsidiary fields and the core discipline. These often revolved around resources and independence, but in other cases, they stemmed from irreconcilable philosophical differences among influential faculty members. At that point, the only option was for the larger organization to splinter into new scientific societies and associations with a particular intellectual or professional focus.

Among the more visible activities undertaken by academic associations are the annual conferences where faculty exchange ideas, junior faculty along with postdoctoral and graduate students hear from the most influential luminaries in the field, and scholars of all ranks present juried papers and symposia. These societal meetings often award prizes for best book and best dissertation, provide recognition for "distinguished fellows," and reward outstanding accomplishments with prestigious lifetime achievement awards.

Often the leading journal in the discipline or profession comes under the auspices of a national academic association. Universities whose faculty are awarded the editorship of these journals – often a competitive process – gain both domestic and international recognition. The work demands significant faculty time and customarily some financial expenditures for the host university, but in return, an editorship brings prestige to the editor, the department, and the university.

Another respected mark of distinction is service as president or officer of a national academic association. In an academic world of competition for ideas and recognition, the status conferred by leadership in a professional association provides both the individual and their academic home with increased visibility. Ambitious departments, where research and scholarly productivity is at a high level already, may encourage members of their department to seek such additional recognition among their peers.

Association accolades, particularly major scholarly awards, are important not only to individual faculty members and their home departments, but also to university administrators who seek greater institutional prominence and distinction. National academic awards factor into individual promotion considerations, merit-based performance compensation, and collegial stature. Recognition from a national professional organization can also help a department chair argue for additional resources for students and faculty.

The existence of both academic societies and broader professional communities helps bind individuals to their field and reinforce department academic priorities. They act as guardrails on centrifugal tendencies, such that faculty do not go too far outside the core subject areas. Of course, these disciplinary and departmental expectations can constrain core faculty members' research, writing, and teaching, serving as a limit to faculty members' personal growth, professional development, and intellectual enrichment. Many elite institutions worry about faculty migrating too far afield from the highest-ranked journals and publishers, fearing that such action might weaken a department's academic comparative performance statistics. A department's ranking can suffer if too many of its members do not regularly publish in the most acclaimed outlets in their field. Nevertheless, there will be faculty members who will follow their research passions and interests despite departmental preferences. Later in this chapter, I will return to the issue of how the university accommodates individual faculty members pursuing research less connected to the core field. This potential for flexibility makes the academic side of the university a bit less tidy compared to other organizations.

Interestingly, departments at aspiring middle-tier universities may be more supportive of faculty working in emerging fields, in part because the top spaces of the core disciplines have long been dominated by the elite universities and have proven difficult to reach. These rising research universities may earn distinction by crossing intellectual frontiers, affording original discoveries or insights.[2] That is not to say that the top-tier universities are incapable of bridging existing fields or disciplines and creating new areas of inquiry. They have been and continue to be major contributors to the creation of new knowledge. That said, it takes both long-term financial support and a culture that welcomes the pursuit of new, speculative work for a department to maintain its existing strength in a core discipline while creating new areas of inquiry.

Traditionally, the national academic association has ensured high academic standards and provided important collegial support and alliances. Faculty use the annual meeting to visit with far-flung colleagues at the precise interface of their work. Those meetings also contribute to the acculturation process for promising doctoral and postdoctoral students as well as junior tenure-track faculty and those faculty on contracts hoping to someday land a more permanent position. These sessions provide implicit and, on occasion, explicit messages about the pathway to tenure and promotion, strategies for job placement, strategic use of time, and identification of high-priority areas of inquiry. While this process can help scholars identify which projects are most likely to be completed and published in a timely fashion, it can also inadvertently discourage faculty from pursuing questions that are more difficult and come with a higher risk, but that are perhaps more important. These expectations of scholarly productivity at research universities may also mitigate against the labor and time-intensive work of mentoring and engaging with undergraduate students.

For many universities, the desire to attain institutional recognition through what are effectively prestigious academic clubs works to keep faculty members tied to the identity of their discipline, profession, and national organization. As I highlighted before, while there may be compelling subfields or multidisciplinary areas of interest to a professor, it is in the interest of the core discipline and home department to attempt to garner territoriality over that academic area rather than have that territory claimed by another discipline or emerge as an entity on its own.[3] Sociologist Jerry A. Jacobs argues that many important and instrumental aspects of the university's organization revolve around these core disciplines; it is through maintaining their primacy that faculty fight for scarce internal resources and recognition.[4] Over the years, in part due to the influence and stature of the national associations and the recognition they foster, departments have built strong walls to protect their identity, their ability to control and attract resources, their academic turf, and their independence from other academic units – walls that still stand today.

For tenured or tenure-track faculty members, the point of attending academic association meetings is to showcase one's work, enjoy the collegial exchange of ideas, attend relevant sessions, and network with peers from across the country and around the world. While teaching remains an important part of a professor's responsibility, it is generally not a high priority for the program of the national academic associations and certainly not a central focus of their annual meetings (which customarily host a limited number of sessions focused on teaching). Some disciplines and professions, such as history, psychology, and education, have focused more on teaching at their conferences, but this is not the prevailing norm among American learned societies. These organizations pay even less attention to the overall student experience, including cocurricular experiences. As past president at two different universities and chancellor at a third, John Lombardi points out about the associations interest in teaching, "few faculty, especially in large research universities, take an interest in this activity, and the guilds do not regard this as part of their primary concern."[5]

The Academic Pipeline and Tenure

The road to faculty jobs in higher education runs primarily through programs, departments, and schools that offer the PhD or the equivalent highest degree in the field. Along that road, a prestigious mentor may be an important guide, well positioned to help a graduate or postdoctoral student in their search for a permanent academic position or helping a graduate student in pursuit of a significant postdoctoral assignment. In today's marketplace, with significantly more doctoral graduates than tenure-track permanent slots, the edge often goes to those who remain close to the luminaries in the core field and establish a strong publication record. The competition for permanent positions is fierce. An opening for a full-time, tenure-track assistant professor can easily draw more than a hundred applications.

Results from the Integrated Postsecondary Education Data System (IPEDS) reveal that, from 1999 to 2018, the number of instructional positions in higher education actually grew from 1 million to 1.5 million. Only 40 percent of the growth, however, was in full-time positions. Part-time positions grew by 72 percent until 2011, before declining by 7 percent by 2018.[6] The overall growth was heavily weighted toward part-time positions. Only 27 percent of the faculty workforce in 2016 were in tenured or tenure-track positions. This varied by type of institution. At research and four-year colleges and universities, approximately one in three faculty hold a tenured or tenure-track position; at two-year institutions, that number drops to one in five.[7] One might expect additional faculty positions to open as more tenured baby boom era faculty retire, but how those openings are to be distributed between tenure-track or contractual faculty remains an open question. However, the indications are not favorable for an expansion of tenure-track openings.

Graduate students' mentorship experiences serve as an important orientation to a future career as a professor. They encounter different role models, observe how the research universities at which they are being trained welcome and treat undergraduate students, and are exposed to the culture, structure, and reward system of both their department and their field. Doctoral students are encouraged to attend the association's annual national meeting, which exposes them to the hierarchy and the competitive milieu in their field. While administrative leaders may, in theory, encourage interdisciplinary work, both graduate students and junior faculty on the tenure track come to learn that too much work outside the home department's priorities can produce negative consequences. The faculty structure sends a strong implicit message that scholars should hew close to the department's academic priorities, keep publishing, and follow existing pathways.

Future faculty members emerge from their doctoral program "apprenticeship" with a worldview, a set of experiences, and an awareness of the behaviors that lead to academic success or may make it less likely. In writing about the "DNA of the University," Christensen and Eyring state:

> Pioneering institutions such as Harvard and Yale first began granting the PhD in the mid-nineteenth century. As graduates of their doctoral programs joined the faculties of other universities, they took their experiences and expectations with them. With the support of ambitious university presidents, they strove to make their new academic environments like those from which they had come. This internal drive was reinforced by external systems for accrediting, classifying, and ranking universities. It also became embedded in a common academic culture. As a result, even the smallest and most obscure universities bear many of the essential traits of the greatest ones.[8]

Tenure brings greater freedom, but by the time tenure comes around, faculty members have been well indoctrinated in their discipline, profession, or field. They may find little incentive to alter how they spend their time. At institutions that prioritize teaching and service, tenured faculty members often increase their engagement with undergraduates. At universities with a tradition of promotion weighted toward scholarship, however, many faculty members continue to monitor the time and attention they provide to the average undergraduate.

Accreditation Reviews

American universities undergo various kinds of accreditation reviews that additionally reinforce traditional academic structure and culture. These include (1) reviews of an entire college or university; (2) professional school or college reviews in such fields as law, medicine, business, engineering, nursing, dentistry, veterinary, osteopathic, architecture, and public affairs/administration; and (3) periodic institutional department or program reviews.

College or University Accreditation Review

The accreditation review is a comprehensive and high-stakes examination of the major functions of the college or university, customarily done every eight to ten years. The United States has both national and regional accreditation agencies, but regional accreditors are the primary accrediting agencies for public and private, nonprofit, four-year colleges and universities. The frequency of the review may vary depending on issues identified in an earlier review; accreditors may review a campus at any time or request an interim review at the halfway mark to the major review.

Of the various types of accreditation reviews, an overall accreditation of the entire institution is the least beholden to the academic associations. Nevertheless, perhaps unintentionally, the process promotes standardization and compliance across colleges and universities. Universities must meet specific accreditation standards promulgated by the accreditors. To lose accreditation would be a serious blow to an institution's operation and even its continuance. The process commands considerable attention on campus.

Take the Middle States Commission on Higher Education's accreditation process, for example. The overall process traditionally takes place over an eighteen- to twenty-four-month cycle. It begins with the university examining and reporting on its progress in meeting the accreditor's published standards. Each standard has a list of specific criteria. Typically, a team of knowledgeable campus faculty and administrators prepares a detailed report citing evidence on progress toward or accomplishment of each of the accreditor's identified standards. The campus self-study committee is composed of subcommittees assigned to write a response to each of the published standards. Once the subcommittee gathers the evidence of the campus's progress to meet the published standard, they prepare a report identifying campus strengths and weaknesses and submit it to the committee's chair. The campus self-study team's chair assembles the reports prepared for each standard into one overall report. The draft is reviewed by the chancellor or president of the institution; once approved, the document is submitted to the accreditation agency. The final document, known as the self-study, can be well over one hundred pages long, not including appendices.

Once submitted to the accreditation agency, the agency then assembles review team members with relevant expertise drawn from multiple different peer institutions. The team, customarily headed by a president or provost from a peer institution, receives a copy of the accreditor's Standards Document, suggested review procedures, and the campus's self-study in advance of a three-day site visit. During that visit, review team members with expertise in each of the different accreditation standards meet with key institutional representatives about the campus' performance. At the end of the visit, the team members provide a preliminary report as feedback to university leadership. The process concludes when the review team prepares a final report and submits it to the accreditation agency for review and action.

The most common topics for review include the institution's mission and goals, along with its governance structure, administration, and leadership. Specific compliance issues include oversight, contracts, performance review, and quality control. Other standards include ethics and integrity throughout the institution; the quality of the academic programs and evidence of learning outcomes; the support structure for the overall student experience; resources and capacity to achieve stated goals; physical, technical, and financial resources; and institutional planning. The accreditation process helps ensure the public that the institution is performing at a high level across all sectors. It guides the college or university on ways to improve the pursuit of its stated goals and identifies areas in need of improvement with specific expectations identified by the accreditation agency.

Institutions must complete a successful accreditation review to qualify for federal funding. As a result of the high stakes involved, accreditation agencies may periodically revise their standards. One standard that has been common across all the regional accreditation agencies focuses on the quality of professional support to students. Notably, accreditation is one of the only times this important topic is addressed by external reviewers as an institution-wide concern.

The information found in the self-study concerning student support is usually prepared by campus personnel from the different professional student services at the campus. Students are often represented on the internal committee preparing the report, but it would be unusual for more than a few students to serve on the self-study committee. However, the committee has access to data on the utilization of campus student services, results from periodic student surveys, and findings from national surveys such as the National Survey of Student Engagement (NSSE). A committee may choose to hold focus groups or meetings on campus with students to discuss their experiences with campus academic and student services. Professionals from a student service area at a peer institution are likely to be the ones to eventually review this standard.

Once the self-study is in the hands of the reviewers, the review team customarily, but not always, schedules open meetings for undergraduate and, if appropriate, graduate students at the campus to comment on their experience. Students who participate are often well prepared for the meeting by staff at the institution under review. But on one memorable site visit in which I participated, only three undergraduate students showed up to meet with our entire team of over a dozen reviewers. Two were student reporters from the campus paper, leaving one student to discuss their experience. No graduate students came to the second session. As a result, there was little student input into the final accreditation report. The student experience was addressed almost entirely from the perspective of the professional staff. While this experience with students may be atypical, the reviewers are heavily guided by the self-study document and meetings with their professional peers.

To better reflect the concern for a holistic approach to learning and the overall student experience, at a minimum, the accreditation agency could add another review standard. The new standard would seek to assess the overall student experience at the college or university from the perspective of the students enrolled and could include recent graduates. To accomplish this, the accreditation agency would require additional information from the campus under review and would develop a survey instrument to collect this information. The campus would then administer the survey to all enrolled students and require at least a 30 percent response rate – if possible it could include feedback from students who have dropped out. The survey would probe more deeply into student encounters with service operations and the curricular components of the campus. It would specifically explore questions on campus climate and sense of inclusion and belongingness that different student identity groups encounter. The campus would prepare a detailed summary of the findings across the student body and delineated by specific underrepresented groups. The survey findings would be included in the campus self-study report along with other information.

The accreditation agency would invite a chief academic officer and the senior executive from student affairs, each from different institutions, to jointly serve as external reviewers and lead the review of this new standard. Before the campus visit, they would review the data provided by the campus and prepare their own interview protocol once on campus. The two reviewers would spend at least a day in meetings with students; recent graduates would also be invited to participate in a separate interview session. This additional standard and the reviewers' written review would help provide a greater understanding of the institutional gestalt as perceived by students. Feedback from the two external reviewers would be shared with the campus leadership along with the other reviewer reports. The overall report would be prepared by the chair and submitted to the accreditation agency.

Departmental or School Accreditation

Many individual departments and schools have their own specific accreditation process undertaken by field-specific national (or international) accreditation associations. For example, in the profession of engineering, the Accreditation Board for Engineering and Technology, Inc., or ABET, is highly respected and involves faculty, industry, and government reviewers. ABET currently accredits 4,301 programs at 846 colleges and universities worldwide.[9] ABET oversees four different commissions for reviews: the Applied and Natural Science Accreditation Commission, the Computer Accreditation Commission, the Engineering Accreditation Commission, and the Engineering Technology Accreditation Commission.

As with university-wide accreditation, these departments and schools undergo reviews of their performance on a regular cycle of five, seven, or ten years. For some professions, reviews are voluntary, but schools that do not pursue review will not be recognized as accredited, potentially hurting student and faculty recruitment. These reviews also require a major self-study report that goes to the accreditation agency and is assigned to an external review team of peer experts. The process parallels the overall accreditation of the institution, but the questions and standards are specific to the professional academic area under review.

Although the review may require evidence of student learning outcomes, more typically it focuses on the extent to which the school or department achieves predetermined academic goals, how it allocates its resources, and whether it meets standards for faculty qualifications and productivity. Reviewers consider the availability of faculty professional development, the relevance of the curricula, the diversity of the faculty, the mix of academic and professionals active in the academic program and the classroom, the quality and availability of equipment and space for conducting research and instruction, the extent of staff support, and the effectiveness of budget management. The review also considers issues related to student outcomes, including whether a program has successfully placed its graduates in jobs in their field and, in some cases, the earning level of graduates six months after having completed their degree. The site visit team meets with the campus senior academic administrators as well as faculty, staff, and students of the unit under review. As professional program accreditation is now customarily structured, an overview of the student experience is often secondary to performance outcomes in student learning, successful job placement, graduate school enrollment (if relevant), assessment of the financial and academic health of the department or school, and the program's overall financial support from the academy.

The accreditation review of a professional school, department, or program is another example of the role of peers in ensuring appropriate academic standards are regularly attained in the profession. Some professions draw upon the specific mission and school goals as a way of assessing progress, whereas others expect units to follow a specific template with identifiable and detailed metrics. But, for the most part, whether intentional or not, the process promotes a level of standardization across the industry.

Periodic Reviews of Departments

Academic departments that are not subject to formal accreditation requirements may undergo periodic reviews at the discretion of individual campus senior administrators. For departments that operate without a specific subject area accreditor, a periodic review, customarily every seven years, is one way for faculty members and administrators alike to gain a fresh external perspective on the state of the academic unit. An external review of a program or department customarily involves a team of two or three senior faculty reviewers from different peer institutions. Again, the program or department prepares a self-study before an external team spends two or three days on campus. The review team provides a written report that assesses areas of strength and suggests improvements. Once again, given the historical traditions and priorities within the academic hierarchy, the external evaluators are unlikely to study the aggregate student experience.

* * *

Of the three types of external reviews, the first two satisfy external accreditation standards. They focus on the overall operation of the organization, including a comprehensive list of items designed to meet overall national or, in some cases, international standards. The internal program review, on the other hand, is designed to provide feedback to the administration and academic unit with the expectation that the assessment and advice of outside experts will help facilitate program improvement no matter how impressive the department may already be.

In all three forms of review, the assessment is heavily weighted toward overall institutional governance, quality of operations, financial support, and academic performance outcomes. Even where the accreditation standards require an assessment of the student experience, the focus is on the services offered or graduation outcomes as presented by professionals within the various units (e.g., resources allocated, staffing, the volume and utilization of services, employment and salary levels, or future educational placement).

When students are invited to meet with the site visit team, it is typically only students who are able and willing to attend (or when the administration has encouraged them to attend) a two-hour meeting to share their experiences. Consequently, these interactions may not reflect the same sort of information that would be captured by targeted interviews conducted by trained interviewers or reflected in student journaling projects. When asked by the site team if they like their college, most students will say they have enjoyed the experience and respect their faculty. A skilled interviewer asking probing questions, however, might elicit very different responses to specific questions about actual incidents the students have encountered. Of course, the valuable insights from students who have left the institution without completing their degree remain unknown. The accreditation process as currently implemented thus misses crucial information about the balance between aggregate student needs and expectations and current institutional processes and operations.

Without this level of detail from a systematic sample of enrolled students, including those who have voluntarily left, the accreditation process must be understood as a review of the performance of units, prepared by leaders of said units, and reviewed by peers with similar professional backgrounds and related duties at peer organizations. In most cases, the operational units under review will be familiar to the reviewers, as they are selected because of their expertise in managing a similar area at a peer institution. In the end, the review is a comprehensive discussion of the parts of the university identified by the review standards, but it lacks an assessment of the whole as encountered by a student. This holistic student perspective of the interaction of academic, cocurricular, extracurricular, and student support services remains absent.

Control over the Curriculum

The undergraduate and graduate curriculum, by tradition, is the purview of the faculty. Departments and program units develop their own curriculum and requirements for their courses, minors, majors, certificates, or programs. New course options and changes are developed by the unit faculty and are then customarily approved by the faculty senate's undergraduate or graduate curriculum committees. New programs would likely require approval by the dean and provost, as well as a review by the campus president and the university's governance board.[10] A new course or program might take a year or more to achieve final approval. The deliberative, multilayered review process helps ensure changes are well justified and thought through. No one wants to create new courses, only to have them closed due to a lack of interest or poor design.

For students, this methodical approach to course development can be frustrating. Undergraduate students are traditionally enrolled for four years (but as I cited in Chapter 1, many take longer to graduate), master's students customarily for two. Given the long time required to update the curriculum, some students may miss out entirely on new content pertinent to their future careers or study. This is particularly true in today's academy, with its more diverse student body. Students who note the absence of historically underrepresented perspectives in the curriculum may get the sense that scholars with a different cultural perspective are not as important. They may extrapolate from this observation to wonder if they as students aren't important either and question to what extent they belong in the setting at all. A sense of belonging is pivotal for students to thrive. Students who have been immersed in discussions concerning institutional racism and the consequences of systemic policies and practices that result in inequities will likely target such practices for change. In response to this emerging issue, several universities have begun allowing new courses to run one or more times while still under review.

The Role of Research Centers and Institutes

One of the internal complexities of the university is its capacity to balance the power and influence of the disciplines, departments, and schools with opportunities for novel exploration and research. The university's roots highlight the tension between centralization and local autonomy. It is known as a setting with insatiable ambition, in constant search for recognition along with new revenue sources. So, to facilitate work that may cross disciplinary lines and provide opportunities for research collaboration among faculty from different units internal or external to the university, or teams of faculty and graduate students within departments, the university has developed organizational structures in the form of centers, institutes, laboratories, or collaboratories.

These are environments where faculty participants work to investigate and solve problems at the interstices of different fields or disciplines. Customarily, these faculty remain affiliated with an academic department that grants them tenure and assigns them their teaching course load. However, they carry out their research under the umbrella of flexible research centers. These freestanding research centers and institutes operate quite differently from academic departments. Generally independent and managed by an entrepreneurial director, research centers typically have the authority to hire staff, build alliances with faculty within or outside the university, and secure external funding. Traditions of shared governance and deliberation are far less common in centers than in academic departments. These centers operate more like independent small businesses headed by a comparatively powerful academic leader. Centers and institutes have proliferated in higher education.[11] They occupy university space and consume faculty time, but it is uncommon for them to have permanent funding from the university's central budget beyond their core operations. Gale Cengage publishes a directory that tracks thousands of such research centers in the United State and across the globe.[12]

In *Beyond Departments: The Story of Institutes and Centers*, Stanley O. Ikenberry and Renee C. Friedman define the various structures and conditions in which these entities rise and set.[13] Some centers and institutes are part of a college or school or multiple schools; some are campus-wide. The college or school-based center or institute relies on the interest and support of the dean(s) for space, infrastructure, and internal resources, but, as entrepreneurial units, they are customarily expected to generate external funding via grants, contracts, fees, or philanthropic support.

The campus-wide center or institute relies on similar benevolence, but from the office of the provost or senior administration. Faculty affiliates are often drawn from across the university, which creates wider visibility for the center and gives the illusion – generally false – of greater stature or significance. Having a university-wide mission can involve delicate arrangements across academic units over issues of faculty time and distribution of grant-funded resources, including any returns from campus indirect charges.

While research centers and institutes are common at research universities, where they provide valuable mechanisms for creative and innovative faculty contributions, they seldom have much to do with the overall undergraduate student experience. Individual students may, however, participate in specific projects or attend high-profile lectures sponsored by these units.

Faculty Ingenuity, Exploration, and Inquiry

Despite the conformity of traditional academic departmental structures as they have developed over the past century, faculty members continue to be a dynamic force at the university. With their home department serving as a relatively stable and secure anchor, faculty members continue to demonstrate a level of restlessness and need for exploration. After all, they have attained their privileged university position because of their penchant for original thinking and their desire to probe deeply into a subject. Faculty members follow their interests and creative instincts wherever they may lead, even when enticed by questions outside the strictures of their discipline or field. With this in mind and in light of the above-mentioned desire to keep faculty tethered to the home unit, campuses make accommodations so as not to lose talent.

The academy, with its considerable decentralized structure, tolerates a level of independence in exchange for faculty members' unique and profound insights and contributions to original research. Compared to organizational structures outside the academy, its administration appears a bit "messy" and complex, yet this very messiness provides some needed flexibility. This is one of many reasons why the academy's intellectual contributions continue to be refreshed and sustained over many generations of scholars.

Sociologist Jason Owen-Smith, in *Research Universities and the Public Good*, argues that this academic structure, based as it is on competing allegiances, provides faculty with opportunities to make discoveries that can make the world a better place. But such discoveries cannot be predicted and are not guaranteed.[14] They depend on a level of serendipity and, therefore, patience. The university's institutional culture is somewhat allergic to change, yet its central stability "allows the clash of different views to be sustained and generate unexpected findings."[15]

In commenting on the vagueness and difficulty in explaining the inner workings of the university, Owen-Smith states:

> More plainly, universities have difficulty clearly describing their aspirations because they have so many of them and because they sometimes conflict. They are unsure about what, precisely, needs to be done to reach those goals because the work they do is uncertain and the materials they work with (people and ideas, mostly) are highly variable. They can't even be certain who will do the work and for how long. These uncertainties necessitate a style of decision-making that fits few commonsense ideas about productivity and planning. They fly in the face of market discipline, and they should. Like the research enterprise that they anchor, universities pose substantial challenges for those who seek clear, direct returns on straightforward investments.[16]

Owen-Smith reminds us that the university is a unique environment that unleashes the creative engagement of faculty in their research, their work with students, and their contributions to society as a whole. The benefits of colleges and universities are enormous. A university, with access to information through a faculty networked locally, nationally, and internationally, and available through its library, is a remarkable and enriching resource for those enrolled, employed, or in its orbit. For students at both graduate and undergraduate levels, the faculty's creative engagement provides an inspirational component of university life, a sense of vitality, and the opportunity to participate.

Students benefit from the amassed prestige and quality of the faculty and academic department. The value of the degree they earn reflects that reputation and will be carried throughout their career. Some top-tier universities and departments have opened their doors and wallets to welcome low-income students, who are often students of color, as an incremental stab at breaking down generational inequality and wealth disparities. Graduates of these esteemed institutions are more likely to advance from these settings into the corridors of power. Nevertheless, the time has come for these leading academic institutions to do more, both in terms of the diversity of their student body and the composition of their faculty. Pressures to do more will continue to intensify.

In the midst of all of this, faculty retain an ever-present focus on the quality of the educational product in their specific area and disseminating that knowledge to students. Their reputation, both as individuals and as a collective, and the quality of their teaching in their field, is a matter of substantial personal pride. For most faculty, however, the overall undergraduate student experience, beyond their own area of inquiry is, at most, peripheral. Faculty take greater notice of students when they protest the curriculum or an aspect of a program, when students gather and make demands, or when student government brings issues to their attention. But that attention can fade quickly. For the most part, students are transient. They are at the university for a limited time and move on. The expectations of the professional guild, however, have lasted for more than a century.

Successfully orienting a university around the concerns and perspectives of students will require some adjustment in faculty assumptions, priorities, and loyalties, particularly for those on the tenure track. And yet, any university leader who hopes to achieve institutional change in deeply held faculty priorities and rewards must be sensitive to the cultural norms, training, preparation, and reputation of its faculty. Faculty are an important constituency in evaluating, assessing, and supporting changes in the academy, and they need to be involved in the dialogue about the overall

13 Stanley O. Ikenberry and Renee C. Friedman, *Beyond Academic Departments: The Story of Institutes and Centers* (San Francisco: Jossey-Bass, 1972).

14 Jason Owen-Smith, *Research Universities and the Public Good: Discovery for an Uncertain Future* (Stanford, CA: Stanford Business Books, 2018), 56, 68.

15 Owen-Smith, *Research Universities*, 60.

16 Owen-Smith, *Research Universities*, 56.

CHAPTER 5

The Evolution of the Student Affairs Profession and the Ethos of Specialization

The historical conditions that shaped the development of student affairs paralleled those that faculty faced during the American university's pivotal years of 1890 through 1910.[1] Societal demands for modernization and professionalism in business and industry operations spilled over to the university. The development of a cadre of experts in the area of student personnel services followed accordingly, with female administrators leading the way.

In the mid-1800s, American colleges and universities began to assume legal responsibility for the students under their supervision. This practice of acting as a temporary guardian, known as *in loco parentis*, originated from British common law. By the turn of the twentieth century, it was fully ensconced in the American university. *In loco parentis* placed in the hands of administrators the ability to "regulate students' personal lives – including speech, association, and movement – and take disciplinary action."[2]

As colleges and universities hired an increasing number of faculty with advanced degrees, they faced this faculty's growing need for additional research time. One way to reallocate time for research was to redistribute faculty responsibility for students' social, psychological, and physical development needs to others.[3] Consequently, colleges and universities needed personnel willing and able to attend to these needs mandated by *in loco parentis*. For a variety of reasons related to conditions both inside and out of the university, the position of dean of students emerged to assist with this needed task.

From the very start, the development of student personnel services was a gendered phenomenon with clear distinctions between men and women professionals and students. For most of the early 1800s, women students were barred from American colleges. Men saw women as having a different role in America, destined for a life of "piety, purity, submissiveness, and domesticity."[4] The establishment of fifty women's colleges between

1836 and 1875 served as a step that began to alter this view.[5] Coeducation remained rare, with Oberlin College becoming the first such college to grant a bachelor's degree to a woman in 1841[6] and Antioch College admitting women from the time it was founded in 1852.[7] The Civil War created enrollment shortages, and with women willing to enroll and pay tuition, the barriers to gender-segregated colleges began to erode. Female enrollments reached 47 percent of total enrollment in 1899–1900 and then declined in the 1920s to 44 percent with a continuing slide to 40 percent in 1929–1930.[8] The challenges women faced both in the classroom and as university employees remained persistent and only began to mitigate when federal legislation required equal treatment among genders. In fact, admission quotas existed for women even as late as 1969 at Yale University.[9]

Male students often reacted negatively to the presence of women at coeducational campuses. At the University of Chicago, male students demanded classes segregated by gender.[10] Men dominated the faculty ranks, while women members encountered additional inequities in compensation, promotion, and recognition. Despite these challenges, it was women who built the field we know today as student affairs. As higher education professor Michael Hevel put it, all of student affairs "from admission and orientation to student activities, to residential housing to career services, can be traced to the work of the deans of women."[11] The first deans of women students were well-educated women who found opportunities in these new openings, but many simultaneously carried faculty teaching obligations. These women served as the bedrock for the emerging profession and helped shape its underlying philosophy. But they were also paid lower salaries, received fewer benefits, and were treated differently than male counterparts who served as deans of men.[12]

In their quest for identity, respect, and stature, and with a desire to develop a new profession, these pioneering women followed the pathways blazed by other faculty and established a new national association for deans of women. It provided for collegiality, dialogue among peers on best practices, and the potential to establish the fundamentals of a profession that drew from such varied fields as human development, management, health care, and psychology. The new association and its members encouraged publishing research in the areas associated with student personnel practice.

Deans of men followed a very different path. Overseeing students based on their own personality and disposition, they balanced the role of disciplinarian against that of an adult guide. While deans of women focused on developing the profession with training and advanced educational preparation, the men for a time rejected such considerations.

As the roaring twenties emerged, deans of men eventually fell into a more professional role and the field developed service specializations, each emulating the pattern and identity of professionalism established by the academic disciplines. Areas of expertise became more sharply defined and distinctions began to emerge between the array of services provided under the umbrella of student affairs. In very short order, universities found themselves with separate offices for advising, extracurricular activities, housing, and numerous other student services.

As student affairs grew to include student health care, oversight of student housing, spiritual life, Greek life, student activities and entertainment, community service, orientation, discipline and judicial affairs, counseling, student government, international exchange, clubs, cocurricular and extracurricular activities, and more, the role of deans of students evolved. Those in the area of student affairs became captains of two of the critical student support domains – psychosocial aspects of the student life and health, including both mental and physical health. While not responsible for all aspects of these domains, the other areas involving academic progress and financial support remained with other offices. In time, these deans of students eventually became vice presidents with significant responsibilities. Today, they are typically an integral part of the university president's cabinet.

In part because of the impetus for professionalization endemic in academic culture, the different units that today comprise the broad range of student services (including student affairs) typically operate as relatively independent enterprises, with their own regulations, data sets, and confidential records and files, not unlike many other offices on campus. That growth led to concerns about how these services are organized, and how they link across specializations to best provide integrated support to students. Historian Brian C. Mitchell and college president W. Joseph King pointedly refer to the office of student affairs as "a collection of fiefdoms jealously guarded through ongoing turf battles, with little sense of common purpose or direction. Fights take place over territory that can be programmatic and facilities-based, over how time and resources are allocated, and over where a particular program or initiative stands in the pecking order."[13] This is perhaps a bit of an overstatement, and it may reflect on a wider array of student support services across the university that, too often, are overly self-protective and independent. Still, the criticism merits attention.

In this chapter, I will discuss the history of student affairs, including the internal and external events that have brought the field to its current state.

The history is riddled with discrimination against women, people of color, people with disabilities, religious groups, and non-heterosexual people. It is a great irony that student service professionals have today become champions and allies of the students who many of their predecessors so avidly persecuted. For this book, the most salient question about the development of student affairs is whether the organizational structures of colleges and universities – which recognize professional staff as essential components of the academic setting that play a pivotal role in student well-being – are capable of providing their services in a way that contributes to an integrated and holistic student experience at the university.

How Student Affairs Became a Profession

Marianne Dascombe may have been the first student affairs officer. Appointed at Oberlin College in 1834, she was the principal and overseer of the "Female Department."[14] But Dascombe remained the exception for most of the rest of the nineteenth century. The professional field of student personnel service did not really emerge until Harvard appointed the first dean of students for its all-male student population in 1890[15] and the University of Chicago appointed its inaugural dean of women, coterminous with a faculty appointment, just before admitting its first female student in 1892.[16] The doctrine of *in loco parentis* provided authority for these new roles and remained in effect until the 1960s.[17]

As I mentioned above, the experiences of student services professionals differed by gender from the very start. Female deans of women were much more focused on developing their role in colleges and universities into a profession than were their male counterparts. Among other things, they hoped to prepare other women to serve as deans of women. These women pioneers saw the role of the dean of students as an opportunity to draw upon new insights from thinkers like Sigmund Freud, Grace Helen Kent, John Watson, and Lewis Terman (who in 1916 released the Stanford-Binet intelligence test to the American public) that were shaping the psychological fields of psychoanalysis, testing and measurement, behaviorism, and human development in the early twentieth century.

These deans saw in new psychosocial perspectives the potential to better assess student capabilities and performance. They developed methods of advising and career counseling that would support and enrich the college experience with the hope of a wider array of choices after graduation, including the possibility of greater financial independence.[18] The deans of women sought to explore the limits and potential of the female college student and added professional goals to the traditional cocurricular and extracurricular programming at women's colleges. These traditional responsibilities of these deans customarily involved housing oversight, including sororities; monitoring student activities and student health;[19] athletics, including basketball, boating, and ice skating; and artistic and creative activities, including music, singing, dancing, journalism, musicals, festivals, and theater performances.[20] The emerging generation of women deans aspired to oversee the overall personal development of the student as an educated and well-rounded woman.[21]

The early deans of women not only enriched the experiences of young women at the elite women's private colleges, but were also on the front lines of coeducational institutions, supporting and advocating for their students as well as establishing their professional standing. By 1910, almost one-third of students enrolled at coeducational institutions were women.[22] Nevertheless, struggles continued for the inclusion of women in previously all-male campuses. Detractors argued that women would distract men from serious study, that their presence would lower educational standards and take away educational spots from men, and that the presence of women was detrimental to both men and women. The most egregious position was that coeducation would produce women who were developmentally stunted and incapable of being effective mothers. This theory was based on the belief that the brain and reproductive organs among young women developed in tandem and that the demands of excessive brain use in coeducational settings would limit their ability to give birth to healthy children.[23]

The first deans of women at coeducational settings confronted issues at every turn, whether in locating appropriate student housing or athletic and recreational spaces; establishing traditions and rituals for women enrollees; or navigating a prejudicial environment that was less than welcoming for themselves and their female students. Deans of women also played pivotal roles for female students at Historically Black Colleges and Universities (HBCUs), as well as at less affluent coeducational nonelite colleges and universities in the South that needed and hired women advocates with skill sets beyond those found in better-funded settings.[24] Over time, their experiences with more diverse and economically challenged students became part of the professional development of the field.

Seeking professional recognition and collegial exchange, in 1903 a group of deans of women began meeting under the auspices of the American Collegiate Alumnae. As early as 1915, Columbia Teachers College began offering graduate summer programs for deans of women, courses that eventually became a full graduate program. In 1916, the National Association of Deans of Women (NADW) was formed. An academic journal soon followed, reflecting the deans' academic focus and determination to shape student affairs in the tradition of other professions. Their meetings were opportunities to explore strategies and practices undertaken at other campuses, cultivate alliances, and shape the intellectual components of a student personnel profession along with its practice.[25]

Early male deans of men, often former professors, saw themselves more as adult role models guiding young men into adulthood; they were less interested in developing their positions into a profession. Their personalities influenced their relationships with students and guided their actions. Each dean found his own style of interaction and, without professional guidelines, relied on his best guess as to which aspect of his role he should emphasize.[26] Their roles included multiple responsibilities, such as overseeing student housing on- and off-campus, supervising fraternal societies, encouraging school spirit, fostering team activities, advising on moral character, nurturing religiosity, maintaining school traditions, monitoring student behavior to ensure that nothing got too out of hand, and maintaining civility among students. For them, areas of concern might include student partying, cheating on exams, excessive alcohol consumption, gambling, card playing, fighting, "lewd" or rambunctious behaviors, and premarital sexual activity. Each dean had his own way of interacting with students, some preferring to mentor, others preferring to be viewed more as a disciplinarian. Deans' authority to impose disciplinary action, including possible suspension or expulsion, complicated their relationships with students.

Many male deans of students aggressively stigmatized behaviors they believed out of the ordinary, particularly sexual behaviors. Some deans hunted down men who showed interest in other men, making their lives difficult with unexpected raids designed to catch and expel gay students. Sometimes their efforts extended even to monitoring the friends of those perceived to be gay. Such aggressive homophobia guided student advising until at least the late 1950s and early 1960s.[27] In at least a few incidents, male deans of men students waited until just before graduation to expel a student for perceived homosexual tendencies as a form of punishment and to teach others a lesson.[28] In 2002, a student reporter at Harvard going through campus archives inadvertently discovered the existence of a "Secret Court" that in 1920 investigated and purged a gay student subculture from the school. Harvard's "Secret Court" is but one example of the aggressive homophobic hunts that took place, and it is one with tragic consequences: one gay student committed suicide and a second followed as a result of the pressures and hostile environment. Other students questioned by the Court, gay or accused of being gay, were immediately dismissed from school and exiled from the city.[29]

In 1919, fourteen years after the deans of women first began meeting to help establish the profession, the first gathering of six deans of men convened. Eventually, this group became the National Association of Deans and Advisors to Men (NADAM). A decade after that meeting, a report by the US Commissioner of Education found gender differences still influencing educational approaches in the area of student affairs:

> in marked contrast with the clear-cut enumeration of the duties of the dean of women and the definition of her functions, the deans of men are apparently groping to discover just what their justification for existence may be. The most illuminating material is found in the proceedings of the National Association of Deans of Men. Here is evident a very masculine sentimentalizing of the work and of the relations with students, which vanished from the discussions held by deans of women a score of years ago.[30]

Women professionals were the cornerstone of the emerging field. By the 1920s, improvements in employee personnel practices began to appear in the corporate and business sectors and caught the attention of the women deans. Soon they began referring to themselves as "student personnel officers" and invested in developing tools to test, measure, and otherwise quantify student activities.[31] The field was maturing into one based on practices shared among female dean colleagues, and lead by women deans of women students.

In the meantime, both the men's and women's deans continued to invest in their own separate professional organizations. In 1922, the NADW expanded its professional membership to include female counselors and began operating under a new name, the National Association of Women Deans and Counselors (NAWDC). This new body soon developed a research committee that published annual collections of research articles, with a journal to follow in 1938. A decade later, in 1948, the NAWDC added administrators to their organization's name (NAWDAC), and in 1991 the name was changed to the National Association for Women in Education. As a result of financial circumstances, its members voted to dissolve the organization on August 13, 2000.[32]

In 1929, Black deans of women exited from the NAWDC and formed their own organization, the National Association of Deans of Women and Advisors to Girls in Colored Schools. This was largely, but not exclusively, in response to the NAWDC's pattern of meeting in hotels that restricted access to women of color. Six years later, in 1935, the Black deans of men formed the National Association of Personnel Deans of Men at Negro Educational Institutions. In 1954 the two organizations merged, becoming the National Association of Personnel Workers. The group is now part of the National Association of Student Affairs Professionals (NASAP).[33]

In 1951, NADAM became the National Association of Student Personnel Administrators (NASPA). In 1963, NASPA established its initial journal, the *Journal of Student Affairs Research and Practice*. Today, NASPA represents fifteen thousand professionals and sponsors seven journals reflecting differing specializations.[34] In recent years it modified its name to NASPA: Student Affairs Administrators in Higher Education. NASPA describes itself as "the professional home for the field of student affairs."[35]

This is not, however, the only national association with a proud history in the field of student affairs. The American College Personnel Association (ACPA) refers to itself as "the leading comprehensive student affairs association that advances student affairs" and has over eight thousand members.[36] ACPA's roots date back to 1924 when the National Association for Appointment Secretaries was formed. At the time, the title of "appointment secretaries" referred to positions in what we might now think of as "career services"; appointment secretaries helped college graduates secure employment, and their field was led by women professionals. In fact, their inaugural gathering was at a NADW meeting with other women. In 1931, the organization changed its name to ACPA. Among its current core values, ACPA lists the "education and development of the total student." This reflects the significance of the seminal statement that the American Council on Education (ACE) issued in 1937, a portion of which is quoted below.[37]

The women who provided the intellectual foundation for student affairs would likely be disappointed at the fragmentation that exists today in the academy and the bifurcation among faculty and other student service professionals. The 1937 ACE publication, *The Student Personnel Point of View* explicitly discusses its perspective on the importance of providing integrated support to the student as a whole person. This landmark document formulated an integrative philosophy of student personnel services in colleges and universities, with an emphasis on the role of all educators in providing an enriched and holistic experience. It particularly reflected the comprehensive view of student support influenced by Esther Lloyd-Jones, a leading figure in the student personnel movement.[38] That philosophy impose[d] upon educational institutions the obligation to consider the student as a whole – his intellectual capacity and achievement, his emotional make up, his physical condition, his social relationships, his vocational aptitudes and skills, his moral and religious values, his economic resources, his aesthetic appreciations. It puts emphasis, in brief, upon the development of the student as a person rather than upon his intellectual training alone.[39]

This historic document – which, despite its use of exclusively male pronouns, reflected expertise developed from working with both female and male undergraduates – discusses the array of professional responsibilities in a holistic collegiate experience and the institution's *obligation* to embrace such a broad view of education. It represented a core philosophy for the academy, explicitly touching on the separate responsibilities of faculty members and staff serving in the area of student personnel and student affairs. An entire section of this document is devoted to the necessary coordination between "all members of the teaching and administrative staff and the student body."[40] But even though this report emphasized as early as 1937 the need to provide a holistic experience for the student, its recommendations have still not been fully actualized.

Less than a decade after the release of the ACE document, men and women began returning from military service after World War II. Having learned from the aftermath of World War I how difficult it was for returning veterans to productively transition back into civilian society without adequate government support, Congress enacted the Serviceman's Readjustment Act of 1944, known as the GI Bill. Nearly two and a quarter million veterans took advantage of this opportunity to earn a college degree.[41] Between 1946 and 1948, veterans represented nearly half of all college students, with about 30 percent being women.[42] As a way of accommodating the demand for a college education from both sexes, to attract new revenue and add mature students (the students were older, commonly around twenty-five years old), and out of a spirit of patriotism, many more universities became coeducational during this period.

Soon the roles of the deans of men and deans of women began to merge at coeducational campuses, many former deans of women or deans of men becoming deans and vice presidents of student affairs. But despite the talented pool of women who had developed the underpinnings of the profession, the top leadership positions became dominated by men. Instead of implementing the student-based philosophy and practices developed by women in the field's formative years and emphasized in the 1937 ACE document, the new generation of male deans and vice presidents applied many of the bureaucratic principles they had learned in the military to their new roles on campus. As historian Robert Schwartz laments, "Deans of women . . . became strangers in a land where a male-oriented culture prevailed."[43] The opening of colleges and universities to large numbers of men and women following World War II wound up excluding many well-qualified women from the leadership positions they had originated and cultivated over many years.

Three Examples of the Expansion of Professionalism

While the office of student affairs has become an identified structure within higher education, questions remain about whether it is a field unto itself or a conglomerate of specialty student service units. The academic community has responded affirmatively with degree programs in student affairs. With slight variations in names, over one hundred master's-level graduate programs in the field exist nationwide.[44] The instructors for these programs are often student affairs professionals or those who have served in student affairs leadership positions. At least two state universities (Ohio State University and the University of Georgia) offer both PhD and EdD degrees in the field of student affairs.

Each of the different specializations under student affairs has its own history, some related to the student personnel movement, some not. Below, I will touch on the history of three different student service specializations often included under the umbrella of offices of student affairs.

Health Care

In 1861, Amherst College became the first institution of higher education to offer health services to its students. Others soon followed.[45] By the late 1800s, universities employed physicians to address student health and physical training,[46] a practice that persisted until college health care became its own distinct service center. The expansion of intercollegiate athletics further intertwined the role of the campus physician with tending to the needs of the collegiate athletes and their physical training, along with delivering health care to the rest of the student body.[47]

Historian Heather Munro Prescott points to the pandemic of 1918–1919, a time when many young men lost their lives to influenza, as the moment when medical professionals in the university first argued that health care was a "right and not a privilege" and should be readily available to all students.[48] In their push for student health care, these physicians initially faced opposition from the American Medical Association, whose members saw the provision of campus medical services as an encroachment on the private-sector medical practice.

However, the campus doctors' vigilance and determination to provide health care for college students proved successful. In 1920, the American College Health Association (ACHA) formed among the growing ranks of professionals serving college and university students through campus health care centers. As intercollegiate athletics became its own juggernaut and hired its own physicians and athletic trainers, athletics and student health centers eventually parted ways, with student health centers typically reporting to the president or the vice president for student affairs.

By the 1960s, college health services had expanded to involve multiple health care professionals and specializations. Over twenty-seven thousand professionals worked in college health services as the 1980s came to an end, with about three thousand physicians providing care alongside licensed nurse practitioners, registered nurses, and physician assistants. But concerns emerged in tandem with this growth, as some critics alleged that college health services delivered subpar care. Some even described college health services as the "backwater of medicine."[49]

As student populations diversified, the role of college health care centers evolved. Sometimes these centers were the only option for lower-income students who needed primary care, injury treatment, contraception, reproductive health services, diagnostic work, and ongoing support for chronic diseases. Pressure from students forced college health centers both to expand services and to ensure continuous quality of health care. Today, in addition to medical services, many student health care centers also provide wellness education programs and mental health services. Approximately 4,400 campuses in the United States operate student health care centers today[50] and ACHA has 3,000 members.[51]

Counseling and Mental Health Care

The first psychiatrist recorded as hired by a campus was at Princeton University in 1910, and his role was focused on "student personality development."[52] However, it was not until the 1960s that colleges and universities began to regularly provide formal counseling services and mental health care to their student population. In 1961 ACHA published standards for college health services, including mental health.[53] Up to that point, colleges and universities had typically left mental health care to private practices of psychiatrists, clinical psychologists, or clinical social workers. College-age individuals with mental illness were not likely to be enrolled in colleges; those who needed more intensive care were likely placed in residential mental health institutions. The expansion of mental health care in colleges and universities reflected modern medicine's success in treating mental health disorders in the late twentieth century and early twenty-first century. It also reflected a cultural shift away from institutionalization toward community-based care and greater public acceptance of neurosis, anxiety, and depression. For the first time, college had become a realistic option for people with mental health challenges. With the proper medication and support, the previously closed doors of the university swung open for them.

With more students seeking mental health services over the last two decades or so, some campus health care centers have merged their psychiatric and mental health services with campus counseling centers run by counselors, clinical psychologists, and social workers. The shifting structure of mental health services reflects the changes to how mental health professionals have categorized the kinds of problems that young people experience. As the American Psychiatric Association periodically updated the *Diagnostic and Statistical Manual of Mental Disorders*, changing its classifications of mental disorders, addiction to drugs or alcohol, eating disorders, learning acquisition problems related to reading and retention, and post-traumatic stress disorder and recognizing that homosexuality was not in fact a mental disorder, so too did the university change its approach to supporting and treating its students.[54]

Today, at least seven national professional organizations have members that may be involved with mental health services in colleges and universities. They include specialized divisions of the American Psychological Association; the National Association of Social Workers; the American Counseling Association; the Association of University and College Counseling Center Directors; the American Mental Health Counselors Association; the American College Health Association; and the American Psychiatric Association. The American College Counseling Association aims to bridge the different professions serving mental health needs in colleges and universities. Its members include psychologists, social workers, and counselors; their organization has published the *Journal of College Counseling* since 1998.

In 2018–2019, an annual survey prepared by the Healthy Minds Network reported that 56 percent of US college students annually receive some sort of mental health professional support, whether on campus or elsewhere.[55] A survey the previous year by the Association for University and College Counseling Center Directors found that about one in every eight students received counseling services directly from their college or university.[56] Mental health support is expected to be in high demand among students after the multiple crucible events of 2020–2021.

Disability Services

Support for college students with disabilities started in 1864 when Edward Miner Gallaudet established the National Deaf-Mute College in Washington, DC. It was renamed after him in 1893 and gained university status as Gallaudet University in 1986. Elsewhere, however, students with disabilities historically received limited support from residential colleges and universities. After World War I, US Congress passed legislation to support veterans with disabilities who sought a college education, but few of these veterans actually enrolled. Disability services greatly expanded after World War II, when large numbers of veterans enrolled at colleges and universities. In 1947, thanks in large part to the GI Bill, 49 percent of all college attendees were veterans.[57] ACE reported in 1950 that the large numbers of college students with single or multiple disabilities required a wide range of support services and appropriate shelter. They included veterans with amputations, many of whom needed assistance with writing. There were veterans with injured voice boxes who were unable to speak; veterans with chronic spinal pain or back and hip injuries; and veterans suffering the chronic consequences of rheumatic fever, malaria, tuberculosis, or heart ailments. Still others had hearing loss or vision loss or suffered psychological stress from the trauma of war.[58]

Through sustained activism, public protests, and many meetings with public officials, people with disabilities fought tirelessly for their civil rights as equal members of society and for appropriate accommodations to allow them access to the built environment. Under considerable public pressure to answer the clarion call of the disability rights community, and facing a clear structural lag between the lack of adequate public accommodations and the needs of vulnerable citizens, Congress provided sweeping protections for individuals with disabilities through the Rehabilitation Act of 1973. Section 504 of the Rehabilitation Act states:

> No otherwise qualified individual with a disability in the United States, as defined in section 705 (20) of this title, shall, solely by reason of his or her disability, be excluded from the participation in, be denied the benefits of,

or be subjected to discrimination under any program or activity receiving
Federal financial assistance or under any program or activity conducted by
any Executive agency or by the United States Postal Service.[59]

The legislation specifically mentioned higher education. However, the
Department of Health, Education, and Welfare (HEW) refused to issue
regulations, fearing the costs associated with making accommodations for
people with disabilities. In the absence of regulations, university administrators, state and local government, and others did not take action. A major
and sustained public outcry from the disability rights community ensued,
including a twenty-six-day occupation of the San Francisco HEW regional
office in 1977. The protesters who refused to leave included paraplegics
and quadriplegics, blind and deaf individuals, and people who needed
oxygen or special medication; the determined activists occupying the
building were widely reflective of the diversity of the disability community.
Reaching as many as 150 strong, they put themselves at risk without
customary health accommodations, hot water, and slept on floors, insistent
on the importance of the regulatory implementation of Section 504.
Under Secretary Joseph A. Califano, HEW finally issued regulations in
1977, and in those regulations, university compliance was required.[60]

Paralleling this landmark 1973 legislation was the 1975 Education of All
Handicapped Children Act, expanded in subsequent years to include
college and university students. Following these laws, colleges and universities expanded their array of services for people with disabilities and
enhanced accommodations in campus facilities.

In 1977, an organization for collegiate professionals serving disabled
students was established – the Association on Handicapped Student
Service Programs in Postsecondary Education, renamed in 1992 as the
Association on Higher Education and Disability (AHEAD).[61] The organization now has over four thousand members.[62]

In the 1980s, after some of their early accomplishments, the disabilities
community demanded that the government implement universal design
principles and additional support services to make it possible for them to
live with greater autonomy and greater acceptance of their presence. To
expand and further clarify the definition of a disability, Congress
passed the Americans with Disabilities Act (ADA) in 1990. For universities, one of the major consequences of the ADA stemmed from its
inclusion of learning disabilities as a recognized form of disability. The
number of students with learning disabilities entering four-year colleges
and universities grew dramatically in the years following the ADA, and
colleges and universities developed new services to support these

students.[63] As a result, the percentage of students with disabilities in undergraduate education grew from 11 percent in 2007–2008 to 19.4 percent just eight years later.[64]

***

By the early 1900s, many colleges and universities had developed programs capable of supporting young adults from prosperous families, whose parents had the resources to guide their children through whatever physical or mental health challenges they might encounter. The original deans of women built personnel services and an associated philosophy of service provision around this constituency. But once the GI Bill welcomed veterans onto college campuses and ushered in the democratization of higher education, the limitations of these existing services began to emerge.

Today's students, more diverse than any prior generation of students, arrive on college campuses with multiple intersecting needs, including questions about their gender and sexual identity; both visible and invisible disabilities; addiction; and mental illness. Over time, campuses have gradually developed a battery of specialized student services to respond to these emerging needs, organized under the umbrella of student affairs. The professionals who work in the student affairs divisions come from a wide range of disciplines and professions, and they affiliate and identify with peers at specialty national associations. Table 6.1, presented in the next chapter, lists some of the most prominent national associations whose members provide services under the umbrella of student affairs and suggests the range of their specialties and constituencies.

Efforts at Collaboration

In 1934, a short-lived coalition of ten different national associations representing a range of student services met to discuss ways for the different professional groups to collaborate. A few years later, in 1938, five associations representing deans and advisors of both men and women students, personnel managers, union representatives, and registrars tried again "to find ways and means for closer coordination."[65] For a variety of reasons, this plan also failed. It was not until the formation of the Inter-Association Coordination Committee in 1959 that such an organization finally took hold. In 1964 it became the Council of Student Personnel Associations of Higher Education and in 1969 it expanded to include sixteen organizations focused on cross-cutting issues in student affairs. But in the early 1970s, different organizations began to peel off, and the organization struggled, finally folding in 1975.

Student affairs practitioners initiated a slightly different effort in 1977 when they joined to create the Council for the Advancement of Standards in Higher Education.[66] This organization successfully established professional standards for forty-five different functional areas. In 2002, ACPA and NASPA formed a Blue Ribbon Committee intended to unify various specializations in student affairs. Six years later, that led to the creation of the Task Force on the Future of Student Affairs, which proposed consolidating the two major national associations in student affairs. In 2011, the effort failed to reach the two-thirds majority of voting members from both organizations required to legally consolidate, leaving ACPA and NASPA, the two largest organizations focused on student affairs, as separate and independent entities.[67]

Student services professionals' earnest attempts to reckon with the segmentation of their professional organizations and the service professionals they represent have not yet borne fruit. From the student perspective, for the most part, integrated student services do not exist today. The units students look to across the university have their own expertise, power bases, and forms of information control, often seeking to serve the same student with too little alignment among their efforts.

Effectiveness of Splintered Services?

Throughout this book, I have emphasized the gap between the university's historic ambition of treating the student as a whole person and its actual service fragmentation. A 2019 report prepared by consultants from Entangled Solutions for NASPA examined the effectiveness of several different service areas. They identified evidence that five areas – academic advising, first-year experience, supplemental instruction, career services, and early warning and early alert systems – "support improvements in academic outcomes, college persistence, and college completion."[68] But it found those services to be fragmented, without adequate integration for the advancement of the student.[69] The Executive Summary states:

> despite growing evidence of the effectiveness of comprehensive advising and other services, the vast majority of students attend institutions that have yet to make the necessary changes to deliver these services well or in a way that is accessible to all students. Despite annual institutional spending of $1 billion on advising, planning, and student support services, we are not seeing a substantial improvement in student outcomes.[70]

Each student service office has a defined set of responsibilities, training, and resources, and each office defines success differently. In most settings, no one has overall accountability for student success. From the student's point of view, the absence of service integration can be frustrating and confusing. The consequences are costly both to students and to the broad mission of the academy.

Not only are the broad array of serves targeted for student support fairly independent, so are the units within student affairs. A study of three different campuses by Mathew Johnson found that despite the independence exhibited, student affairs offices can operate along very different philosophies and cultures.[71] On one campus, according to Johnson, students are viewed as "customers." In this example, the office of student affairs has a management-oriented staff focused on professional service delivery. It follows established policies and procedures and uses an approach that assumes students are familiar with navigating university functions and services. The office is well run and efficient, but not known for empathy and deeper personal relationships. The second campus is described as a "party school," where professional staff in the office of student affairs seek to ensure that students have a good time in college. The staff devotes considerable time to organizing events and entertainment, but interpersonal development and cocurricular programming are low priorities. In the third campus Johnson studied, the staff emphasize the importance of controlling student behavior and containing partying, drinking, indiscretion, and conflict. This more authoritarian approach to student services, Johnson notes, stifles student voices, with the result that they are only heard if and when students turn to protest and confrontation. Undoubtedly, other campuses display further variations and combinations of approaches.

Johnson's research reveals wide variability in the foci of offices dedicated to enriching and managing student affairs and experiences. If the overall student experience is a combination of all interactions, certainly interaction with the institutional offices and personnel focused on student affairs contributes significantly to that experience and college students' eventual success.

The Rising Costs of Student Services

The disruption of on-campus programming in the early months of the COVID-19 pandemic limited students' access to student services to electronic communication. Some services, such as mental health support, successfully migrated online in various forms. At the moment of crisis, however, university administrators' primary focus was the question of how faculty would teach their courses at a distance. Now that the immediacy of the crisis has passed, the pandemic offers an opportunity for administrators to reflect on which parts of student services are essential, and which are merely desirable. The demand for student services was rising before the pandemic, as was the cost for staffing such services. Demand will likely continue to increase based on student needs, particularly for mental health support. What services are best provided in-house, as part of the institution's core mission, and which could be contracted out? Which services can be amalgamated, integrated, or linked to be more efficient and accessible? Is the university currently providing services that might better be covered by student insurance? And finally, should some services institute a charge or an additional fee?

Wisconsin has experimented with adding student fees to pass on the costs associated with specific services. As a result of declining state resources at a time when the state had frozen the price of tuition, four public university campuses attempted to raise revenue by increasing mandatory fees for select services or improved facilities.[72] For example, fee increases could be tagged to popular services, such as mental health services, health care, or wellness programs. Many of the services associated with student affairs are designed to enhance student well-being and, in the search for new revenue, could be subject to a universal fee. The same could be said for funding for a new student center or new or remodeled residence halls. The university can amortize these brick-and-mortar projects, generally of great interest to the student community, over many years, yielding a modest individual fee per term.

In Wisconsin, each campus administration had the discretion to propose the amount of a new fee or to increase an existing fee. Some campuses passed their fee increases onto all students, while others exempted some students, such as commuters, or allocated the fee based on the credit hours enrolled. The University of Wisconsin System Office had to approve any additional fees or changes for an existing service.

The imposition of fees affects students differently, depending on their ability to pay. Nancy Kendall et al., based on their research at four public four-year colleges in Wisconsin from 2014 to 2016, devote an entire chapter to the impact of student fees on low-income students in their book, *The True Costs of College*.[73] Let's say, for example, that a university began levying a new student fee to help cover the construction cost of a new student center. The new student center may be an attractive and cheerful place for students to relax, but students with jobs may not have the time to enjoy the new building for which their fees help pay. As Kendall et al. point out, these students may feel excluded and develop a sense of resentment about their fees helping other, wealthier students to use and "own" the space.[74]

In other cases, Kendall et al. note that the "free" services that universities provide may turn out to have limited capacity to address student demand. The most obvious case being experienced nationwide is the availability of mental health services. The offerings available without an additional charge may fall short of meeting demand; limited staff capacity might create long wait times for an appointment, or the service might limit the number of visits to less than what a more intensive (but more expensive) off-campus treatment option could offer. While the campus provides some mental health services, they may be inadequate to protect at-risk students. This can have serious consequences for classroom performance and, even more importantly, for the students' personal safety. In this case, the campus needs to assign charges for additional care beyond budgeted amounts. If tuition is frozen, universities have few choices other than limiting services or instituting a student fee for service.[75]

Health care is another good example that Kendall et al. cite as a service that many campuses advertise as "free," with the costs for limited services built into student fees or tuition. Low-income students receive this as welcome news, as they may have previously been relying on public health services or emergency rooms for immediate care. They soon find out, however, that their needs may exceed what the health care center is willing to provide without additional charges. Specialized lab work, some medicines, selected forms of birth control, third-party medical services, or orthopedic devices, to name only a few examples, often come with a bill.[76] In the meantime, low-income students may have canceled other forms of health insurance to cut expenses, while their more affluent peers will have likely retained health coverage through their family's insurance plan. What may seem like a reasonable financial strategy from the perspective of the administration can have devastating consequences for students without deeper financial resources.

The point is that student services, no matter how professionally offered or well designed, require someone to pay for them. Universities have experimented with different ways of containing these costs, from adding or increasing fees to simply reducing the level of services previously offered. Many students will be able to absorb the extra fees and take advantage of the services offered, but for others, an additional fee can become one more hidden barrier, one more marker of difference, and one more way to loosen low-income students' ties to the institution. What has yet to be explored as a strategy for saving costs in student affairs is a substantial modernization of the student service infrastructure, including the possibility of integrating the functions associated with student success and well-being with the guidance and mentoring responsibilities of the faculty.

Dividing Lines

The evolution of student affairs cannot be considered separately from the influence of faculty culture on student service professionals seeking their place in the university. The fragmentation of student services, and student services professionals' impulse for specialization, is the inevitable result of organizational expectations deeply rooted in the institution itself.

Since the turn of the twentieth century, educators at residential colleges and universities have repeatedly emphasized the importance of a holistic approach to the educational and social development of the college student. The authors of *How College Affects Students: 21st Century Evidence That Higher Education Works*, arguably the single most comprehensive collection of research on the student experience in higher education, insist on the importance of a comprehensive view of student development. The team of researchers who prepared the volume write, "Regardless of the individual student's path or purpose, we contend that the traditional outcomes of college – knowledge acquisition, academic achievement, degree attainment, and occupational success – are a central part of a college education but do not entirely fulfill what it means to be an educated person." Becoming an educated person, they argue, involves "growth in self-understanding; development of personal, intellectual, cultural, and social interests; critical reflection on one's worldview, attitudes, and values; cultivation of moral and ethical standards; and preparation for global citizenship in a diverse nation and world."[77] There appears to be little disagreement as to the broad goal of student success and well-being from the perspective of the learner, the teacher, the researcher, and those in roles of support. But somehow the goals are thwarted and lost in operation.

Unfortunately, the atomistic approach to students' well-being is in evidence across the university, including in the clear cleavage between the faculty and other service professionals. Of this bifurcation, K. Patricia Cross remarked: "At best, this division of labor represents an administrative convenience; at worst, it depicts an erroneous and even dangerous conception of education."[78] One result of this schism between the cognitive and affective domains in colleges and universities is a diminution of faculty guidance in the moral and ethical development of the student, both inside and outside the classroom. Discussions of justice, equity, truth, duty, and humanity that might originate in the classroom and necessitate further dialogue outside of the classroom have been curtailed in many settings due to other faculty obligations.[79] Instead, this kind of discourse is passed on to staff or the students themselves, or is possibly lost entirely. With reductions in humanities programs, even curricular options for such discussion have been curtailed. For the most part, long gone is the expectation that students would study, debate, and discuss these issues and examine their personal character and role as moral citizens in society with their faculty outside class hours.[80]

The loss is palpable, as modern-day challenges exacerbated by social media raise questions as to what is fact, opinion, or falsehood. Students, like the general public, gravitate to preferred sources of information. The precariousness and messiness of the democratic process, which involves dialogue, compromise, and the right of all citizens to vote and express their opinions, are topics that too many people with more recent college degrees clearly have missed, ignored, or abandoned. Such concerns are on the mind of many academic leaders.

Other than out of convenience, why has such a division evolved between academic matters and the rest of the student experience? Some have argued the division merely represents the reallocation of responsibilities from faculty to staff. Once this reallocation took place, however, some faculty distanced themselves from student service personnel. There are faculty members who take umbrage at the sustained expansion and the increasing costs of the work of student affairs professionals. On many campuses, the use of the budget for student activities and events, derived from student fees, can rankle some faculty who see this as a drain of precious resources.[81] Faculty express concern at the allocation of additional resources to student affairs or other student services, particularly when resources are taken from the core campus budget. For their part, student affairs personnel come armed with utilization and demand metrics when they make their case for increased resources. It is rare, however, for such requests to be accompanied by service quality and student impact metrics, as these are often elusive to measure.[82]

These are delicate and complicated internal issues within the university. In offices of student affairs, we see multifaceted administrative units undertaking an essential set of services. In academic affairs, we see faculty providing essential teaching and guidance in their field. This separateness is hardly in the best interest of the student or the institution. As we contemplate a more student-centered university, clearly there needs to be a better balancing of roles, responsibilities, and respect between faculty and student service professionals. In particular, faculty need to take increased ownership of student intellectual engagement around citizenship and public responsibility in a democratic society.

While student affairs professionals may cooperate, there is no structural mechanism to formally align their tasks from the student perspective. Each area of specialization has hardened itself, making it more resilient to outside interference and less vulnerable to changes proposed by senior administrators; just as faculty have armed themselves with protections to safeguard their turf and authority, so have student and administrative service professionals secured themselves to protect their way of doing business. Anyone seeking ways to meld, align, or integrate services within student affairs and the broader array of student services needs to be fully aware of the multiple previous unsuccessful attempts to connect the related national service organizations and their constituencies. At the college or university level, however, there may be ways to provide a more holistic approach to student services and I will explore this further in Chapter 10.

Notes

1 I extend considerable appreciation to Robert Schwartz for his work on the history of student services, *Deans of Men and the Shaping of Modern College Culture* (New York: Palgrave Macmillan, 2010). This, like the development of other administrative functions in the university, is an area that has received far less scholarly attention than it merits. For further reading about campus life in the formative age of the university from 1890 to 1910, there are several original articles about college life at the turn of the century in James C. Stone and Donald P. DeNevi's *Portraits of the American University, 1890–1910* (San Francisco: Jossey-Bass, 1971). Readers interested in student culture and activities of the period, in particular school spirit and sports, should refer to James A. Henretta et al., *America: A Concise History, Vol. 2: Since 1865*, 6th ed. (Boston, MA: Bedford/St. Martin's, 2015), 530.

2 Phillip Lee, "The Curious Life of in Loco Parentis at American Universities," *Higher Education in Review* 8 (Spring 2011): 66, accessed May 3, 2021, https://papers.ssrn.com/sol3/papers.cfm?abstract_id=1967912.

3 Chad Wellmon, "The Amoral University: How Professors Ceded Their Authority," *Chronicle of Higher Education*, November 30, 2018, B11.

4 Patricia Albjerg Graham, "Expansion and Exclusion: A History of Women in American Higher Education," *Signs* 3, no. 4 (Summer 1978): 767, accessed May 3, 2021, www.jstor.org/stable/3173112.

5 Patsy Parker, "The Historical Role of Women in Higher Education," *Administrative Issues Journal* 5, no. 1 (Spring 2015): 7, accessed May 3, 2021, doi.org/10.5929/2015.5.1.1.

6 "Oberlin History," Oberlin College & Conservatory, accessed May 6, 2021, www.oberlin.edu/about-oberlin/oberlin-history.

7 "Antioch College," Ohio History Central, accessed May 6, 2021, https://ohiohistorycentral.org/w/Antioch_College.

8 Thomas D. Snyder, ed., *120 Years of American Education: A Statistical Portrait* (Washington, DC: National Center for Educational Statistics, 1993), 65, figure 14, accessed May 6, 2021, https://nces.ed.gov/pubs93/93442.pdf.

9 Parker, "Historical Role," 4.

10 Robert A. Schwartz, "Reconceptualizing the Leadership Roles of Women in Higher Education: A Brief History on the Importance of Deans of Women," *Journal of Higher Education* 68, no. 5 (September–October 1997): 504, accessed March 31, 2021, doi.org/10.2307/2959944.

11 Schwartz, "Leadership Roles," 505.

12 Michael S. Hevel, "Toward a History of Student Affairs: A Synthesis of Research, 1996–2015," *Journal of College Student Development* 57, no. 7 (October 2016): 852, accessed June 5, 2021, doi.org/10.1353/csd.2016.0082.

13 Brian C. Mitchell and W. Joseph King, *How to Run a College: A Practical Guide for Trustees, Faculty, Administrators, and Policymakers* (Baltimore: Johns Hopkins University Press, 2018), 85.

14 Hevel, "Toward a History," 847.

15 Schwartz, *Deans of Men*, 3.

16 Schwartz, *Deans of Men*, 141.

17 Lee, "*In Loco Parentis*," 66.

18 Carolyn Terry Bashaw, *"Stalwart Women": A Historical Analysis of Deans of Women in the South* (New York: Teachers College Press, 1999), 14.

19 Hevel, "Toward a History," 850.

20 Abbe Carter Goodloe, "Undergraduate Life at Wellesley," in *Portraits of the American University, 1890–1910*, ed. James C. Stone and Donald P. DeNevi (San Francisco: Jossey-Bass, 1971), 311–334; John R. Thelin, *A History of American Higher Education*, 2nd ed. (Baltimore: Johns Hopkins University Press, 2011), 181.

21 See Schwartz, "Leadership Roles," 502–522.

22 Bashaw, *"Stalwart Women,"* 70.

23 Bashaw, *"Stalwart Women,"* 70.

24 Bashaw, *"Stalwart Women,"* 1–17.

25 Janice Joyce Gerda, "A History of the Conferences of Deans of Women, 1903–1922" (PhD diss., Bowling Green State University, 2004), 24–25, accessed January 13, 2020, http://rave.ohiolink.edu/etdc/view?acc_num=bgsu1100290629.

26 Schwartz, *Deans of Men*, 142.

27 Patrick Dilley, "20th Century Postsecondary Practices and Policies to Control Gay Students," *Review of Higher Education* 25, no. 4 (Summer 2002): 416, accessed March 18, 2021, doi.org/10.1353/rhe.2002.0018.

28 Dilley, "Practices and Policies," 416.

29 Amit R. Paley, "The Secret Court of 1920," *Harvard Crimson*, November 21, 2002, accessed April 3, 2021, www.thecrimson.com/article/2002/11/21/the -secret-court-of-1920-at/; "Harvard Secret Court Expelled Gay Students in 1920," *Washington Post*, December 1, 2002, accessed May 3, 2021, www.washingtonpost.com/archive/politics/2002/12/01/harvard-secret-court -expelled-gay-students-in-1920/5633e721–67b4–426b-954f-4f25fc415c00/.

30 Arthur Jay Klein, *Survey of Land-Grant Colleges and Universities*, Vol. 1 (Washington, DC: United States Government Printing Office, 1930), 416.

31 Hevel, "Toward a History," 847.

32 Lynn M. Gangone, "The National Association for Women in Education: An Enduring Legacy," *NASPA Journal about Women in Higher Education* 1, no. 1 (2009): 3, accessed June 5, 2021, https://nces.ed.gov/pubs2020/2020144.pdf.

33 "History," National Association of Student Affairs Professionals, accessed April 2, 2021, www.nasap.net/about/history/.

34 These seven journals are *Journal of First-Generation Student Success, Community College Journal of Research and Practice, Journal of Student Affairs Research and Practice, Journal of Women and Gender in Higher Education, Journal of College and Character, Change: The Magazine of Higher Learning,* and *Technology & Higher Education: Emerging Practice.*

35 "About NASPA," NASPA: Student Affairs Administrators in Higher Education, accessed March 8, 2021, www.naspa.org/about.

36 "Who We Are," American College Personnel Association, accessed March 8, 2021, www.myacpa.org/who-we-are.

37 "The History of ACPA," American College Personnel Association, accessed March 8, 2021, www.myacpa.org/history.

38 Hannah Certis, "The Emergence of Esther Lloyd-Jones," *Journal of Student Affairs Research and Practice* 51, no. 3 (2014): 259, accessed March 11, 2021, doi.org/10.1515/jsarp-2014-0027.

39 American Council on Education, *The Student Personnel Point of View* (Washington, DC: American Council on Education, 1937), 1.

40 American Council on Education, *Student Personnel*, 5.

41 Roger L. Geiger, *American Higher Education Since World War II: A History* (Princeton, NJ: Princeton University Press, 2019), 5.

42 Geiger, *American Higher Education*, 6.

43 Robert A. Schwartz, "The Rise and Demise of Deans of Men," *Review of Higher Education* 26, no. 2 (Winter 2003): 234.

44 "Graduate Program Directory," NASPA: Student Affairs Administrators in Higher Education, accessed September 28, 2020, http://apps.naspa.org/grad programs/srchres.cfm.

45 "A Brief History of ACHA," American College Health Association, accessed March 18, 2021, www.acha.org/ACHA/About/History/Brief_History /ACHA/About/Brief_History.aspx.

46 H. Spencer Turner and Janet L. Hurley, "The History and Development of College Health," in *The History and Practice of College Health*, ed. H. Spencer Turner and Janet L. Hurley (Lexington, KY: University Press of Kentucky, 2002), 3.

47 Turner and Hurley, "College Health," 4.
48 Heather Munro Prescott, "Student Bodies, Past and Present," *Journal of American College Health* 59, no. 6 (2011): 466.
49 Turner and Hurley, "College Health," 16.
50 David R. McBride et al., *ACHA Benchmarking Committee Report: 2010 Survey on the Utilization of Student Health Services* (Silver Spring, MD: American College Health Association, 2010), 2, accessed March 19, 2021, www.acha.org/documents/resources/survey_data/benchmarking/ACHA_Benchmarking_Report_2010_Utilization_Survey.pdf.
51 American College Personnel Association, "History of ACPA."
52 David P. Kraft, "One Hundred Years of College Mental Health," *Journal of American College Health* 59, no. 6 (June 2011): 478, accessed March 18, 2021, doi.org/10.1080/07448481.2011.569964.
53 Kraft, "One Hundred Years," 479.
54 Kraft, "One Hundred Years," 479.
55 Daniel Eisenberg and Sarah Ketchen Lipson, *The Healthy Minds Study: 2018–2019 Data Report* (Ann Arbor, MI: Healthy Minds Network, 2019), 3, accessed March 19, 2021, https://healthymindsnetwork.org/wp-content/uploads/2019/09/HMS_national-2018-19.pdf.
56 Peter LeViness et al., *The Association for University and College Counseling Center Directors Annual Survey 2018* (Indianapolis: Association for University and College Counseling Center Directors, 2019), 26, accessed March 18, 2021, www.aucccd.org/assets/documents/Survey/2018%20aucccd%20survey-public-revised.pdf.
57 Villanova University, "From $60 to a College Education: Origins and Development of the GI Bill: The Servicemen's Readjustment Act of 1944 (GI Bill of Rights)," updated January 14, 2021, accessed February 4, 2022, www.villanovau.com/resources/military/origins-of-the-gi-bill/.
58 Ralph J. Strom, *The Disabled College Veteran of World War II* (Washington, DC: American Council on Education, 1950), 39–40, accessed November 5, 2019, https://hdl.handle.net/2027/uc1.b4237151.
59 Section 504 of the Rehabilitation Act of 1973, 29 U.S.C. § 794 (1973).
60 "Patient No More: 1977 Occupation of Federal Offices in San Francisco," FoundSF, accessed May 7, 2021, www.foundsf.org/index.php?title=Patient_No_More:_1977_Occupation_of_Federal_Offices_in_San_Francisco. "Patient No More" also gives a day-by-day description of the occupation. For further information on the disability rights movement and occupations, I recommend Nicole Newnham and James LeBrecht's 2020 documentary, *Crip Camp: A Disability Revolution* (Los Angeles: Higher Ground Productions), available on Netflix at www.netflix.com/title/81001496.
61 Joseph W. Madaus, "The History of Disability Services in Higher Education," *New Directions for Higher Education* 2011, no. 154 (Summer 2011): 10–11.
62 "Home Page," Association on Higher Education and Disability, accessed November 4, 2019, www.ahead.org/home.
63 Madaus, "Disability Services," 11–12.

64 National Center for Education Statistics, "Number and Percentage Distribution of Students Enrolled in Postsecondary Institutions, by Level, Disability Status, and Selected Student Characteristics: 2003–04 and 2007–08," table 240, accessed April 7, 2021, https://nces.ed.gov/programs/digest/d10/tables/dt10_240.asp; National Center for Education Statistics, "Number and Percentage Distribution of Students Enrolled in Postsecondary Institutions, by Level, Disability Status, and Selected Student Characteristics: 2015–16," table 311.10, accessed April 7, 2021, https://nces.ed.gov/programs/digest/d19/tables/dt19_311.10.asp.

65 Jared T. Tuberty, "The Council of Student Personnel Associations in Higher Education: A Historical Analysis of Inter-Association Collaboration in Student Affairs" (PhD diss., Bowling Green State University, 2018), 2, accessed March 4, 2021, http://rave.ohiolink.edu/etdc/view?acc_num=bgsu1539097186242367.

66 Tuberty, "Student Personnel Associations," 9.

67 Tuberty, "Student Personnel Associations," 11–13.

68 NASPA: Student Affairs Administrators in Higher Education and Entangled Solutions, *Accelerating the Growth of Institutional Success Services: Working Together to Scale and Sustain Integrated Advising and Holistic Student Support* (working paper, NASPA: Student Affairs Administrators in Higher Education and Entangled Solutions, Washington, DC, 2019), 49.

69 NASPA: Student Affairs Administrators in Higher Education and Entangled Solutions, *Accelerating the Growth*, 17.

70 NASPA: Student Affairs Administrators in Higher Education and Entangled Solutions, *Accelerating the Growth*, 5.

71 Mathew B. Johnson, "Social Class and Cultural (Re)production in Higher Education: An Ethnographic Look at the Culture of Student Affairs Offices" (PhD diss., Brandeis University, 2002), accessed April 4, 2021, https://search.proquest.com/docview/305343824?pq-origsite=primo.

72 For more information, see the chapter "The True Costs of Student Fees" in Nancy Kendall et al.'s *The True Costs of College* (Cham, Switzerland: Palgrave Macmillan, 2020), 91–122.

73 Kendall et al., "True Costs," 91–122.

74 Kendall et al., "True Costs," 101.

75 Kendall et al., "True Costs," 113–117.

76 Kendall et al., "True Costs," 110.

77 Matthew J. Mayhew et al., *How College Affects Students, Vol. 3: 21st Century Evidence That Higher Education Works* (San Francisco: Jossey-Bass, 2016), 159.

78 Robert M. Hendrickson et al., *Academic Leadership and Governance of Higher Education: A Guide for Trustees, Leaders, and Aspiring Leaders of Two- and Four-Year Institutions* (Sterling, VA: Stylus, 2013), 363.

79 Wellmon, "Amoral University," B11.

80 Wellmon, "Amoral University," B11–B12.

81 Mitchell and King, *How to Run*, 88–89.

82 John V. Lombardi, *How Universities Work* (Baltimore: Johns Hopkins University Press, 2013), 124.

CHAPTER 6

Decision-Making, Governance, and the Distribution of Power: Implications for the Student Experience

At first glance, the typical American nonprofit four-year residential college or university appears to be a classic hierarchy, with organizational unit personnel reporting through their supervisors to the president or chancellor, who in turn reports to a board of governors. In this model, decisions flow back and forth from reporting units and the central administration. In fact, the hierarchy and decision-making process at a typical university is far more complex and nuanced than this, often encompassing other complex organizations with their own processes, traditions, and subcultures. A university might be associated with a hospital system or manage a conference center, for instance, each with its own semiautonomous management structure and organizational culture. Even within the university proper, different divisions may operate in distinctive ways. As discussed earlier, the university is a conglomeration of different semiautonomous operational units linked together to assist with a multiplicity of purposes.

Written nearly half a century ago, J. Victor Baldridge's insightful reflections on New York University's academic social structure remain true today at many universities:

> The university is fractured, divided, and complicated by interlaced networks of authority, status, professional outlook, and special interests. There are common values and concerns, of course, that hold the university together as a relatively cohesive enterprise, but this is indeed remarkable in light of the divisions and conflicts of interest that permeate the campus. Power is loose and ambiguous, in large measure because of the complex social framework: there is extreme specialization among the university's participants, extreme fragmentation of its values, and extreme complexity in its structural arrangements.[1]

This chapter will examine the unique decision-making, governance, and distribution of power in the university and the implications for the student experience. Comparing the different approaches of the academic and administrative units reveals markedly different organizational styles.

Faculty are afforded unique privileges in terms of oversight of their activities, their decision-making processes, and overall governance compared to the rest of the campus. Within academic departments, even faculty and staff within the same unit are governed differently. A department chair, who is a member of the faculty unit, might report to a dean who reports to a senior academic administrator in typical hierarchical form, while the faculty in the department may be overseen in a more collaborative or networked manner via a committee structure. Meanwhile, the department's administrative staff associates are accountable to the department chair and do not share in the more collaborative shared governance structure and flexibility in the use of time and duties that faculty enjoy.

The university has a wide range of internal groups with differential access to power and authority. Some have influence because of the tradition of shared faculty governance, others by the nature of their work and title. Others find a voice in decision-making through a function of their personality or circumstantial factors, while still others, customarily staff, have far less voice in their duties and assignments. Any agenda designed to improve responses to a changing student body must take these dynamics and unique internal operations into account.

To add to the complexity, the faculty itself includes members with at least four different levels of autonomy and authority. There are faculty members who have earned tenure; those who are still on the tenure track; those who are full-time, but not on the tenure track, who serve on annual or multiyear contracts; and, finally, adjunct faculty hired on a per-course basis. Those with tenure have a level of employment security without equal in the university. They have considerable authority over faculty hiring and the curriculum. Those on the tenure track are at risk of termination until and unless they earn tenure. They have less authority, influence, and voice as a consequence of their precarious standing. Those on contracts are vulnerable to falling enrollment, fiscal challenges, or performance concerns at the time of contract renewal; they often have less voice in shared governance. Those hired to teach specific courses, meanwhile, have little or no voice in shared governance. In contrast, all staff, even those working in academic units, are governed by traditional employment rules and regulations. Their formal authority is related to their position in the hierarchy.

These powerful structural and cultural dynamics are the legacies of more than a century's worth of decisions that, collectively, have established the politics and distribution of power on campus. The question before us is whether fundamental change is possible within such an entrenched, decentralized structure and culture. I believe such change is possible but not without a clear understanding of internal processes that govern the current form of the American four-year college.[2]

The starting point for changes emphasizing student success and well-being involves a close look at university governance, starting with the power historically delegated to the faculty. But because the university is much more than its faculty, the chapter also examines the role of staff within academic affairs, professional staff in nonacademic units, professionals in student affairs, and, of course, the power and authority of the president. After this survey of university governance, I provide a broader theoretical examination of the university as an institution as the necessary context for what it will take to modernize and reform the student experience.

Shared Governance and Faculty Power

Faculty members occupy a unique position within university governance by virtue of three traditions: shared governance, tenure, and academic freedom,[3] concepts that have evolved in the USA over the last century. While final authority, delegated by the board of directors, remains with the institution's executive, shared governance gives faculty a role in consultation and decision-making on matters of university-wide policy.[4] That said, the implementation of shared governance varies considerably across colleges and universities.

The American Association of University Professors (AAUP) officially codified shared governance as an expectation of university management in 1920.[5] As now understood, the concept encompasses a wide range of obligations and expectations, including that university administrators consult with faculty members on the hiring of leadership and on major decisions that affect the future of the university. Many administrators and board members perceive this deliberative and consultative process as cumbersome and slow, at times even an obstacle to rapid modernization.[6]

Faculty moreover play pivotal roles in hiring and evaluating peer scholars and, eventually, in recommending tenure, a contractual status that reinforces their intellectual freedom and employment security. Faculty also make recommendations regarding the curriculum and, commonly, the creation of new academic programs – all matters dear to students. At most universities, their recommendations are not necessarily binding but rarely denied, even though new programs customarily are reviewed by the provost and president and formally approved by a board of overseers.

Many universities also include faculty representatives on the governance committees involved in developing campus budgets.

Faculty manage the day-to-day operations of their respective academic departments, schools, or colleges. The department chair is a member of the faculty with a specified term of service that often comes with the option of reappointment at the end of the term. Departmental traditions vary, with some having long-serving chairs, while others prefer a routine and regular change of leadership. In some departments, the dean is involved in selecting the chair, while in others faculty elections select chairs. The person serving as chair may or may not have prior supervisory experience, but is nevertheless responsible for overseeing the budget, unit planning, course assignments, new curricula, faculty personnel matters, day-to-day operations, and supervising unit staff. The chair usually receives some form of compensation, whether in the form of a teaching release or additional pay or benefits, in exchange for the extra responsibility.

Beyond the department, faculty typically exercise their influence on university governance through faculty committees. At the university level, these include standing committees formalized by a faculty senate as well as ad hoc committees created for specific purposes. Faculty committees address curricular, personnel, budgetary, research, and operational issues at the school, college, and department level. This consultative approach to decision-making at various levels complicates the locus of authority at the university. Even in the most favorable circumstances, a university's capacity for swift decision-making is limited; it can be further constrained as committee assignments, attendance, and membership change over time.[7] We have seen a public health crisis or natural disasters force decisive action, but those events are distinct from the deliberative process customarily associated with faculty governance.

To further compound the complexity, a hierarchy of faculty committees typically engage sequentially on any given decision. For example, an academic review that culminates in a tenure decision may require independent reviews at multiple levels. The process begins in the home department or school, with the candidate creating a file that reflects their body of academic work. The review then customarily involves a written independent analysis of that work by expert scholars from other universities. The file is then reviewed by the home department or school, where individual tenured faculty members vote to affirm or deny tenure. It then goes to the department chair for a separate and independent review, and then to the dean for yet another review. It would not be unusual for a standing committee of faculty members drawn from across the university to conduct still another review. All of that information and the varying opinions regarding the candidate's accomplishments then goes to the provost and president for a decision that will ultimately be reviewed by the board (in some settings a denial at the academic unit terminates the process). Customarily, the board officially makes the tenure appointment, but the earlier reviews and the final decision by the provost and/or president are crucial. Should a faculty member appeal a tenure denial, another faculty committee often composed of campus-wide representatives might review the grievance and pass it to the president for a final decision. The entire tenure process can take a year or more.

Such an elaborate process, involving such high stakes, can be very stressful for candidates. A faculty member denied tenure will, in most cases, need to find another job at a different institution, which is not easily done in today's market. Imagine being denied a permanent position after spending an average of 7.8 years from the start of graduate school to its finish,[8] possibly 3–5 years as a postdoctoral fellow, several years on the faculty job market, and 6 years in a probationary faculty position. The anguish and trauma can be significant. Nevertheless, tenured faculty members tend to see the process as a way to ensure high academic standards and strengthen their department's future rather than as an inappropriate hazing ritual, a perception probably related to the fact that they primarily control it.

Awarding tenure dates back to the turn of the twentieth century when faculty at too many campuses found their appointments held hostage to the personal preferences of individual donors or board members. In the late 1800s, universities fought retention battles on behalf of faculty whose ideas were viewed as controversial or otherwise threatening to the status quo. The AAUP declared a set of principles that began to lay the ground-work for tenure as we know it at its founding in 1915. A quarter of a century later, the AAUP officially codified the practice in its "Statement of Principles of Academic Freedom and Tenure."[9] At that time, the AAUP specified that the terms of initial employment were to be in writing, the probationary period for review of tenure should be no more than seven years, and that universities must have explicit parameters for the (rare) dismissal of a tenured faculty member.

The process and procedures of tenure have evolved since that time, but the basic principles remain.[10] In general, only faculty members who are already tenured and at least one rank above the candidate may vote on tenure cases. While the process of earning tenure can be arduous, once achieved, it provides faculty members with a cherished level of security, as well as with protections for academic freedom in faculty research, creative output, and classroom teaching.

The process is not without flaws. Individual faculty members may have personal grudges against a tenure candidate independent of the candidate's academic merit. External letters assessing the candidate's scholarly contributions can land on the desk of another scholar who has an intellectual disagreement with the written work; their negative review can influence a decision. The tenure system can also disadvantage those who have taken on subjects that traverse traditional disciplinary lines and may have fewer distinguished colleagues in these new fields able to prepare the sort of letters justifying the significance of the work. This burden may fall most heavily on women and people of color of any gender working in selected fields. Hopefully, a careful review of a tenure file by the final decision-maker(s) can determine the validity of the criticism and make a fair and independent decision in the best interest of the university.

At leading research universities, a faculty member who is an excellent instructor, but lacks quantity and quality of publications, will likely be denied tenure. Students who have benefited from the teaching and mentorship of this individual might question how an excellent teacher could be removed when others, perhaps not as gifted in the classroom, receive tenure. The decision to dismiss a popular teacher is always painful for students, and it is particularly egregious when the faculty member is a person of color. It runs counter to the notion of diversity, inclusion, student-centeredness, and the goal of building relationships between students and faculty. These contradictions, conflicts, and difficult decisions reflect some of the challenges for board members and senior officials in managing an institution that practices shared governance, expects its faculty to maintain a distinguished and even international reputation, and, at the same time, desires to become more inclusive, diverse, and student-centered.

Since its introduction, the tenure system has been under constant assault from critics both within and outside the university. Tenure reduces administrators' capacity to make strategic cuts in the faculty workforce, putting pretenured and nontenure-track faculty at risk in times of budgetary crisis – even if they are not the faculty members working in subject areas with declining enrollments or other signs of declining productivity. The internal tenure process consumes so much faculty energy and time that might be directed in other ways, raising questions of appropriateness and balance. Within the public university system, recent incidents reveal examples of legislators, boards, and university presidents seeking to dismiss tenured faculty, whether for ideological or fiscal reasons (tenured faculty may be terminated based on "just cause" or should an institution declare "financial exigency"[11]). In defiance of tenure, different state legislatures have advanced bills that seek to restrict faculty opinions in the classroom, or even more directly eliminate tenure, giving administrators greater latitude to terminate faculty based on their ideology.[12] Further, individual legislators have demanded documentation from campus officials of speci-fied themes prevalent in courses seeking to purge topics they find objec-tionable.[13] For a few states, the national political vitriol has inspired some elected officials to target their concerns on local colleges and universities, their curriculum, and the faculty who teach. Interestingly enough, this is precisely why prior generations of scholars fought for tenure and academic freedom. The AAUP continues to support those at risk of losing tenure, including through lawsuits challenging universities' attempts to dismiss faculty members without due process and just cause.

Since its codification, tenure has played a demonstrable role in the university. In a special issue on tenure prepared nationally for college and university trustee members, *Trusteeship* described how tenure, and the sense of job security it entails, grants faculty a level of freedom to disagree with or even resist directives that might not be as easily expressed in other organizations. The special issue also observed that, among faculty, a "systematic skepticism pervades the academy."[14] Indeed, faculty mem-bers have spent their careers honing their critical thinking skills, learning to be skeptical of information in their area of study, even of luminaries in their own fields. This inherent skepticism is essential in understanding the role of the faculty in the governance of the university. An administrator who hopes to implement a change agenda must develop comfort with this dynamic and patience in engaging in thoughtful interchanges with faculty members. Technically, all internal governance processes that involve fac-ulty consultation are advisory to the president; most university by-laws delegate a board's authority for administrative decision-making to the president. Nevertheless, a shrewd president needs to be mindful of the faculty's sense of ownership of curricular and personnel matters. While the process flows in a bottom-up hierarchical manner, it is infused with considerable deliberation and discussion.

Shared faculty governance, whether in questions of hiring, tenure, or curriculum development, involves a sequence of processes that switch on and off at different administrative levels, deliberately including different points of view, moving like a gear that hits a cog, pauses, then jumps forward to the next committee process. It begins with the set of academic players best informed on the case in question. Next, it moves to another group of faculty, deliberately situated at some distance from the subject, and so on, inching forward along a hierarchy toward eventual resolution. Though time-consuming and labor-intensive, the shared governance process ensures that academic decisions are vetted thoroughly, reflecting the high standards of the community. It may produce strains in the power relationship between faculty and administration, but as Baldridge observes, "[d]uality of authority and ambiguity of power are the price of ensuring that faculty expertise will have its say."[15]

Despite the power and influence that shared governance and tenure give faculty, many faculty are reluctant to become too involved in the granular details of university operations. From elementary school through to the PhD, faculty members participate in a system that rewards them for individual excellence and personal achievement. They are primed to focus on their personal work and its contribution to their area of study. Some faculty see ties to the broader university, and in some cases even to their home department, as a responsibility that can conflict with their individual career ambition, leaving service duties and nurturing undergraduate students to those faculty with a particular calling or those faculty hired on contracts without tenure, or for certain tasks, professional staff. This dynamic is particularly damaging for women in selected disciplines and minority candidates on the path to tenure, as students looking to connect with faculty with backgrounds similar to their own turn to these faculty members for support and advice. The students may feel there is no one else to turn to – and they may be right. Too many talented junior faculty members have been denied tenure precisely because they chose to spend their time caring for their students and building community on campus. It is hard to say no to a needy student – and they should not have to.

Tenured faculty members are particularly reluctant to participate in governance issues that deal with the more bureaucratic and technical – rather than academic – aspects of the university. Many faculty members see the administrative processes and rules on such matters as purchasing, local or state or federal government regulations, student financial aid or registration procedures, and cumbersome bureaucratic transactions as a drain on their time and, possibly, their academic productivity. Not only do they shirk committees wrestling with such issues, but they may also, on occasion, actively circumvent these same rules. While faculty can be harsh critics of time-consuming university procedures and red tape, too few are willing to dive into the types of technical details that might ameliorate processes they see as vexing and unnecessary.

Over the years, I have known a handful of productive faculty members who left one university for another over issues of bureaucratic unresponsiveness, ranging from errors in the timely processing of grants, to inadequate staff support, to frustrations over frequently lost paperwork and inaccurate reports. I also know faculty members who have intentionally submitted a grant through another university due to its favorable submission process – denying the home institution the recognition and use of the generated indirect funding. Despite these frustrations and attempted endruns, some faculty find it easier to leave for another university promising better support than attempt to fix the problem, seeing the bureaucratic functions of the university as outside their area of responsibility or expertise. Too many faculty consider the university as a vehicle for their teaching and research, and its wider administrative operations, as well as the people involved in projects beyond their immediate sphere, as less important to their daily life. Given the rewards system in place, this is not an unreasonable response.

At the same time, faculty go to great lengths to defend traditions of shared governance when it comes to the university's academic operations. They see the decision-making process as important, if not more important, than the decision itself. A perceived violation of process threatens shared governance, a tradition and a source of authority that faculty seek to protect. They complain of a "lack of transparency" or "process" when they feel an administrative decision has been made too hastily or without appropriate consultation.

We have, then, a faculty culture that values shared governance, teaching and research, academic freedom, intellectual honesty and pursuit of truth, a commitment to excellence, and a tradition of mentoring the next generation of scholars. But beyond these broad statements, multiple conflicting priorities break swiftly into subcultures, both within departments and across academic units.[16] At the same time, individual faculty members must constantly and almost daily weigh their use of time for their own career advancement as well as for the collective good of the unit. From the perspective of a faculty member who has seen campus presidents and their strategic plans come and go, there is reason to be skeptical about the next administration's ambitious plans to transform the university. This is particularly true in an era when transitions at the top occur so frequently – even within three to five years. Given how faculty governance really works, administrators must understand the faculty's points of view, their inherent skepticism, and their reward structure. They must involve faculty in a manner that respects the decision-making process. Serious changes that promote greater student well-being cannot be fully achieved without engaging the faculty.

The Role of Professional Staff Reporting to Academic Affairs

University faculty, as well as the entire college or university, could not function without the support of a host of staff members and offices, from financial business operations to the office of human resources to the library. Each and every staff member has an important role to play. Here, I examine the role of the staff within the university's academic affairs unit – customarily the largest unit in the university, typically under the supervision of the provost, the chief academic officer reporting to the president.

As mentioned previously, staff within academic departments lack many of the privileges accorded faculty. Faculty come and go from their campus offices frequently and as they choose; they are often less visible during breaks between terms or in the summer. Even before the pandemic, it was not unusual for faculty to work from home, a lab, or off-site, sometimes during odd hours of the day or night, largely unseen by staff or students. In contrast, staff members – especially administrative support staff – are generally expected to show up in person with predetermined office hours. Some opt for telework, but this requires supervisory review and approval. It remains to be seen what will happen to these expectations as universities return to something resembling their normal operations after the pandemic subsides, but in all likelihood, supervisors will once again expect staff to be present on campus during business hours, particularly those who work directly with students or provide direct services. Departmental staff members often report to the department chair, but the supervisory attention provided to them will vary depending on who is serving in the role.

Moving up the hierarchy, each professional staff person employed at the college or school level likely reports to either an assistant dean, associate dean, or dean. The governance and flexibility accorded to these staff can often be different from those reporting directly to the faculty, as faculty may not be available to constantly oversee or hold them accountable in the same manner. Staff are not part of the shared governance tradition and are expected, as in any hierarchical organization, to follow the duties of their job description and undergo an annual performance review. Their engagement with students varies depending on their job descriptions.

The gulf in status between staff and faculty is reinforced regularly, and misunderstandings between the two are not uncommon. Faculty have been known to be condescending to staff and, understandably, staff members have been miffed at the arrogance of faculty. Within a given school or college, staff members have their own separate subculture or subcultures, depending on their various functions. Such fragmentation across professional categories with defined roles, of course, is not unique to universities. It can be seen in organizations like hospitals, law firms, real estate companies, large corporations, and even performing arts organizations.

Further up the academic ladder, the office of provost oversees all the academic units and their related professional units. These may include the library (some campuses also have tenured librarians), the registrar, institutional research, financial aid, admissions and enrollment management, study abroad, faculty personnel, academic financial management, online and/or continuing education (which may include faculty members), career services, veterans' services, academic support, one-stop business services, graduate studies, research administration, technology transfer, IT, and sponsored programs. The list is neither definitive nor exhaustive, as units reporting to the office of the chief academic officer vary across campuses. Nevertheless, each of these administrative offices eventually reports to the provost or their designated senior supervisor. These unit directors oversee a staff trained in their respective fields and are often affiliated with a national professional association. There may be a staff senate, but these are customarily weak committees that serve as a source of input and information to the campus leadership rather than as formal decision-making bodies. Some of these reporting units in academic affairs directly serve students.

The duties of personnel in undergraduate admissions, for example, give a sense of the complexity of the tasks undertaken by these specialists. Each year, starting more than a year before students would put down a deposit for enrollment, the admissions staff must calculate and obtain approval for target enrollment numbers for the next first-year class. Admitting too many students can create a housing problem; too few, a revenue shortfall. Admissions staff must consider the changing competitive market forces, the distribution of enrollment by region, diversity, the mix of income brackets, the amount of institutional financial aid available, and the match to areas of study.

The culture of the admissions staff is focused on building an incoming class, keeping in mind all possible permutations. With assistance from faculty and administrators, the team sets an admit and discount rate to meet the incoming class targets within budget. In the end, the admissions team builds a class, assists with the awarding of financial aid, and works to retain the right proportion of admitted students. Enrollment management is a high-stress operation that requires both analytical tools and personal communication skills. The success of everyone at the university depends on the success of enrollment managers. Their selection criteria contribute to admitted students' sense of being wanted. For many students and parents, their encounters with admissions staff provide the first impression of the college or university.

Similarly, each of the administrative units or offices provides services to the broader university and the various faculty groups. Each unit perceives itself to be accountable within a standard shared by their professional peers and enshrined by their national professional association. For example, in some university settings, the enrollment management group has little to do with the academic program. Their primary task is to recruit, vet, and enroll future students. However, the more successful admissions offices reach beyond their own specialization, provide feedback, and share with other academic units what they have learned in meetings with prospective students and their families about potential students' academic interests, perceptions of campus safety and housing, and possible curricular enhancements that might influence subsequent enrollment. Nevertheless, it is more common for administrative units and their staff to see their roles narrowly, and within their area of expertise.

The university provost's office contains a wide array of professional staff units that operate independently from the schools and colleges. Given the scope of the office's responsibilities, provosts need to cultivate the flow of information as well as shape policy. At American University (AU), at the suggestions of the deans, I began holding regular monthly meetings with staff leaders of the professional academic units reporting to the Office of the Provost as well as the associate deans within the schools and colleges. This "Provost's Operational Council" dived into the university's daily operations, regulations, practices, and policies at a level of granularity that allowed each of the units to report on their own practices, while also allowing them to learn from what others were doing. This dialogue across and among the units not only provided a venue for continuous improvement, but also kept me informed of salient administrative issues. Because of the provost's authority over all academic administrative functions, the council also provided me a forum to resolve disputes across units and to challenge administrators to consider more student-centric operations. I highlight some of these challenges in Chapter 8.

Other College and University Staff and Their Influence on the Student Experience

Another large set of offices maintains critical parts of the university's operations, such as information technology, budget and finance, facilities, human resources, legal affairs, student affairs, athletics, development, alumni relations, health care, and public safety, to name only a few. Many of these administrative functions are commonplace in other large organizations. In the case of the university, the overall senior directors of these units eventually report to the president or chancellor, and each unit has its own departments, power bases, traditions, functions, and subcultures. They fit more clearly into a linear bureaucratic structure than do the faculty.

The goals, databases, lines of communication, resources, and accountability of the different administrative offices are distinct and separate from one another. Universities typically establish cross-division committees to meet the obvious need for communication and coordination. For example, the president's office might establish a committee on campus-wide space planning, business intelligence, online learning, or risk management. In addition to permanent standing committees, universities might also establish specific task forces and working groups as needed, involving members from the different units. Most university presidents also maintain some form of "cabinet meetings" to gather input from and discuss strategy with the leadership of the various administrative divisions. The cabinet typically includes the key vice presidents, the provost, the general counsel, and the chief of staff who, together, represent the administration. These various administrative groups also coordinate their efforts through a complex web of regular meetings involving combinations of vice presidents, provost, and deans. The meetings foster shared dialogue and coordination and provide an opportunity for leadership to explore and test ideas. As routine parts of university operations, however, these meetings are unlikely to be the venue for large-scale organizational change.

Though understudied and perhaps underappreciated, these administrative units, their personnel, and their interactions have significant consequences in the lives of students. They are responsible for essential administrative tasks and, with the support of the president, wield significant power and authority, from overseeing the budget and managing the endowment, to the quality and condition of facilities, to the influence of legal considerations on campus policies and practices. Nonacademic units manage university communications, keep the data flowing, hire and retain staff, procure goods and services, keep the community safe, help build institutional identity and pride, manage athletics programs, and directly oversee student services (a topic to which I will return below). In one way or another, each of these offices influences the overall student experience, yet (except for those in student services) the responsibility for the overall student experience is unlikely to be part of a staff member's job description in most, but not all, of these administrative offices.

Each division of the university, while functioning independently and reporting to the university president, has its own set of external professional associations with opportunities for professional development. For example, university business officers often belong to the National Association of College and University Business Officers (NACUBO), which represents over 1,900 US colleges and universities. NACUBO's educational materials are designed to help business officers manage such issues as finance, advancement, facilities, endowments, energy, investments, risk, tuition discounting, taxation, procurement, and student financial service budgeting.[17]

In addition to relationships with peers in national associations, some members of the president's cabinet have external constituencies and pressures that may influence their decision-making. As one president told me, "I feel like I am at a meeting where ghosts are whispering in the ear of different members of my leadership team." For example, when discussions of debt service for necessary facility expenditures come up, the chief financial officer may feel the tug of Moody's Investors Service or Standard and Poor's ratings on creditworthiness. The legal counsel is preoccupied with fears of liability risk, and the communications officer worries about the local press's reporters and consequences for enrollment.

Each of these administrative unit's decisions has consequences for students and the overall university experience. For example, the chief financial officer's attitude toward risk can influence the composition of the endowment's investments and, ultimately, the availability of funds for university operations or financial aid to students. Decisions about facilities management can influence both academic programs and the services that support students, including those with disabilities. A CFO too focused on business priorities can become isolated from the university's distinctive mission and the priorities of academic and student life. An overly fearful general counsel can cause a president to move too cautiously, costing market positioning and visibility among prospective students and their families. The administrators in the president's cabinet, often invisible to students, have a significant influence on the student experience – and they need to be included in any plan to enhance that experience.

University-Wide Student Services

Student services deserve special attention for their direct relationship to students and potential role in institutional change. In its broadest sense, the term includes a wide swath of programs, offices, and activities that interact or involve students, many of which come under different administrative authorities across the university. While the exact categories and groupings vary from university to university, this can include everything from dining, health, mental health, supplemental instruction, financial aid, registration, orientation, resident student advisors, student judicial affairs, career planning, advising, admissions, campus security, aspects of technological support, library services, spiritual support, community services, recreation and entertainment, housing, Greek life, international services, retention, and intramural and collegiate team athletics.

The specific services within this group have distinctly different histories, identities, and reporting lines. Some, like dining and campus security, are considered auxiliary services and are accountable to the fiscal side of the institution. Others, such as advising, supplemental instruction, the library, and sometimes financial aid, are linked to academics. Still others, like health services, fitness, exercise, recreation and athletics, and more recently IT, have distinct histories and their reporting lines have evolved over time. Many of these service professions have developed their own identity, national organizations, professional standards, and support groups. Table 6.1 lists some of these national organizations, the year they were founded, their membership size, and whether they publish a journal(s).

Nevertheless, the widest array of direct services offered to students today typically come under the heading of "student affairs." As described in the previous chapter, this administrative unit often oversees student government, clubs, fraternities and sororities, spiritual life, housing, social support for first-year and transfer students, orientation, student behavior, counseling services, entertainment, cocurricular and extracurricular activities, health care, and resources for diverse populations – whether diversity is defined through ethnicity, religion, race, prior military service, disability, political affiliation, nationality, gender or sexual identity, or income – to name some of the areas. Customarily student affairs units house the dean of students and manage disciplinary actions. It would not be unusual for psychological counseling and health care to be included under this

Table 6.1 *Examples of national associations for personnel providing student services customarily outside the office of student affairs*

National Association	Founding Year	Membership	Journal
American Association of Collegiate Registrars and Admissions Officers	1910	11,000	Yes
Association for Student Conduct Administration	1987	3,000	Yes
Association of College & Research Libraries	1940	11,000	Yes
Association of International Educators (NAFSA)	1948	10,000	Yes
Association of Research Libraries	1932	125 libraries	No
Association of Title IX Administrators	1972	6,800	Yes
EDUCAUSE	1998	100,000	Yes
International Association of Campus Law Enforcement Administrators	1958	4,200	Yes
National Academic Advising Association (NACADA)	1979	10,000	Yes
National Association of Campus Safety Administrators	2015	–	No
National Association of College and University Business Officers (NACUBO)	1962	1,900 campuses	Magazine
National Association of College Auxiliary Services	1969	7,000	Magazine
National Association of College University Food Services	1958	–	Yes
National Association of Student Financial Aid Administrators	1966	28,000	Yes
National Career Development Association	1913	3,800	Yes

Sources: Association websites and contacts

umbrella, but that function could also be part of a different portfolio. Student affairs often oversee student activities and behavior in the residence hall and social activities and student entertainment on campus.

The office of student affairs, or its equivalent unit, customarily either reports to the office of the provost or the president, depending on the campus. As observed in Table 6.2, its staff members participate in a potpourri of national and regional associations allied with their area of specialization, with their own publications, conferences, and mechanisms to provide professional development and recognition. It would not be unusual to have professional staff involved with more than one national association. As a result of a desire for permanence on campus, they have

Table 6.2 *Examples of national associations for personnel customarily affiliated with the office of student affairs*

National Association	Founding Year	Membership	Journal
American College Counseling Association (A Division of the American Counseling Association)	1991	56,000 (within ACA)	Yes
American College Counseling Directors Association	1950	900 colleges	No
American College Health Association	1920	3,000	Yes
American College Personnel Association	1924	7,500	Yes
American Psychiatric Association	1844	38,500	Yes
American Psychological Association, Division 17, Society of Counseling Psychology, College and University Counseling Centers section	1892 (APA)	122,000	Yes
Association for Chaplaincy and Spiritual Life in Higher Education	2020	(merger)	–
Association for Orientation, Transition, and Retention in Higher Education	1976	1,900	Yes
Association for Student Conduct Administration	1987	3,000	Yes
Association of College and University Housing Officers	1949	17,000	Yes
Association of Recovery in Higher Education	2011	138 colleges	Yes
Association on Higher Education and Disability	1977	3,000	Yes
NASPA: Student Affairs Administrators in Higher Education	1919	13,000	Yes
National Association of Social Workers	1955	140,000	Yes
National Association of Student Affairs Professionals	1954	15,000 individuals & 1,200 institutions	Yes
National Association for Campus Activities	1960	892 schools, 436 associations, & 16 affiliates	Yes
National Campus Activities Association	1960	1,000 campuses	Yes
National Career Development Association	1913	4,700	Yes
National Intermural-Recreation Sports Association	1950	700 campuses	Yes
The American Mental Health Counselors Association (A Division of the American Counseling Association)	1976	56,000 (within ACA)	Yes
The Mental Health Section of the American College Health Association	1979	3,000 (within ACHA)	Yes

Sources: Association websites and contacts

become institutionalized in the academy, with increasing responsibility for the well-being of students.

For example, when conflict comes to campus through student protests or actions, confrontations, or individual or collective misbehavior, the relationship between student affairs and the student population is pivotal in the university's ability to manage the situation. These situations may also involve the office of public safety, which, depending on how prudently it acts, can actually escalate a tense situation. Hence, the president's office generally relies heavily on professional staff in student affairs who know how to manage crises involving students. When a student is rushed to the hospital in the middle of the night due to possible alcohol poisoning or when tragedy befalls a student at the hands of fellow fraternal brothers, it is the frontline staff in student affairs who rush in to help and, if necessary, console a parent.

On some campuses, student affairs' unique ability to solve – or at least manage – difficult problems has put the office in a position to earn additional resources and a bigger voice at the leadership level. Nationwide, the area of student affairs is among the fastest-growing budgets on campuses, due not only to its role in direct support of students, but because in recent years, students and parents alike have advocated for increased levels of services on campus, in particular in the area of mental health. Hence, student affairs represent another important constituency vying for resources and influence in the modern academy.

On many campuses, it would be customary for units of student affairs to produce an annual report highlighting the demand and utilization of its services. However, an assessment of the effectiveness of these services is less common, partly due to the difficulty of such measurement and the cost if an independent evaluation were commissioned. In other administrative areas, such as financial services, for example, independent assessments can be a routine part of the university governance process, typically overseen as at AU by the Board of Trustees. Each year an external auditing firm is hired to review AU's internal business procedures and operations to ferret out potential areas of risk, inefficiency, or inadequate operational procedures. The auditing firm recommends to the Board seven to nine areas in which it proposes to undertake a detailed operational audit. With Board approval, the firm assigns evaluators to complete a detailed review of each area, which might take two or three months.

Upon completion of the audit, the firm presents a summary report of its findings to the unit (or units) primarily responsible for the area in question. The report lists any issues that merit further attention, identifies recommendations for improvements, and categorizes the issues identified as low risk, medium risk, or high risk to the institution. The unit(s) can then prepare a management response and propose a timeline to make the changes. The complete report and unit response is an item for review by the Board of Trustees. Depending on the recommendation, the unit is responsible for making changes as proposed. No one wants an identified area of risk to appear a second time before the Board. This is a best practice to ensure quality business and financial practices.

Such periodic independent examination and detailed analysis of internal processes are surprisingly absent among such an important area as student services, so important to the well-being of students. Financial operations require – and receive – constant and careful scrutiny. Why would a similar set of operational service practices that have direct consequences for student success (and university revenue) be left without a comparable independent assessment of effectiveness, efficiency, and execution?

Change Management and Presidential Leadership

Heading this loose conglomeration of operational units and an independent-minded faculty is the university president, who has responsibilities to multiple constituencies: a board, elected officials (if the university is a public institution), donors, alumni, students and their parents, faculty, staff, neighbors, possibly unions, accreditors, financial rating agencies, auditors, and sometimes watchdog groups and the media. Those who have served in other sectors often say there is no more difficult executive job than that of a university president. Given the structure and complexity of the university, the president's executive authority is often more limited than one might find in a private corporation. Still, numerous presidents have managed this convoluted, politicized, entrenched, and Rube Goldbergesque set of operations effectively. Reflecting on his experience at Northeastern University, Richard Freeland observes that the need for a strong presidency varies with circumstances. A relatively healthy university, one with "a well-defined educational paradigm and a successful operating mode, and when the component parts are generally strong,"[18] can function well and even improve under a fairly wide range of capable transactional presidential leaders. When circumstances call for larger-scale and more complex changes, however, stronger and transformational leadership is required.

The president is the voice of the institution and ceremonial figurehead. Should things go awry, which is not uncommon, it is the president who ultimately speaks for the campus, assisted by personnel skilled in public and governmental relations, communication, speech writing, legal, development, and finance. The president is accountable for the periodic accreditation review, the strategic plan, the long-range facilities and grounds planning, audits, and the annual budget. One of the most vital of the modern responsibilities of the office is fundraising. External funds raised by the president can be a mark of excellence that helps support activities and facilities at the campus, well beyond what is garnered by tuition and fees. Athletics is one area that may report to the president and can be a vehicle for building community pride and informally engaging with alumni around institutional support and gift-giving. The president's cabinet, including all the vice presidents and provost, is the direct line of communication and accountability for all the different divisions of the university. The provost, as the chief academic officer, is the "first among equals" in the president's cabinet and maintains a close working relationship with the president.[19]

A president can identify a direction and, in consultation with the board of trustees, set multiyear stretch goals for the organization, understanding that implementing them relies on talented individuals within the organization. The president can provide direction, incentives, resources, and support to those deeply invested in carrying out appropriate institution-building efforts and reform. Leaders at various levels of the organization – those who are accepted and well respected by others in the community – can be a galvanizing force in making change. But it bears repeating that this is hard and challenging work in a decentralized organization reluctant to change. A president intent on change must present a convincing case for it to various constituencies, including the board of trustees. If change is to occur, the campus community members eventually have to accept and genuinely own the rationale for it.

The experience of the University of Maryland, Baltimore County (UMBC) under President Freeman Hrabowski is a case in point. Hrabowski has led UMBC since 1992 with remarkable outcomes in research productivity, diversity, and student academic accomplishments. His success in effecting transformational change across the university can largely be credited to his ability to build shared goals and aspirations. On presidential leadership, he writes,

> Most experienced presidents know firsthand how difficult it is to lead substantive change in a university. Indeed, most presidents will be the first to tell you that if a proposed change at a university is perceived as top-

down, it has a high likelihood of being dead on arrival for the faculty and staff who must implement it. Forcing change, while sometimes expedient, often undermines long-term sustainable impact.[20]

It is insufficient for university presidents to simply invoke formal authority to create change. They must motivate and engage others and earn a level of authentic authority and respect for their message. In the case of Northeastern University, Freeland writes that the campus, under his leadership, "marshaled its organizational resources, accepted the need for dramatic change, and within a remarkably short period of time, emerged as a transformed and competitive university."[21]

Such is the reality for traditional nonprofit four-year colleges and universities. The case for change must be compelling, consistently repeated, and carried deep into the organization so that virtually every employee is aware of the goal. Faculty and staff – whatever their unit affiliation – must see how their area fits into the proposed changes as well as the benefit of supporting them. With resources and institutional support from the top and the engagement of talented people deep in the organization, a president and their cabinet, with the full backing of the board, can go from being mired in entrenched turf battles to moving quickly with sustained and long-lasting change.

Presidents have a university-wide view. But the national median tenure for a university president is 6.5 years and declining; as mentioned above, it is no longer surprising to see transitions after only 3–5 years.[22] Consequently, a president has relatively little time to make changes, even when the situation is dire. At times, they encounter intransigency, reflecting the distinctly different views of the university held by faculty and administrative leadership. Faculty see themselves as having to deal with any changes administrators make, perhaps long after the administrator has moved on. The largest barrier to transforming the university into a more student-centered experience remains an institutional structure routinely accepted and protected by faculty and staff that too often fails to align with the best interests of students.

Theorizing the University as an Organization

John V. Lombardi writes that "complexity and bureaucracy, especially in the public sector, tend to absorb initiatives for change and dissipate them across a wide estuary of bureaucratic swamps and regulatory tributaries so that the flow of change slows to a virtual stop."[23] This complexity and uniqueness of university structure and culture, particularly surrounding the faculty, have attracted the interest of scholars who study organizations. Robert Hendrickson et al. have drawn from the conceptual literature on organizations and structures and applied them to university settings. They organized the literature into three distinctive theories about the university as a complex organization, which I summarize below.[24]

One theory describes organizations as fluid with multiple unconnected components and functions – universities as "organized anarchies."[25] In their classic essay, Cohen, March, and Olsen argue that universities are complex organized anarchies with poorly articulated and unclear preferences, a setting where the technology remains uncertain and participation of decision-makers can vary. They developed a theory known as the "garbage can model of organizational choice" to describe decision-making within such organizations. It sees universities as settings "in which problems, solutions, and participants move from one choice opportunity to another in such a way that the nature of the choice, the time it takes, and the problems it solves all depend on a relatively complicated intermeshing of elements."[26] Instead of determining solutions through a linear and efficient process, university decision-makers rely on a convoluted process involving multiple participants that may change over time, and too often leaps from one choice to another inefficiently and unpredictably in search of problems.[27] They see decisions in universities as spasmodic, inconsistent, and prone to change over time, depending on who is participating at any given moment.

In contrast, Robert B. Glassman (as interpreted by Hendrickson et al.) views the university as a "loosely coupled federation"[28] whose interactions vary by unit, topic, and intensity. He argues that while some units act as fairly autonomous bureaucracies whose decisions have little impact on other units, others are more interconnected, with linkages that might be considered a tightly coupled alliance. For example, faculty in the physics and electrical engineering departments might partner to build and maintain lasers for collaborative work in photonics, but performing artists and mathematicians might have little interaction with one another beyond their shared role as faculty. The relationship between admissions officers and financial aid officers is an example of a loosely coupled alliance. According to Hendrickson et al., Glassman's coupling and alliances are factors in mapping decision-making and interventions in university settings. Hence, the label "coupling theory."[29] In my own experience, the autonomy of units remains paramount, and conflicts between units covering related subjects are far more common than coupling. Nevertheless, such coupling does occur on campuses.

Hendrickson et al. offer a third classification of the university as a "professional bureaucracy" with a division of labor centered on a core faculty,[30] an analysis based on Henry Mintzberg's typology of structural configurations, which explores a wide range of different organizational structural models, from simple to more complex.[31] Mintzberg notes that, as organizations and their problems become more complex, individuals from a given field of expertise come together for a certain time to address an issue. The ad hoc, transient nature of these interactions across professional specializations led Mintzberg to characterize them as an "adhocracy."[32] Hendrickson et al. identify the modern university as an adhocracy in the aforementioned typology.[33] The university works through formal standing committees as well as through temporary ad hoc committees, raising questions about the universality of the theory for colleges and universities. The university is a politicized and fragmented system that tolerates highly individualized decision-making, perpetuates tensions between the centralization and decentralization of functions, and is known for competitiveness and territoriality between university functional units. Within that setting, individuals and groups continuously struggle for prestige, enhanced reputation, and distinctiveness.

The three grand theories all have applications to understanding the organization and decision-making at the contemporary university, depending on the circumstance, the level within the organization, and time allotted for the decision. Cohen, March, and Olsen's garbage can theory is spot on in characterizing many decisions at the university, but on other occasions, decisions, particularly at the unit level, can be rational, thoughtful, and sequential, involving the same participants within the resources available. Other incidents occur that follow the logic of coupling theory. As a grand theory, however, Glassman's approach fails to capture the centrifugal forces that pull administrative units apart, particularly those based on distrust of one another's groups. Other types of decisions follow the ad hoc process described by Mintzberg. While no one of these three theories perfectly captures the decision-making process at universities, each merits consideration as an aspect of university decision-making and organization.

To understand the possibilities for changing how universities might better serve the needs of their students, I return to the insights from Baldridge introduced at the beginning of this chapter. As he noted, both academic and administrative units primarily function as siloed operations. While there are of course exceptions, any framework for organizational change within the university must account for this central characteristic.

As self-protective units, the various administrative components of the university define their turf and territory in ways that shape their responsibility and narrow their duties, producing outcomes that few of the principals would envision as ideal. To begin a meaningful dialogue between faculty and administrative stakeholders about the unanticipated consequences of fragmented services on students' lives, we must begin by confronting the reality of university structure.

These siloed enterprises can create problems for students, ranging from stress, frustration, lost time, and dropping out – and worse. Indeed, the university's acceptance of a decentralized and specialized administrative structure can have unexpected consequences including evidence of heinous crimes inflicted on students, including sexual abuse and athletic exploitation. The extreme cases discussed below involve predatory individuals, illegal behavior, and alcohol, drugs, or just bad judgment. But while extreme, each emanates from a common organizational structure and culture that allowed the incidents to take place, knowingly did not report them to authorities, and in some cases tried to keep them secret. Specifically, each case was made possible by a managerial structure with loose reporting lines, operating within a broader university culture that respects independence and professional autonomy and seeks national recognition, sometimes at too great a cost. In each case, we see how a university's attempt to protect its reputation by withholding damaging information or simply looking the other way eventually backfired.

Pennsylvania State University, Michigan State University, and the University of Southern California, to name three, have acknowledged situations that allowed the large-scale sexual abuse of female athletes to continue for years. Ohio State reported sexual abuse toward at least 177 male athletes,[34] a case in which 22 coaches admitted to knowing of the sexual misconduct but did nothing to stop it.[35] Despite the awareness among multiple employees including at least one senior official who had received complaints of misconduct on multiple occasions, a physician at the University of Michigan continued to molest male and female students in his practice over a span of 37 years. According to an independent investigation commissioned by the university nearly 20 years after the physician had retired, at final count over one-thousand former students came forward to tell their stories of the doctor's predatory behavior.[36] In other cases, individual faculty members have been identified as having abusive sexual relationships with their students. Often, these abhorrent behaviors, discussed among faculty in hushed tones, have been tolerated for years.

In some cases, athletic coaches have demanded more from athletes than their bodies are capable of, resulting in tragedy. The relationship between a student and their coach, physician, or professor is based on an enormous power imbalance. When students want to do well in their course or their sport, they try to please their professor or coach. When a coach derides, harasses, or unfairly punishes a student, the student may have little recourse but to tolerate the situation or eventually leave the team – losing an athletic scholarship and possibly having to leave the university. A physician may inappropriately touch or otherwise violate a student's body, leaving the student unsure of where to turn for help. Colleagues may be uncertain about how to discuss or manage a coach, doctor, or professor with a substance abuse problem. A setting built on loose oversight of semi-independent decentralized units provides plenty of room for a range of abusive behaviors.

Students who find themselves in uncomfortable or inappropriate situations involving faculty or staff may fear that reporting the issue will jeopardize their grades or even their future careers. As victims, they may fear physical harm or reprisal, or worry about being put in a situation where the adult authority figure denies the charges, placing them on the defensive and forcing them to relive their anguish and trauma. Or they may feel ashamed to acknowledge that they had sexual relations with an older adult, even if it was without their full consent. Student-athletes bear the additional burden of expectations of toughness, of stoicism, of "sticking it out."

These incidents are a testament to major shortcomings in the university structure. They are not exclusive to large state or private universities. They take place in public and private colleges, large and small. Too frequently, students, alumni, and members of the public only learn about incidents years later because the victims' silence was bought through nondisclosure agreements and perpetrators' departures handled through retirements designed to avoid scandal.

These are terrible things ... whatever ancillary benefits faculty independence and athletic victories bring, they cannot be at the expense of inflicting trauma on students. Faculty, coaches, physicians, and other administrators cannot be allowed to engage with students without clear rules, boundaries, procedures, and penalties aimed at fostering oversight and accountability. The power imbalance is simply too great. Change does not come easy to the residential university, and yet, it must.

What Path Forward?

There is a growing dialogue among scholars that the American university is both poorly run and highly effective – a combination that confounds logic.[37] There is evidence that it is highly effective in supporting research and development, but, with 40 percent or more of students not completing a degree within six years from the institution they entered, a chorus of critics are questioning the university's effectiveness in its educational mission. No matter how successful the university may be from the perspective of faculty accomplishments, the question for this book is whether its structure effectively serves the current generation of students?

The contemporary four-year residential college and university faces increased criticism for its perceived pandering to the wealthy and well-connected, its management of conflicts of ideas and political positions, and even its underlying value proposition. Universities with large endowments face questions about their use. Advocates have raised concerns about safeguarding students from various forms of harm (violence, sexual harassment, racial insults and attacks, bullying). I am suggesting that all of these questions and criticisms relate to the university's underlying dated structure and culture, which limit its capacity to respond to shifting expectations that have become commonplace in other contemporary settings. Enhancing the university's performance in providing today's students, diverse and grappling with global and domestic crises, with an enriched holistic educational experience, based on the strategic alignment of resources, is the first step in quelling the critics.

If we value the quality of the student experience, then we need to reach beyond the existing structure, with its stovepiped administrative units. We need to unite faculty, staff, and administrators around a shared goal of a holistic approach to the educational and services students expect, deserve, and need if they are to be successful.

University faculty and professional staff alike need both support and room to experiment. This may be the most likely path to change in the university. University leaders have to strike a balance between setting the direction for the institution and leaving implementation details to the parties closest to the students. All parties must remain in continuous dialogue with the leadership, as final decisions and choices ultimately rest with the president (or the president's designate) and board.

Those who tend to be most successful in making changes in an organization have a deep awareness of the different needs, desires, and sources of power for their various constituencies. Successful leaders have the patience to engage in sustained dialogue on goals and direction. Freeman Hrabowski writes, "The most effective means of [changing the institution] is by clearly articulating a vision for the future through a collaborative process with others – faculty, staff, administrators, and students – who broadly embrace it and, as positions turn over, selecting or developing new colleagues who align with the culture, mission, and work."[38] Continuously doing "precinct work" with individual power brokers and influential faculty is part of an academic leader's obligation and pathway to success. Change management is part art and part science – with an emphasis on art. A president or provost may have the final authority – and faculty and staff understand this – but they are more likely to successfully implement policies if they incorporate faculty and staff into the process. Rather than telling others what to do, leadership motivates, energizes, and empowers individuals and groups through inclusion.

Notes

1 J. Victor Baldridge, *Power and Conflict in the University: Research in the Sociology of Complex Organizations* (New York: John Wiley & Sons, 1971), 105.

2 Other works, such as David J. Staley's *Alternative Universities: Speculative Design for Innovation in Higher Education* (Baltimore: Johns Hopkins University Press, 2019), offer creative concepts for modeling the future that emphasize the development of smaller-scale alternative organizations that can eventually serve as models for the larger organization.

3 William G. Bowen and Eugene M. Tobin, *Locus of Authority: The Evolution of Faculty Roles in the Governance of Higher Education* (Princeton, NJ: Princeton University Press, 2015), 34, 49–52, 143–145.

4 Bowen and Tobin, *Locus of Authority*, 207.

5 "Shared Governance," American Association of University Professors, accessed March 4, 2021, www.aaup.org/our-programs/shared-governance.

6 Susan Whealler Johnston, "Sharing Governance," *Trusteeship*, Summer 2018, 2.

7 See Bowen and Tobin, *Locus of Authority*.

8 National Center for Science and Engineering Statistics, *National Science Foundation, Doctorate Recipients from US Universities: 2018: Data Tables and Resources*, special report NSF 20-301 (Alexandria, VA: National Center for Science and Engineering Statistics, National Science Foundation, 2019), 186–188, table 54, accessed March 5, 2020, https://ncses.nsf.gov/pubs/nsf20301/downloads.

9 American Association of University Professors, "1940 Statement of Principles on Academic Freedom and Tenure with 1970 Interpretive Comments," in

Policy Documents and Reports, 11th ed. (Baltimore: Johns Hopkins University Press, 2015), 13.

10 American Association of University Professors, "1940 Statement," 15–16.

11 Donna R. Euben, "Termination & Discipline (2004)" (presentation, 14th Annual Legal Issues in Higher Education Conference, University of Vermont, Burlington, VT, October 24, 2004), 4–6, accessed May 14, 2021, www.aaup .org/file/Termination_Discipline_2004.pdf.

12 Eric Kelderman, "Iowa Ideologues: Tenure under Siege," *Chronicle of Higher Education*, March 5, 2021, 7.

13 Lindsay Ellis, "Thought Control: When Politicians Probe Teaching," *Chronicle of Higher Education*, March 5, 2021, 8.

14 Terrence MacTaggart, "Nontraditional Presidents: A New Wave of Enterprise Leadership," *Trusteeship* 26, Summer 2018, 12.

15 Baldridge, *Power and Conflict*, 144.

16 Baldridge, *Power and Conflict*, 118–123.

17 "Welcome to the NACUBO Product Center," National Association of College and University Business Officers, accessed May 10, 2019, http:// products.nacubo.org.

18 Richard M. Freeland, *Transforming the Urban University: Northeastern, 1996–2006* (Philadelphia: University of Pennsylvania Press, 2019), 183.

19 James Martin and James E. Samels, "First among Equals: The Current Roles of the Chief Academic Officer," in *First among Equals: The Role of the Chief Academic Officer*, ed. James Martin and James E. Samels (Baltimore: Johns Hopkins University Press, 1997), 3.

20 Freeman A. Hrabowski III with Philip J. Rous and Peter H. Henderson, *The Empowered University: Shared Leadership, Culture Change, and Academic Success* (Baltimore: Johns Hopkins University Press, 2019), 37.

21 Freeland, *Transforming*, 184.

22 Andy Thomason, "Is College President 'the Toughest Job in the Nation'?," *Chronicle of Higher Education*, May 1, 2018, accessed March 24, 2020, www .chronicle.com/article/is-college-president-the-toughest-job-in-the-nation/.

23 John V. Lombardi, *How Universities Work* (Baltimore: Johns Hopkins University Press, 2013), 170.

24 Robert M. Hendrickson et al., *Academic Leadership and Governance of Higher Education: A Guide for Trustees, Leaders, and Aspiring Leaders of Two-Year and Four-Year Institutions* (Sterling, VA: Stylus, 2013), 29–31.

25 Michael D. Cohen, James G. March, and Johan P. Olsen, "A Garbage Can Model of Organizational Choice," *Administrative Science Quarterly* 17, no. 1 (March 1972): 16.

26 Cohen, March, and Olsen, "Garbage Can Model," 1.

27 Cohen, March, and Olsen, "Garbage Can Model," 1.

28 Hendrickson et al., *Academic Leadership*, 29–30.

29 Hendrickson et al., *Academic Leadership*, 30.

30 Hendrickson et al., *Academic Leadership*, 30–31.

31 Henry Mintzberg, "The Adhocracy," in *The Structuring of Organizations: A Synthesis of the Research* (Englewood Cliffs, NJ: Prentice-Hall, 1979), 431–467.

32 Mintzberg, "Adhocracy," 432–433.

33 Hendrickson et al., *Academic Leadership*, 30–31.

34 Rick Maese, "Ohio State Team Doctor Sexually Abused 177 Students over Decades, Report Finds," *Washington Post*, May 17, 2019, 7:27 p.m. EDT, accessed March 24, 2020, www.washingtonpost.com/sports/2019/05/17/ohio-state-team-doctor-sexually-abused-students-over-decades-report-finds/.

35 Jeremy Bauer-Wolf, "2 Decades of Abuse, 177 Victims, No Action," *Inside Higher Ed*, May 20, 2019, accessed March 24, 2020, www.insidehighered.com/news/2019/05/20/former-ohio-state-doctor-abused-nearly-200-young-men-no-consequences-decades.

36 Bruce Berman et al., *Report of Independent Investigation: Allegations of Sexual Misconduct against Robert E. Anderson* (Washington, DC: Wilmer Cutler Pickering Hale and Dorr LLP, 2021), 10, accessed May 12, 2021, https://regents.umich.edu/files/meetings/01-01/WH_Anderson_Report.pdf. Also see, Alan Blinder, "University of Michigan will Pay $490 Million to Settle Abuse Cases," *The New York Times*, January 19, 2022, updated January 20, 2022, accessed January 25, 2022, www.nytimes.com/2022/01/19/sports/ncaafootball/michigan-abuse-settlement-robert-anderson.html.

37 Robert Birnbaum, *How Colleges Work: The Cybernetics of Academic Organization and Leadership* (San Francisco: Jossey-Bass, 1988), 3.

38 Hrabowski, *Empowered University*, 37.

CHAPTER 7

Lost among the Silos: Students and Information Systems

In previous chapters, I explored the technological expectations of a generation of students whose interactions with organizations and services had been generally seamless, until they enrolled in college. In the outside world, the information they sought was integrated, personalized, and responsive. For the most part, that is not the case in their interactions with the university.

As a result, students, and even younger faculty and staff, find the university sluggish, bogged down with wasteful, time-consuming red tape, and highly bureaucratic in comparison to the more stakeholder-centric responses of other institutions. User-friendly tools developed by the tech giants are ubiquitous, but the university remains flat-footed. At most colleges and universities, even such a basic action as finding information about activities, programs, lectures, policies, and courses through the campus portal is not particularly intuitive. The portal does not correct for search entry misspellings and too often requires multiple clicks. Some students and others more accustomed to accessing information nearly instantaneously are unwilling to spend time sorting through information irrelevant (and sometimes even relevant) to their quest.

I recently had my own frustrating experience with the user-unfriendly nature of campus operations while reserving a meeting room through the university portal. The process required that I: (1) go to the portal; (2) enter a twelve-digit password; (3) click on "search links"; (4) click on "team sites"; then (5) select "school team sites"; (6) select the "school" housing the room; (7) select the administrative unit responsible for room management in the school; (8) select the room number from a list; and finally (9) complete a reservation form listing name, location, start time, end time, description, and click "save." I should mention that my office shares a wall with the conference room I had just reserved. Now imagine a student governance group needing to reserve a room for a meeting – they simply would not bother.

But the digital distance between the world today's students are accustomed to and what is available through the university is more than a frustrating inconvenience; it can be a real gap that hinders access to vital information and the rich resources of the academy. Worse, for some students, inevitable encounters with staff who rely on the university's existing software systems and policies can cause unnecessary stress. Take a student we will call Adena, who is concerned about her ability to pay her college bills. A sophomore in good standing, she manages her time well and has a part-time job in the library, but worries that college costs are too great a burden on her family. Her mother is a seamstress, her father works at a national chain hardware store. Over the years, they have saved a modest nest egg for Adena's college expenses. Adena is their only child, but even with university financial aid, her campus job, and loans, the family has trouble making ends meet. Adena worries that following her dream is causing her family additional hardship.

Early in the term, Adena learns her father has been diagnosed with a chronic disease and can no longer work full-time. Soon, the family's income will be significantly reduced. Adena meets with her university financial aid officer to seek increased support due to the changing financial situation. After a review of her request, she learns that it has been denied because of data on record about the family's assets – specifically, the savings her parents have accrued over the years to help pay for her college expenses. Anxious and agitated about her father's health and the drain on her family's savings, Adena begins having difficulty sleeping and becomes increasingly irritable. She feels guilty about taking money from her family's savings, given the changed circumstances at home. To help her parents with chores, she begins going home on the weekend. Her classroom performance wanes, and her grades start to tumble.

For reasons of confidentiality, her financial aid counselor does not share the information about Adena's situation with other administrators. Nor does Adena speak to any other university official about it. Neither her academic advisor nor the dean of students is aware of anything that might be affecting her academic performance. She soon finds herself on academic probation; unless she brings up her grades quickly, she will face dismissal.

Somehow, Adena struggles through this crisis, finding the funds to pay an additional $4,400 for a three-credit-hour course during the summer term to improve her grade point average and eventually graduate. Despite an ultimately positive outcome, it is reasonable to ask whether the confidentiality policy regarding financial matters, enforced through information management practices, was truly helpful in Adena's situation. Did she receive the guidance she needed?

Another student, Jamal, called the Office of Student Accounts to point out that his bill did not reflect funds transferred to the university from a loan he had secured. The erroneous bill was much more than he had anticipated or could afford. The staff person said the office's records did not show processing of the external loan and suggested Jamal speak with the Financial Aid Office. But until the error was settled, Jamal would be expected to pay the entire bill. Otherwise, he would accrue penalty fees and at some point would be blocked from registering for the next term.

At the Financial Aid Office, a counselor explained that the external loan would not show up in its database because it was from a private vendor and not the federal government. Therefore, she would not be able to verify the loan or its amount to Student Accounts. She told Jamal it was a "system" issue and he should speak with the Office of Information Technology for help updating the records. But the staff person at the IT Help Desk said there was nothing he could do. He suggested Jamal try to work it out with Student Accounts, advising him that the system would block his access to registration for the next term if he did not resolve this matter soon.

Despite multiple attempts with Student Accounts, Jamal was unable to resolve the issue. Three weeks passed, the tuition payment was now overdue, and a late fee was attached. He was now worried about being blocked from registration. Jamal was frustrated and angry with the way the university was treating him. Eventually, Student Accounts received and recorded the payment from the loan, but Jamal still had to pay the late fee. Such situations occur all too frequently on university campuses, creating unnecessary stress for students and their families.

These two examples both resulted in mostly successful resolutions. They were serious irritants, not of the tragic magnitude that push some students to emotionally break down or leave school – but incidents of tragic magnitude do occur. This chapter will explore how today's campuses arrived at their current configuration of information flow, why it can be ineffective, frustrating, and at times harmful for today's students, and what can be done to improve it.

A Tale of Two Data Strategies

Like all large and complex organizations, American universities and colleges need a flow of accurate and timely information for planning, decision-making, running their operations effectively, and meeting their institutional goals. Universities have two broad responsibilities involving data management: to oversee their resources, including facilities, personnel, and budget; and to support and nurture their students.

Most colleges have a centralized data system that provides decision-makers with accurate and timely information on business, finance, personnel, payroll, enrollment, and budget functions. Reliable data from the participating units are typically linked through an integrated Enterprise Resource Planning (ERP) software system. An ERP system is a business software system that provides campus leaders with timely business intelligence that can assist them in making strategic decisions based on enrollments, revenues, expenses, and other factors.

But the flow of information about student interactions such as academic support services, psychosocial behavior, or direct service provision is usually independent of the ERP system and lives within a different set of data systems and repositories often designed for individual service areas. Typically, these systems lack interoperability. Few universities have developed a digital strategy for a holistic support system for the entire student experience. I would argue that the existing configuration of student data on most college campuses is one more obstacle to effective guidance of the student as a whole person.

Essentially, there are two different campus digital strategies, one for business and finance-related operations, the other for student service programs. That divergence can be traced to the evolving software systems from business and industry adopted by colleges and universities in the early 1990s, as well as to the internal data preferences among student service providers. The combination of three factors helped create the framework for the software systems we see in use at universities today: first, the desire of the specialized student units to house their own private records; second, the belief that any integration of this private student information with other service units could potentially violate confidentiality and create unwanted risks to the student; and third, the limitations of the existing foci of the evolving collegiate ERP systems. These factors, among others, have resulted in an absence of a coherent and comprehensive digital strategy among the diverse array of student service providers.

As a result, most direct student service units, programs, or functions operate with their own information systems and software packages. These packages are periodically updated and serve their intended independent functions. However, segmentation across data sectors is now well entrenched. At American University, for example, there are more than forty-nine different databases for various aspects of the undergraduate student experience, housed in five different university divisions. When

I showed an early graphic representation of those databases in Figure 7.1 – initially containing thirty-five different software products – to university leaders around the country, the disconnected information silos elicited murmurs of recognition.[1] This single image shows the compartmentalization of student services and functions based on the needs of the record-keeper or office – something that is implicitly understood, but rarely presented visually. While fragmentation of information in the university is a familiar and daunting problem, in the area of student services, many have accepted it as the norm.

Figure 7.1 reveals that the Office of Campus Life maintains databases for the counseling center, event scheduling, campus housing, volunteer tracking, community service, internships, new student orientation, judicial activity, the student care network, student health, the meal plan portal, Eaglebucks and dining dollars, Title IX, student worker schedules and timesheets, and international student services. The Division of Alumni Relations has one database for alumni management and engagement and a second for fundraising. The Office of the President also maintains two databases, both related to athletics: one for the fitness center and another for athletics. The largest cluster of units and databases belongs to the Office of Academic Affairs. Here, the several business-related databases linked to the central ERP include the student information system, student advising, financial aid, recruitment, registration, grading, graduation, the student early warning system, student planning, and enrollment. Other autonomous databases cover study abroad, student support services, retention, online education, graduate employment outcomes, institutional research and student surveys, career services, the one-stop service center, the university library, printing, transcripts, student course evaluations, noncredit registration and payment, the online math placement exam, and advisor appointment scheduling. In many cases, these offices, services, or functions utilize more than one software product. The Office of Finance and Treasurer oversees three databases: student accounts (linked to the ERP), ID cards and electronic door access, and parking permits and citations.

All this means that student data – while plentiful – is not easily accessible to professionals working with the same student in different parts of the university. It would be difficult, for instance, for the intermural sports supervisor to share a recorded incident of serious student misbehavior with that student's academic advisor. Likely, the supervisor would not even know who the academic advisor is. Similarly, due to federal confidentiality requirements for most universities, it is difficult if not impossible

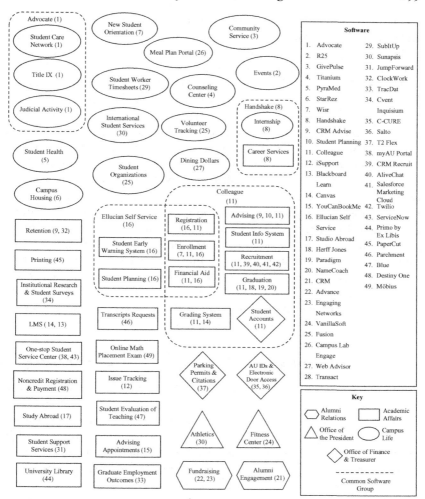

Figure 7.1   Student services at AU: navigating silos

to link individual student health with financial aid records. I will discuss this topic further below. There is nothing like an automobile's electronic control unit to oversee and integrate the range of computers and software products. And even if universities could somehow link all the existing student-related databases, it would be difficult to overcome confidentiality regulations or provide integrated information that would be actionable. In addition, prior turf battles, internal competition for resources, and the use of information to maintain influence and importance all act as disincentives for sharing student information on campus.

The consequence is that information about four key components of the student experience – academic support and progress, social experiences, health (physical and emotional), and economic support – remains separated, cutting off a critical source of timely insight into the student's aggregate experience. The separation is mutually reinforced by privacy and confidentiality requirements and the specialized functions in the different domains. Without a skilled person explicitly tasked to gain an overview of the data collected across the four key components, the information remains segregated, available only to those authorized to examine or record it. In the absence of a capability to connect these experiences that are separate for the university but inextricably linked for the student, both university and student struggle to tap into the necessary flow of information on students' needs. Unless students inform someone of their interconnected problems – and even sometimes when they do – administrators and advisors may be unable to respond to challenges to the student's wellbeing outside of their own specific responsibilities.

The Early Digital Strategy for Campus Business and Finance

For too many campuses, the transition to the various ERP systems in the early 1990s did not go as smoothly as anticipated. Immediate issues included the mismatch between the unique organizational structure of universities and the centralized business and finance expectations of ERP systems. There were technical challenges in implementing the system, cost overruns in installation, and a desire to customize the existing software to the unique characteristics and needs of a specific campus creating unanticipated downstream effects.[2] The systems were not designed with the existing collegiate unit staff user in mind; they required considerable training, often demanding a higher technical skill level than many staff possessed. Staff capability in implementing the system varied significantly across university offices, causing delays, confusion, and tension. Some staff members compared the experience of interacting with the database to learning a new language. In some instances, the implementation was a near disaster, leaving administrators and faculty considerably frustrated by their inability to access essential information. Whether in the office of the registrar or the office of financial aid, university staff members require regular and immediate access to information to better serve students. When this ability is compromised, it has an immediate impact on campus life.

I was party to an ERP transition that resulted in a crisis for the university. While there were implementation problems across the campus, the system created an immediate issue for faculty running federal research grants. They found themselves cut off from information on how much money remained in their grants, including money to pay students and the funds to pay for their summer salaries. They had been told to abandon their old "shadow systems" – their personal grant records of spending and anticipated expenditures – for the more precise ERP grants management system. No one wanted to overspend, and certainly not underspend on their grant. The information did exist on the university's ERP research database, but too few faculty or staff knew how to access it. The problems with the transition to the new ERP went on for months, possibly as long as two years. Affected faculty directed their ire at the president for what appeared to be an expensive botched operation. Eventually, staff members were able to operate the system, but most were limited to its more basic functions, unable to fully access the far more complex analyses the system could provide. This rough-and-rocky transition tested the leadership of the campus, with consequences for all members of the community, including students. Early adopter universities typically encountered problems with bugs during operation and at times required software patches to fix problems. If they had customized their systems they found it difficult to implement ERP upgrades.

Universities that came later to the ERP transition had the advantage of learning from others' experiences. They could provide enhanced training for personnel responsible for operating the ERP before going live with it, and they increased the salaries of the IT staff who were now responsible for making sure that every business, administrative, and academic unit had the support it needed. It became apparent that implementing an ERP was a multiyear operation that involved extensive staff training, piloting, and testing and the complete engagement of the line workers. In some cases, offices were allowed to remain on their old but trusted systems until they were confident enough to make the transition and "go live." The universities that took more time and provided additional direct support to the personnel operating these systems were more successful than those who rushed in headlong – but even in the best-case scenario, the transition was challenging.

Campuses that delayed acquiring these systems may have had the advantage of market testing. But on the other hand, they also had to provide considerable reassurance to faculty and staff who had heard the horror stories elsewhere. These historic incidents surrounding the introduction of new data systems remain lodged in the memory of the college and university community, influencing its willingness to welcome new products when existing ones may be cumbersome, but still functional. Tight budgets, fear of losing data, and the opportunity costs of implementing a new system all delay the acquisition of more modern systems.

At a conference in 2019 where I presented an early version of Figure 7.1, I met a senior administrator for student recruitment and enrollment. Recruitment and enrollment administration is a priority task in private universities for the simple reason that enrolling too many first-year students would create a housing shortage while enrolling too few would endanger the university's financial health. Getting to the right number of new enrollments, with the correct balance between those with tuition discounts and those paying full tuition, involves considerable analytical planning and reliable data. The administrator said the software system she was then using was at least twenty years old and had been highly customized to meet the unit's needs. But the company that produced the software was no longer in business, and the key IT staff that had helped customize it and kept it running had long since retired or left the university. The system had to be replaced, or it would eventually fail.

The university IT team recommended that the senior administrator buy a new product designed specifically for recruitment and admissions from the company that hosts the campus ERP. She understood the need to update but was happy with her current system and leery of the transition. She feared the consequences if anything went wrong with a new system. The IT team agreed to delay implementation for a year to allow her unit to become familiar with the new product. Later, when I inquired how the new system was working, she replied forcefully, "It is a system designed in hell!" Not all products on the market work as advertised for frontline workers.

Now, after a quarter-century, many campuses find themselves relying on aging and patched ERP systems. At some point, replacement becomes inevitable. It is also costly. A flagship state research university, for example, might spend $150 million or more on a new ERP system, and the change might take years to fully implement. These new systems are marketed as more efficient, more integrated, and easier to operate. They offer better reporting tools, greater functionality, fewer steps in the execution of tasks, and opportunities to reduce the number of transaction approvals. Often cloud-based, the new ERP systems include tools to monitor all major business, financial, and administrative transactions on campus, including many of those associated with student administrative information. They can integrate all student recruiting operations, admissions, curriculum, enrollment, academic record-keeping, advising, financial aid, and student accounts. But critics remind us that while these new systems are better compared to earlier versions, they still rely on computational concepts developed more than four decades ago.

Even the best, most up-to-date, easy-to-use ERP system can only aggregate and report on what has been entered into them. If one office enters information using a slightly different definition or parameter than another, the resulting aggregated information is imprecise or inaccurate. In one recent case at American University, anomalies appeared in the weekly admissions, enrollment, and tuition revenue executive reports. The president could not understand why the admissions and enrollment reports showed slight differences in their numbers. It took a team of four senior administrators from different units meeting regularly over several months to trace and correct the source of the confusion: a relatively minor technical problem. In another case, senior managers reviewing the deposit figures for the upcoming Fall Term were unaware that the processing of admissions deposits had changed from a rolling system, in which they were registered as they came in, to a batch system, in which multiple deposits were registered together at scheduled time intervals. As a result, the managers panicked when they compared "current" deposit figures with those from the same time the previous year. In each case, the ERP system was capable of accurately reporting the data entered, but it could not discern entry errors or distinguish administrative policy changes from one year to the next.

These experiences highlighted the essential need for an enterprise system for managing business and financial functions, but also raised concerns about what digital strategy should be introduced for the myriad of student services.

The Office of Information Technology

As universities take up the challenge of improving their information systems, the now ubiquitous Office of Information Technology (IT) is at the center of the action. IT's expanding role on campus is relatively recent. Campus computer support emerged in the 1970s, at which point it was typically divided by function. Areas associated with academic and research oversight reported to the chief academic officer, while those connected to the university's administrative functions typically reported to the chief financial officer. That all changed in the 1980s with the growing responsibilities associated with information technology. Not only was there a campus mainframe computer to oversee, but there also were multiple software packages and legacy systems to support. Personal computers became more common, and collaboration networks, including email, became necessary. The early 1990s brought the World Wide Web to college campuses, while in the later 1990s, many IT offices were busy introducing or maintaining ERP systems. As universities became accustomed to these systems, demand for personal computers mushroomed and student expectations for greater bandwidth emerged. To meet these multiple demands, IT offices required additional resources and personnel. Their responsibilities just before the turn of the century also included overseeing data portals, developing learning management systems for online education, connectivity for digitizing library collections, providing data security from hackers, ensuring the systems would not crash as the century turned to the year 2000, staffing twenty-four-hour help desks, and a growing list of other data services, software, hardware, and institutional operations. Today, IT offices typically manage all of a university's information and data systems. Nationally, about a third of them report to the vice president for finance and administration, a third to the provost, and the other third to the president.[3]

Technology is ubiquitous on college campuses; the demand for more and better technological applications and wireless connectivity is unrelenting. It is not unusual for students to arrive on campus with a handheld device, a laptop computer, a TV, and a gaming console, and expect to have the capability to live-stream films, games, and large data files. The library has transitioned from stacks of books to a digitized world of information. A 2015 incident at American University is telling: student activists demanded the installation of more electrical outlets in the library for their portable electronic devices. Imagine, activism around electrical outlets! Today, the library is lined with strips of electrical outlets. Around the same time, faculty became more vocal about their need for powerful desktop computers to process large amounts of information and cloud storage became the expectation. In all cases, the task of ensuring that faculty, staff, and students have access to quality equipment, bandwidth, software, and data falls to the office of IT.

The Evolution of Information Systems

Not long after ERP systems were introduced, software companies began developing and refining a new product that focused on managing customer data, a package that eventually became known as customer relationship management (CRM) software.[4] One of the leading companies was Salesforce, which provided statistical techniques to better obtain and analyze customer data and promised that its software could be integrated with the ERP. As smartphones became available, Salesforce and other software companies developed apps to make customer information more readily accessible. CRM systems provided organizations with a better understanding of the customer's needs, with the idea that vendors could improve the customer experience based on the intelligence provided by the system.

It soon became clear that a variation of the CRM system could be useful for nonprofit organizations, including colleges and universities. The rebranded name for use in the academy – which remains averse to referring to students as customers – became constituent relationship management.[5] In 2017, the worldwide market for CRM systems, including both commercial and nonprofit variations, reached $39.5 billion, leading all other software products in sales.[6]

CRM systems in academic settings are designed to provide centralized and integrated data about student and college interactions, from the time a student is a prospect, through the college experience, and beyond graduation. The CRM can store information about prospective students, compile data on periodic student interactions with administrators, and create a personalized record of every pertinent exchange between students and designated officials. Companies providing ERP systems have been integrating multiple database components within an overall networked system, including CRM, allowing the flow and sharing of information across systems. By integrating functions across these powerful systems, multiple individuals can accurately enter data and share it across units, helping to ensure that the data is accurate and current.

Service providers claim that CRM systems allow managers to make better predictions of future behavior based on past performance and provide students with more informed, timely, and targeted information about career planning, cocurricular events, and more, fostering a more personalized student–institution relationship. The CRM can also follow graduates as alumni and potential donors with a more informed and customized approach. Campuses using CRM systems have reported improvements in student retention. Yet, despite the enthusiasm of system advocates, the jury is still out on the effectiveness of CRM systems. For example, according to a study by McKinsey & Company, there remain questions as to the effectiveness of system utilization by frontline staff.[7]

The CRM system is designed to assist the university in improving communication with students, prod students to follow through on designated tasks, and eventually, engage them in a lifelong relationship. While there may be benefits for students, the central appeal is to administrators. Initially developed for businesses, a CRM system is designed to work for the benefit of the institution providing information to better manage the customer. At bottom, CRM systems are another example of products designed for corporate needs being customized for higher education.

Quite different from the history of applications transitioning from the private sector to the colleges and universities, in 2015 two national academic associations, the American Association of Collegiate Registrars (AACRAO) and NASPA: Student Affairs Administrators in Higher Education, partnered with the nonprofit IMS Global Learning Consortium to develop a national standard for a comprehensive student record system. With funding from the Lumina Foundation, it developed the comprehensive learner record (CLR), which offered a public standard for a secure and verifiable student data record system capable of housing all academic records, achievements, and milestones. This might include video productions, recitals, portfolios, research papers, evaluations and assessments, internship reviews, cocurricular materials, awards, badges, credentials, competencies, and extracurricular achievements of the student's choosing. In 2020, AACRAO approved IMS's CLR as the recommended standard for academic records. This established the first data information standard for student records developed by the academic industry itself that provides verifiable academic information that can be shared among different educational or employment settings.[8] Most campuses will use an existing software system to support this new standard.

Another student–faculty system that proved essential during the pandemic is the learning management system (LMS), a platform for online instruction offered by numerous companies. It provides a modular breakdown of the course syllabus, serves as an interface for assignments, and allows instructors to provide content and discussion with their entire class of students online. The grade book, course readings, announcements, and record of performance are all part of the LMS platform. Though its principal functionality is to assist in synchronous and asynchronous instruction, an LMS can also provide data analytics to better support student progress. In a report exploring integrative options to enhance student learning, Alan D. Greenberg, senior analyst and partner at Wainhouse Research, writes that "most technology platforms are siloed, designed for specific administrative, functional, or teacher needs."[9] LMS systems developed in the late twentieth century are already dated, he says, and "are structured from the point of view of the instructor's needs, but neglect the needs of the learner and, in some instances, the institution."[10] In this context, Greenberg introduces the learning relationship management platform, which is designed to assist the learner with information customized around their personal learning pathway.[11] I discuss this further in Chapter 10.

Another emerging use of student data involves data analytics and data mining. The combination of the available data, additional information provided by the student, and subsequent analysis can provide stakeholders with what Baer and Campbell call "actionable intelligence" regarding the overall student experience.[12] Data analytics enable advisors to monitor a student's course selection, examine current academic performance, and explore preferable academic pathways, all based on the historic performance patterns of other students with similar profiles.[13] For example, Georgia State University tracks data on eight hundred different academic risk factors per student as well as financial, class performance, and even class attendance information.[14] This allows it to make a probabilistic prediction of any given student's likelihood of success, based on the historic academic performance patterns of a large number of similar students. The system seems to be working: at the same time, the school increased enrollments of underrepresented minority and low-income students, and graduation rates improved by 23 percent. Administrators partly attributed this to advisors' effective use of information, which led to early intervention and timely student support.[15]

At the Univerity of Iowa, researchers used dining hall participation as a proxy measure of student social interaction. In this case, researchers analyzed individual meal-time card swipes to assess the likelihood that students encountered different lunchtime partners. They developed a meal index to see the variety of friends who would be sharing a meal over several weeks. The researchers found that a wider array of meal partners correlated with higher rates of retention and graduation compared with the same or no partners.[16] Other universities have created student success dashboards to better understand student pathways and progressions.

Much of the evidence on the use of data analytics is in the form of case studies and has had limited independent research review. A review of the literature on data analytics in higher education by Carly Foster and Peter Francis identified thirty-four rigorous research studies published between 2007 and 2018. In their analysis of these studies, they find evidence that data analytics in higher education has demonstrated an enhancement in student outcomes. However, most of the studies analyzed by the authors assume the improved student outcomes were caused by the data analytics intervention, but clear causality between the intervention and subsequent student outcomes remains a subject for further research.[17]

Predictive analytics allow universities to identify students at academic risk early on and provide the support necessary for success. While there are verifiable examples of increased student retention using predictive analytics, the tool is not without its critics. Some argue that predictive analytics can create a self-fulfilling prophecy, where a student's current academic performance, based on the experience of similar previous students, is believed to serve as an estimate of the student's future performance. A result is some advisors might counsel students away from their preferred academic field, steering them away from character-building opportunities to meet challenges, overcome obstacles, and beat the odds. The argument in favor of predictive analytics is that they can serve as a way of intervening and assisting a student whose prior academic performance reveals a proclivity or academic risk. Timely assistance can be provided through nudges, academic support, or other strategies designed to enhance eventual success. The concept of actionable intelligence is indeed a planning tool that universities may further explore, but like all predictions, it is based on general patterns from which individuals may vary.

The levels of student surveillance implicit in some approaches to data analytics raise questions about the appropriateness of monitoring what might be previously considered private interactions. While it is useful for administrators to collect data about students' lunch partners, for example, the students themselves might find this data collection to be an overreach. Such system capabilities raise ethical questions about student autonomy, possible information leaks, and the value of data as a monetized commodity of information. Perhaps students should be able to opt out of a system that involves surveillance, even if it is implemented with the best of intentions and ultimately used to improve the student experience.

Technological capabilities now being developed make current systems look like a Model-T. Remarkable computational advances have the potential to change entire industries, including aspects of higher education management. Google recently announced that its sixty-four-bit quantum computer had completed a task that would have taken what was previously the world's most powerful supercomputer ten thousand years to calculate in an unbelievable two hundred seconds. Critics have suggested that Google overestimated the comparison, but the development of a high-performing quantum computer could rank among the most significant technological breakthroughs in history.[18] (Instead of using the two digits 0 and 1 – the basis of digital computing – quantum computing uses quantum bits known as qubits. For example, a sixty-four-bit quantum computer is capable of processing thirty-six billion-billion bytes per step, in comparison to a typical personal computer, which processes eight bytes per step.)[19] A reality that will require increasing computational speed is the increasing volume of information available. According to the International Data Corporation, we are at the threshold of a staggering increase in data worldwide. By 2025, it predicts, global data will grow from the 2018 figure of 33 zettabytes to 175 zettabytes – more than a five-fold increase of the information currently available.[20] The demand for data access along with storage by the campus community, particularly faculty and students, will need to respond to this challenge.

Another important and promising development has been the development of blockchain technology, also known as distributed ledger technology. Blockchain technology creates a digital record of information that is distributed and shared with other participants in a network. Data can be entered by any authorized participant at any "block" in the networked system and shared with all members in the network. The data entry becomes a permanent record of a transaction. This system is designed to allow participants in a decentralized environment to enter data anywhere along the chain. Once data is entered, it is nearly impossible to alter the source information.[21]

Universities have begun using blockchain technology, starting with student records. It allows digital information, such as student grades and credentials, to be securely entered, instantly updated, reconciled with a database, and distributed, but not copied. This allows a student or college graduate, for example, to access and share stored information without having to request a copy of a transcript from a registrar. The security of blockchain technology may allow universities to expand the content of student performance data, for instance, collating an e-portfolio that can be updated, but not altered. Several institutions, including several members of the American Association of Universities, are currently testing blockchain for records.[22]

Except for the CLR standard, the products I have described previously are designed to primarily serve the needs of administrators and are valuable in their own right. The basic concept of the ERP, so fundamental to data management and analysis, was a product of the late twentieth-century technology revolution. With the price tag of new systems reaching well over $100 million and many university systems entering their second or third decade, we are at a crossroads. Could artificial intelligence and creative design circumvent what is currently a labor-intensive management tool requiring an extensive cadre of trained professionals? Could the equivalent of an ERP be contracted out to a provider that stores and manages the information, giving the university access through a search engine like Google? Rather than owning a system that eventually needs replacement or updating, could data management systems be leased like SaaS (software as a service), the responsibility for updates falling to savvy technology experts?

Information Privacy and Regulations

Beyond the technological aspects of data integration across different student services, there remain territorial, jurisdictional, and legal considerations. Let's say that a student's involvement in an altercation in a residence hall is logged into a database administered by the office of campus housing or the dean of students. Would sharing this information with the student's academic advisor negatively and unfairly predispose the advisor to the student? Does the value of the information mitigate that risk? Might knowledge of the incident assist the advisor in understanding the student's performance in the classroom? Could this information unintentionally leak to others in a way that might harm the student? Does sharing it entail legal risks to the university? Currently, such digital information remains with the originating unit; it is customarily not shared with personnel in other university divisions.

Adding to the complexity, a campus also works within multiple external regulatory environments. Local or state regulations may restrict universities' ability to share vital information across administrative units, and federal law requires that universities protect certain kinds of information from unauthorized disclosure. The Family Educational Rights and Privacy Act (FERPA) restricts disclosure to parents of information on students over eighteen, including grades, without the student's express written permission. FERPA also requires educational institutions to protect their students' identifying information, which includes date of birth, Social Security number, identification photographs, home address, academic performance, academic records, disciplinary records, special education program enrollment, all medical and health records, enrollment and attendance records, awards received, and degrees earned.[23]

Given the threat of significant penalties on institutions violating federal law, university administrators are understandably protective of student records. But FERPA is not intended to interfere with the ability to counsel or advise individual students. When administrators restrict access to information essential to students' academic success, they may be impeding needed assistance rather than protecting privacy. The consequences can be dire; there are times when sharing information might prevent students from harming themselves or others. As I noted in Chapter 2, the students of Generation Z are reporting significant levels of stress; the increase in youth suicidal ideation requires institutional vigilance. These situations lack clearly defined boundaries and involve professional judgment on what information may be shared, under what circumstances, and with whom, a conversation that should include university counsel to ensure proper protections for both students and the university at large.

Information obtained by campus public safety is regulated by the US Department of Education under the Crime Awareness and Campus Security Act of 1990. This law requires the institution to disclose crime statistics for the campus and the surrounding area. An amendment in 1992 was made to protect the rights of those who are victims of sexual assault. The act was renamed in 1998 as the Clery Act (The Jeanne Clery Disclosure of Campus Security Police and Campus Crime Statistics Act) in memory of a college student, Jeanne Clery, who was sexually assaulted and brutally murdered in a Lehigh University residence hall.[24]

Another relevant federal law is the Health Insurance Portability and Accountability Act of 1996 (HIPAA), which limits the electronic transfer of health care information and grants patients rights over their personal health records. Absent a written release from a student, a health care provider is permitted, but not required, to use and disclose information only in clearly defined circumstances[25] – "(1) To the individual (unless required for access or accounting of disclosures); (2) for treatment, payment, and health care operations; (3) opportunity to agree or object; (4) incident to an otherwise permitted use and disclosure; (5) public interest and benefit activities; and (6) limited data set for the purposes of research, public health, and health care operations."[26] Institutions may confidentially distribute the minimum necessary information to assist an individual for "quality assessment and improvement activities, including case management and care coordination."[27]

HIPAA regulations do not require that institutions eliminate every risk of incidental use or disclosure of protected health information; only that all reasonable safeguards are adopted and that information-sharing be limited to the "minimum necessary" as required by the aforementioned Privacy Rule.[28] In the case of a serious threat to a student's or the public's health or safety, a provision in the Privacy Rule permits covered entities to disclose protected health information to others they believe can prevent, protect, or lessen a serious and imminent threat to a person or the public, and to law enforcement if the information is needed to identify or apprehend an escapee or violent criminal.[29]

The Privacy Rule also covers the use of confidential data for research, defined as any systematic investigation designed to develop or contribute to generalizable knowledge. Protected health information may be used and disclosed for research purposes without an individual student's authorization if the researcher obtains approval from an institutional review board (IRB) or privacy board. The researcher must provide specific documentation on how the information will be protected. Similarly, a limited data set of protected health information may be used or disclosed for research purposes without an individual's authorization, provided that specified direct identifiers have been removed[30] and that the researcher agrees to specified safeguards for the information.[31]

These provisions give the university and its personnel some discretion and flexibility. Nevertheless, the best way to make sure that students' confidential health information is distributed appropriately is to secure students' written consent in advance of an emergency, perhaps as part of standard university orientation procedures. At that time, students can opt to share certain kinds of personal information for advising, counseling, or participation in research. However, students reluctant to allow personal information to be shared with their parents may opt out of signing a release, precluding the university from sharing information, even if viewed as in the student's best interest. Some campuses provide a more customized set of options for confidential information such that a specific individual can have access to some information but others may not. There are likely times when involving parents is in the best interest of the student. The balance between protecting the university from liability and a student's or the community's best interest is a difficult one.

University personnel should work with their legal counsel to develop specific protocols for the release of information governed by FERPA, HIPAA, and other local and state regulations.[32] The legal team should moreover provide professional in-service training to ensure that faculty and staff understand how information may and may not be shared. These activities should be done independently of any specific incident and repeated periodically as new staff members arrive on campus and as regulations are amended. Students should also be briefed on information-sharing and confidentiality as part of the admissions, orientation, or registration process.[33]

Other reasons for university personnel's reluctance to share relevant student information have more to do with institutional structure and culture than with government regulations. Classic issues of turf, interpersonal conflicts, intentional control of information, poor staff performance, unjustified fear of risk, or dated and misguided traditions all limit information-sharing. Whether because of a murky view of the law or university policy, or other human dynamics, conflicts, and interpersonal factors, timely information regarding at-risk students often may not reach the appropriate professional in certain circumstances. Technology alone cannot solve this problem.

Rethinking Information Services

A student's experiences both in and outside the classroom are intimately connected. From the perspective of numerous university professionals, however, a student's life is segmented according to the areas for which they hold responsibility. With no one unit responsible for all aspects of advising and guidance, a student can be bounced around like a ball in a pinball machine, careening from one unit to another. Separate and relatively autonomous administrative units, each focused on their own area of specialization, can produce unanticipated outcomes for students. When individual students become stuck between administrative divisions, or when significant delays occur among decision-makers, it is not uncommon for one specialist to blame another for the student's problem. These are not simply technical problems to be solved by new software. They reflect unresolved management issues emerging from the historic tension between a desire for some centralization of authority and the tug of decentralization and unit flexibility.

While IT can supply and implement a technological application, it is people who will interact with or operate it. For example, the university can provide different departments and administrative units with web-based templates, but if the unit does not update the information on its website, a search can return misinformation, dated information, dead links, or no information at all. Systems intended to provide responsive feedback are dependent on the person or persons using them. For example, an academic early warning system that too many faculty do not use, or only use too late in the term, fails its purpose. A campus that sends out over one hundred messages to recently accepted and soon to enroll first-year students can produce information overload causing some students to inevitably miss pertinent communications. A technology-enabled one-stop support center that isn't actually one stop is but one more gate to hurdle. Updating information important for students and others on websites depends on the routine activity of staff at the unit level, which can be uneven and uncertain. And staff with access to certain data sets are limited in what they can do to solve a problem that reaches beyond their sphere of influence.

These sorts of frustrations and irritants can affect students who follow the appropriate process only to find that the information has changed and they have missed a deadline, opportunity, or task. In a decentralized system, such oversight exceeds the capability of an IT team.

People select, install, operate, support, and utilize these complex systems that are relied upon for many administrative functions including supporting students. Problems with data operations may result in periodic hiccups, delays, errors, or misinformation that can pile up across different interactions and become overwhelming to an at-risk student.

There is no magic bullet to resolve human interface issues. Nor is there a simple replacement for the separate student service databases identified in Figure 7.1. The path to providing a digital strategy for student services involves deciding what information is needed to provide effective support to a student, and what information and in what form is most useful to the student. This is a different question from what the university would like to know, or must know, about a student. It is again a different question from which software system to buy.

The university has not yet set its own agenda of what is necessary for an integrated and comprehensive digital student service strategy, what is important to know about student progression, and what is helpful for students to be successful and promote their well-being. But university administrators must ask themselves: what information should students have available on their handheld devices, beyond academic achievements and milestones? And how can colleges and universities better organize their balkanized service sector and selectively draw upon new technological capabilities to enhance the flow of information for student well-being and success?

To successfully provide the information that reflects the whole person, well beyond academic progress, will involve administrative redesign, letting go of unit ownership of data, and even reorganizing day-to-day procedures. Once a university has a coherent concept as to who has the authority and responsibility to receive information related to the overall progress of a student, including academic progress, social interactions, physical and psychological health, and financial circumstances, then a digital strategy may commence that ensures data standards, protects confidentiality, and governs data such that the content entering from different units can be meaningfully shared.

Organizational problems involving information flow, or the lack thereof, are not new. Technology can be a transformative tool, but making the most of it requires that universities examine their existing management practices and procedures. Layering technology over inefficient and unco-ordinated operations is not a best practice. Technology can harden silos or can help break them down. Many large organizations have shifted from previously siloed management operations to more integrated service systems. While university leaders would like to embrace similar principles, they are often hindered by historic organizational alignments, resistance to change, interpretation of regulations, and service unit independence at universities.

Change will not come easily. The process requires nothing less than the wholesale reconceptualization of student support, followed by a digital strategy. It is here where universities have a real opportunity to improve student well-being, and possibly reduce costs. To my knowledge, no university has yet attempted such a radical rethinking of its approach to information management and a student service digital strategy. Students need not be passive actors in a digital student support strategy. A shift must be made from the view of what the professional needs to know to what the student needs to know. Giving students timely information adds to their sense of agency and ownership of their college experience and is part of the institutional transition to being more student-centric. This remains a priority task for the post-pandemic era of university leadership.

Notes

1 The initial version of Figure 7.1, which listed thirty-five software products, was originally developed by Kamalika Sandell, a former associate vice president at AU's Office of Information Technology. The current listing of software products in Figure 7.1 was updated on March 26, 2021, by Laurie Ambach, senior director of planning and delivery for AU's Office of Information Technology.

2 Aaron Charles Marterer, "Enterprise Resource Planning in Higher Education: A Comparative Case Study" (PhD diss., University of North Florida, 2008), 2, accessed March 25, 2021, https://digitalcommons.unf.edu/etd/360/.

3 Jeffrey Pomerantz, "C-Level Reporting Lines," *EDUCAUSE Review*, April 5, 2018, accessed April 25, 2021, https://er.educause.edu/blogs/2018/4/c-level-reporting-lines.

4 Tetiana Girchenko, Yana Ovsiannikova, and Liudmyla Girchenko, "CRM System as a Keystone of Successful Business Activity," in *Knowledge, Economy, Society: Management in the Face of Contemporary Challenges and Dilemmas*, ed. Andrzej Jaki and Bogusz Mikuła (Cracow: Foundation of the Cracow University of Economics, 2017), 251, accessed March 18, 2021, https://cfm.uek.krakow.pl/media/files/36/ff/MANAGEMENT_%20CFM%202017.pdf.

5 Carrie Hancock Marcinkevage, "Critical Success Factors of Constituent Relationship Management (CRM) Strategy in a Higher Education Institution" (PhD diss., Pennsylvania State University, 2020), 4, accessed March 28, 2021, https://etda.libraries.psu.edu/files/final_submissions/20995.

6 Renee Rui Chen et al., "Moving beyond the Direct Impact of Using CRM Systems on Frontline Employees' Service Performance: The Mediating Role of Adaptive Behaviour," *Information Systems Journal* 30, no. 3 (May 2020): 458, accessed March 29, 2021, doi.org/10.1111/isj.12265.

7 Chen et al., "Moving Beyond," 458.

8 Jeff Bohrer, "New Ways of Documenting Student Success: Comprehensive Learner Records," *EvoLLLution*, February 24, 2021, accessed May 17, 2021, https://evolllution.com/programming/applied-and-experiential-learning/new-ways-of-documenting-student-success-comprehensive-learner-records/.

9 Alan D. Greenberg, *Learning Relationship Management: Ending the Expectation of Average While Getting Back to Basics* (Duxbury, MA: Wainhouse Research, 2016), 5.

10 Greenberg, *Learning Relationship Management*, 5.

11 Greenberg, *Learning Relationship Management*, 6.

12 Marcinkevage, "Critical Success Factors," 4.

13 Jonathan S. Gagliardi, "The Analytics Revolution in Higher Education," in *The Analytics Revolution in Higher Education: Big Data, Organizational Learning, and Student Success*, ed. Jonathan S. Gagliardi, Amelia Parnell, and Julia Carpenter-Hubin (Sterling, VA: Stylus, 2018), 5–6.

14 Kimberly Hefling, "The 'Moneyball' Solution for Higher Education," *Politico*, January 16, 2019, 5:04 a.m. EST, accessed June 17, 2020, www.politico.com/agenda/story/2019/01/16/tracking-student-data-graduation-000868/. Also see Andrew Gumbel, *Won't Lose this Dream: How an Upstart Urban University Rewrote the Rules of a Broken System* (New York: The New Press, 2020).

15 Timothy M. Renick, "Predictive Analytics, Academic Advising, Early Alerts, and Student Success," in *Big Data on Campus: Data Analytics and Decision Making in Higher Education*, ed. Karen L. Webber and Henry Y. Zheng (Baltimore: Johns Hopkins University Press, 2020), 180.

16 Vimal Patel, "Are Students Socially Connected? Check Their Dining-Hall Swipe-Data," *Chronicle of Higher Education*, April 26, 2019, A35.

17 Carly Foster and Peter Francis, "A Systematic Review on the Deployment and Effectiveness of Data Analytics in Higher Education to Improve Student Outcomes," *Assessment & Evaluation in Higher Education* 45, no. 6 (2020): 822–841, accessed June 2, 2021, doi.org/10.1080/02602938.2019.1696945.

18 Deborah Netburn, "Q&A: Google Claims 'Quantum Supremacy.' What Could That Mean for the Future of Computing?," *Los Angeles Times*, October 23, 2019, 6:47 p.m. PST, accessed October 28, 2019, www.latimes.com/science/story/2019-10-23/quantum-supremacy-google-computers.

19 Kumaresan Ramanathan, "QC101: Quantum Computing & Quantum Physics for Beginners," *Udemy* (website), accessed October 28, 2019, www.udemy.com/course/qc101-introduction-to-quantum-computing-quantum-physics-for-beginners/.

20 Andy Patrizio, "IDC: Expect 175 Zettabytes of Data Worldwide by 2025," *Network World*, December 3, 2018, 2:30 a.m. PST, accessed April 25, 2021, www.networkworld.com/article/3325397/idc-expect-175-zettabytes-of-data-worldwide-by-2025.html.

21 Marco Iansiti and Karim R. Lakhani, "The Truth about Blockchain," *Harvard Business Review*, January–February 2017, accessed March 29, 2021, https://hbr.org/2017/01/the-truth-about-blockchain.

22 Ray Schroeder, "Emergence of Blockchain," *Inside Higher Ed*, June 5, 2019, accessed July 17, 2019, www.insidehighered.com/digital-learning/blogs/online-trending-now/emergence-blockchain.

23 "Protecting the Privacy of Student Education Records," National Center for Educational Statistics, accessed May 6, 2019, https://nces.ed.gov/pubs97/web/97859.asp.

24 Gail McCallion, *History of the Clery Act: Fact Sheet* (Washington, DC: Congressional Research Service, 2014), 1, accessed March 24, 2021, https://crsreports.congress.gov/product/pdf/R/R43759.

25 "Summary of the HIPAA Privacy Rule," United States Department of Health and Human Services, accessed May 6, 2019, www.hhs.gov/hipaa/for-professionals/privacy/laws-regulations/index.html.

26 United States Department of Health and Human Services, "HIPAA Privacy Rule."

27 United States Department of Health and Human Services, "HIPAA Privacy Rule."

28 United States Department of Health and Human Services, "HIPAA Privacy Rule."

29 United States Department of Health and Human Services, "HIPAA Privacy Rule."

30 United States Department of Health and Human Services, "HIPAA Privacy Rule."

31 United States Department of Health and Human Services, "HIPAA Privacy Rule."

32 See, for instance, the guidance in Angela Burnette and Julia Dempewolf, "Clarity Instead of Confusion; Available Solutions under the HIPAA Privacy Rule and FERPA to Prevent Student Violence," *Health Care Law Monthly* 2014, no. 3 (March 2014): 2–13, accessed June 6, 2021, www.alston.com/-/media/files/insights/publications/2014/04/clarity-instead-of-confusion-available-solutions-u/files/march2014_health-care-law-monthly-article/fileattachment/march2014_health-care-law-monthly-article.pdf.

33 Burnette and Dempewolf, "Clarity," 11–13.

CHAPTER 8

*Pinch Points and More: Insights from the
Student's Perspective*

At most four-year residential colleges and universities, students used to interacting with a personalized, convenient digital world confront an inefficient, fragmented environment that some perceive as unwelcoming, aloof, and bureaucratic. Hundreds of YouTube videos produced by undergraduates show an unfiltered view of the first year of college, revealing frustrations large and small. In one example from Cornell University, a first-year student describes the challenges of connecting with others, missing high school friends, and feeling lonely, disconnected from peers, and generally unwelcomed.[1] Her video reflects the experiences of so many other first-year students who describe feeling almost like "imposters" out of place in a foreign land.[2] With nearly half a million views already, the video is so expressive that I have urged the entire American University (AU) campus community to watch it as a reminder to faculty and staff of the challenges students face and their responsibility to assist with the transition to college. Not all students are extroverts or arrive with friends on campus. The community can fill the critical role of helping students connect to others (this topic will receive additional attention in Chapter 10).

University administrators, as a rule, tend to avoid public discussions of internal problems in their own institutions, focusing instead on its accomplishments. I spend time almost every day explaining why AU is such a dynamic educational setting for faculty, staff, and students. Located in one of the world's great cities, AU has emerged as an educational powerhouse. My great admiration for AU's faculty, staff, students, and leadership should be obvious in this chapter.

However, success is never final, and no matter how accomplished or prized, an institution can and must reach beyond its grasp. For a university to grow stronger and continually improve, it must first understand its weaknesses. If it rests on its laurels, it withers. Like so many other residential universities, AU can fall short of its aspirations. As provost,

I shared these concerns with the AU community, its Board of Trustees, and its president, Neil Kerwin. Out of a desire to build an institution focused on improving the undergraduate experience, in 2015 I initiated a program to systematically examine the university from the students' point of view – an essential first step in becoming a more student-centered university.

This journey to better understand how we are viewed by our students, and to use the insights gained to reflect on ourselves and improve our administrative and student services, was an opportunity to ask how might we reinvent the university from the inside out to better serve our students.

To make the process work, we needed input from students, faculty, staff, and administrators. Among students, we conducted focus groups, surveys, meetings, workshops, and retreats, and we invited them to join a journaling project to periodically write about their encounters at the university. Students participating agreed that administrators could later read and use their anonymous entries. We then asked a team of faculty, staff, and administrators to review this material and talk with undergraduates, and with each other, about the student experience.

For the most part, students who participated in the journaling project reported high levels of success and engagement – they were doing well in college, enjoying the experience, and generally spoke highly of their professors. Of course, this might be a case of self-selection bias; students who volunteered to write journals were more likely to be thriving while struggling students might be reluctant to take on one more responsibility, even if it might help other students like themselves. But even "successful" students reported frustrating moments incongruent with their expectations of the university.

In other sessions, team members listened to interviews and meetings as students told unvarnished stories of their experiences on campus. These sessions could have easily slipped into gripe sessions. Yet for the most part, they did not (the only exception being some heated exchanges about dining options). The sheer number and variety of challenges revealed that our academic community was at sea on a burning raft and had not even noticed the fire.

We dubbed the areas that particularly chafed students "pinch points." Some occurred in single administrative areas, while others crossed several. Specific pinch points, of course, will vary from university to university and change over time. They might concern academic regulations, or communications between university offices, or residential life; be experienced by all students or only by certain individuals or groups; be caused by a lack of professionalism, mistakes by ill-informed individuals, poor communication within or across offices, underlying conflicts over policies, inadequate staffing, vague priorities, or just simply poor service.

Over time, AU leadership attempted to ease or eliminate our pinch points by identifying an individual or group to work on resolving the problem or to mitigate it within a defined time frame. Some issues were easy to fix; some more difficult ones took longer than expected, and some remain unresolved. While a few are unique to AU, many will resonate on other campuses. Our overall goal was to institute changes that would tell AU students that they belong, that we genuinely care about their success, that the institution can adapt, and that we want them not only to be successful but to thrive. Institutional change takes time, but we hope our actions and messages will improve student institutional identity, strengthen academic performance, and eventually enhance retention and graduation rates. But we also hope that what AU undertook will prove meaningful, in both method and content, to other colleges and universities seeking to be more student-centered and holistic in their educational approach.

We identified over sixty pinch points falling into five general categories, starting with initial encounters with the university bureaucracy. To provide some continuity to the narrative, I draw repeatedly on excerpts from the journal of a single student, with all identifying data except gender removed. This student, the first in her family to attend college, had transferred from a community college. Her story could be that of thousands of students across the United States. It is revealing for its candor about her encounters and interaction with the university – none of her words have been edited (although any identification of the student and her organizational affiliations have been altered for anonymity). When appropriate, excerpts from her journal are woven into the exploration of related pinch points drawn from surveys and interviews of other students.

Some of the specific items raised might seem minor, but they collectively paint a portrait of an institution less responsive to students' needs than intended. A large number of problems grew out of faulty communication across the university's many offices and functions. The data strongly confirmed this book's central point: that *all* campus encounters, not just those in the classroom, powerfully affect students' educational success. While this is a story about a particular moment in time at AU, it has relevance for other residential colleges and universities.

Initial Bureaucratic Pinch Points

The first experience of our transfer student's journal suggests the positive impact that initial communication from the university can have, even before a student reaches campus.

> *My transfer process was great. When I started the application, I received an email from [a staff member] from the office of Admissions requesting my transcripts from my previous institution. I was very surprised when I realized that [the same staff member] would remain in contact with me throughout the whole process. Any time the University needed a new form or anything from my part [she] would be the one to email me and so she was the person I contacted whenever I had a question or concern. There is something very comforting about becoming familiar with one name and one person throughout the whole process and so I greatly appreciate that AU works this way.*

Unfortunately, we soon learned from interviews with other students and university administrators that this student's experience was atypical. New students and their families typically receive a large number of uncoordinated communications from different university offices between the student's first deposit and their actual arrival on campus. One year, before this study, we convened the leaders of every office that reaches out to incoming first-year students, put up large sheets of blank paper on the walls, and asked each to list what they send to students and family members before the students arrive on campus. The resulting lists of correspondence, calls, emails, and mailed materials filled all of the sheets. No one was aware of what the other offices were sending out, what the print material looked like, or when it was being sent.

With this information, we sought to better coordinate the sequencing and flow of materials to incoming students from the various offices, and to reduce the total number of messages. Four years later, a follow-up review revealed that the flow of materials had quickly swelled back to (at least) its original volume. Collectively, AU had issued an overwhelming 130 different communications to students and parents *before the start* of classes.

For students and parents, this deluge of uncoordinated messages was the first sustained encounter with the university bureaucracy – a harbinger of what was to come. We learned that some students cope with the barrage by simply ignoring it, only opening messages from individuals whose names they recognized. In our interviews, many students complained of an apparent lack of coordination of university information, particularly between Financial Aid and other offices. They reported feeling bounced around between offices for answers to their questions before they had even arrived on campus.

We took several actions to resolve these unanticipated problems. First, we enhanced AU's web presence to consolidate some communications to students and their families. We created a "Services for New Students" webpage, managed by the Office of Undergraduate Enrollment, to assemble information for new students in one place. A new calendar on the webpage shows important dates, deadlines, and events. Over the summer, the same office sends a monthly newsletter featuring information collected from student services offices across the campus. A more comprehensive review of the 130 different materials distributed, including an assessment of their relevance, presentation, and timing and sequencing, is a much larger task and remains a work in progress.

An issue of data governance lurks beneath this problem. Currently, all student administrative units have access to the incoming student database and can communicate with them and their families at will, without any coordination. This structure reflects the historic balance between centralization of authority and unit independence highlighted in earlier chapters.

Academic Pinch Points

The largest number of pinch points concerned AU's core mission: the administration of student academic policies. Student concerns ranged from course schedules and registration to problems with advising, course loads, regulations and codes, progress reports, final grading, and even faculty hiring. Despite these concerns, it should be emphasized that students voiced high praise for faculty and the quality of the teaching. As our transfer student wrote:

> I am truly amazed at the "classroom experience." All my professors look like they want to be here teaching the subjects that they teach and working with the students. I feel like I have learned more this past month than what I learned in my previous institution. Academically, I feel more challenged and there is an overall increase in engagement between the professors and the students. This is great because I look forward to all of my classes and to the material that I am learning.

As administrators, we found it encouraging that students enjoyed their time in the classroom and respected their professors. Unfortunately, interviews revealed numerous academic pinch points external to the classroom experiences. A number of these complaints involved the use of paper form equivalents, especially forms requiring original signatures. Students need signatures from administrators or professors to change a major, drop or add a course, register for classes, withdraw from a class, approve an internship, register for an independent study, participate in study abroad, or register for a consortium course (AU and other regional campuses are members of a consortium that allows students to take individual courses at other colleges and universities). While faculty and administrators saw this as a bit of a relic, it was a routine and tolerated procedure; students, however, were completely stunned that a university would require an original signature in the digital age. The lag between the expectations of Gen Z and the university procedures could not have been more evident.

One professor told of a student seeking to add her course as an elective, which required an original signature on an approval form. The professor received an email with the form attached just before she was to board a cross-country flight. She informed the student she was traveling and would not be near a printer for several days, and asked the student to print the form and leave it in her faculty mailbox so that she could sign it upon her return to campus the next week. The student replied that she was in another state herself, living with her parents at home while taking only a few online courses that semester. The professor was stumped for an easy solution; electronic signatures were not authorized. She forwarded the form to a department administrator from her phone, asking the administrator to print it, sign it on her behalf with the email attached as authorization, and forward the printed form to the appropriate office for authorization. This solution worked but was unwieldy. The professor, like the student, wondered why there was not an app that would allow her to approve requests like this from her smartphone.

As a first step, we began examining the rules about who signs off on various forms and questioning whether the various signatures are really necessary. Students insisted that many forms could be updated and further automated. It does seem that these processes could be made simpler, with fewer steps required for students, and so we continue to digitize forms and review sign-off requirements at AU.

Students also identified problems and suggested improvements to the process of registering for classes. The campus registration website, for example, showed waitlisted courses as open, which really meant the *waitlist* was open if someone wanted to add their name. The class itself was filled and closed. This confusion meant that some students dropped classes in which they were already enrolled, only to discover that they could not register for the one on the waitlist. The solution was to provide a numbered list to let students see where they were on the list along with the total seat cap for the classroom, thereby giving them a more realistic assessment of their likelihood of being admitted to the course. Students also suggested the university post two terms of class offerings per year rather than one, allowing them to look further ahead when planning their schedules – a recommendation that was implemented.

Students face additional challenges enrolling in courses that require prerequisites. The point of a prerequisite is to ensure that students are adequately prepared before they are admitted to a course. A student wishing to circumvent a prerequisite can seek an advisor's waiver with credible evidence of comparable prior work. But this delays registration; by the time the advisor approves the evidence, the course may no longer be open. Advisors recommended that students meet early with their advisor, but this does not fully resolve student concerns.

Our review found shortcomings in advisors' overall academic planning advice, leaving some students vulnerable to peer pressure to take on a heavier load of classes and activities than some could handle. Students cited a culture at AU that says "you can do it all." Some said they had chosen double majors, for example, because it was part of the culture established by previous cohorts of students. Similar pressures surround internships. At AU, both faculty and advisors encourage students to take on one or two quality internships with academic oversight over the duration of their undergraduate education. Only two supervised, fifteen-week internships may be used for credit. Nevertheless, students experience pressure from other students to do more. Some AU students take as many as four such internships by the time they graduate.

AU has looked to academic advisors to help students establish reasonable workload expectations. At the time of this study, first-year students were assigned to advisors located in their initial school or college of choice. For the most part, these advisors, located in an individual school or college, are immersed in the priorities of the student's major and specialization and so a student's overall academic pathway may not receive the same attention. Based on feedback from students, AU has shifted to a dedicated team of first-year advisors independent of any school or college who now counsel incoming students about pacing themselves when they choose their courses, warn against the message that "you can do it all," and recommend up to two well-supervised internships as the ideal. While AU has centralized first-year advising to provide a consistent message to all students, no matter their school or college, an entrenched culture set by students themselves is difficult to change.

I have had a very eventful week! I was accepted to participate in the [name] competition, working with a team of students. I wanted something that would force me outside my comfort zone. I was also elected President of my Residence Hall Council. Today I attended a 9–3 orientation and was given a lot more information about how it works. I also interviewed for a position as a tutor and I was hired on the spot! I receive federal work study and I wanted a job that would be rewarding and help me gain more experience. I haven't left the campus much since I got here and so I feel that being a tutor will help me feel more confident with working and traveling outside of the AU area. I had my training yesterday from 9–1 and it was very exciting to learn about the amazing work the [program] does.

I also got a part time babysitting job I found on the AUSG [student government] Job board and the family seems very nice. I am really looking forward to interacting with the children.

While this may seem overwhelming, I have carefully planned out all these commitments and fit them into my schedule. I can wake up early [to] take charge of my day. Right now, I am just setting my alarm, only to hit the snooze button a million times. I am trying different approaches to make sure I can stop doing this.

Here, in full flower, is the "you can do it all" attitude that permeates student culture. While our student does not acknowledge feeling overwhelmed, she already recognizes that she is coping by "hitting the snooze button."

When students realize that they have overcommitted and decide to reduce their courses below a full load, they have to get the requested schedule approved by their advisor and the Academic Support and Access Center. Even then, problems arise around notifying other relevant offices, such as Financial Aid, the Writing Center, the Math Center, athletics, or even faculty instructors. This lack of communication creates other problems, including limiting access to specific academic support services, inadvertently derailing a student's graduation plans, endangering financial aid eligibility, and restricting access to required course sequences. At AU, we have attempted to rectify this through additional and timely notices. Specifically, the Academic Support and Access Center now notifies the Writing Center, the Math Center, and the Dean of Undergraduate Studies to keep an eye out for individual students to ensure they receive the help they need.

I haven't been getting the grades that I am used to getting at my previous institution and that has been a little difficult to adjust to. Here I have to study harder and longer, read more, and prepare better. I am taking all these things into consideration to make sure that I get the grades that I want. My professors are great and I don't think I am utilizing them enough. I want to start attending their office hours to make sure that I am putting all the effort into my work. I think putting their office hours into my weekly schedule will make it more likely that I will attend their office hours.

Our student's journal reveals her newfound awareness of the level of work expected and the importance of meeting with faculty members about assignments. When academic problems show up in the classroom, instructors are the first to know about them. Faculty can detect academic difficulties early in the term so that the student can receive timely tutoring and support. With this said, students raised multiple concerns about the effectiveness of the university's early warning system, which is meant to alert them and their advisors if their academic progress is in jeopardy. In this case, the student has not been meeting with her professors during office hours. Nor have her professors suggested she make an appointment or triggered an "early warning."

Under AU's early warning system, a faculty member emails an advisor or designated administrator to signal that a student is struggling and may need tutoring. Often, such a notification comes after an examination or a major assignment. But even if that comes comparatively early in the term, perhaps in week five of a fifteen-week course, it might take another week or more for an instructor to analyze the results and return them to the student. The advisor needs time to contact the student and arrange necessary tutoring or support services. It is often week seven or later before the student receives any direct help – around the time of the midterm exam. Another two weeks could easily fly by before a tutor has diagnosed the source of the problem and begun to help. At this point, in all likelihood, the student is so far behind that success in the course is unlikely. The only realistic options are an incomplete grade, a low grade, or repeating the course in the summer or the following term, at an additional cost.

Students asked for earlier, more personalized, and specific information regarding their progress before being notified that they are at risk in a course. They also wanted access to information on how shortcomings in their academic progress might put their financial aid and scholarships at risk, and they asked that their advisors also be alerted to that connection. For some students, the early warning system has worked, but for too many others, it is like pulling a fire alarm only to find it disconnected.

At AU, we encourage faculty to provide assessments early and often to swiftly detect when students are struggling with assignments and arrange for the help they need. Not all faculty do so. Beyond changing faculty behavior, an app could be used to simultaneously send early warning messages to student, advisor, and tutor, along with available time slots for the student to meet with a tutor. This particular system does not currently exist at AU, but the university has introduced a new CRM Advise software program that allows instructors to file an early warning notice with a few clicks. This generates simultaneous emails to the student, the academic advisor, the Office of the Registrar, and the Academic Support and Access Center.

The system is a good start, but implementation has been rocky. In a course where I required weekly writing assignments, I was able to tell a student by the second week that their written work was difficult to understand and they needed to get assistance at the campus Writing Center. By the next week, it was clear that the student was still struggling. For a second time, I indicated they needed support because they might not pass the course. I also verbally informed the student's advisor of the situation and reiterated my recommendation about immediate writing assistance. The advisor responded that she would contact the student, but I don't know if that ever happened. After my third notice, letting the student know that there had been little improvement, I issued an early warning notice through the website. That generated a notice, copied to me. But instead of referring the student to writing help, the notice directed the student to meet with me. We were running in circles.

> *I think partially that the school should not only provide academic counseling but also a form of "progress" counseling for transfer students. It would be nice to have someone reach out to us as students, even if it is just once a month, to ask how we are doing, if we have any questions, if we need help with anything. Most students would probably ignore and disregard this assistance, but a student like me would greatly appreciate that. I have yet to put AU on a face on campus. What this means is that aside of faculty, whom I see as direct employees of the school, I have yet to meet someone that I consider fully represents AU. Someone that I can go to and ask, "hey how can I do this?" or "Do you have some advice for how I am feeling right now?" I am not sure if I am getting my point across or if I am making this clear enough, but so far this campus feels very lonely. I mean lonely in that sense that it's hard to identify who here cares enough about our transition progress.*

Here we have a failure of the academic support system, its advisors and support staff, as well as those in the unit designed specifically to help transfer students. AU is adequately staffed with trained employees who know best practices for addressing emerging concerns from transfer students. Nevertheless, no one reached out to the author of this journal. She was feeling disconnected and had the sense that no one cared about her success at AU. From an administrative perspective, AU had provided the resources, but the skilled staff, in this case, did not execute their duties well.

> *This week I had two papers due, one in-class writing assignment and one test. I felt very overwhelmed and missed a total of two classes. Partially because I was not feeling well and partially because I have been feeling very down and am constantly in the mood of just wanting to hide under my blankets and avoid all types of responsibilities. I don't doubt my abilities. I know I can study well and I know I can write good papers, so I am not exactly sure why I have taken this "careless" attitude towards my work. I am hoping that by resting this weekend I will be better to begin next week with a brand-new mindset and work ethic.*

At this point, our student is clearly overwhelmed. One support system on campus that might have helped her is the CARE Network, which over many years has reached out to students who are feeling depressed or evidencing psychological or potential medical issues. Faculty and academic advisors may enter comments and observations about potential "at-risk" students – students they notice having difficulties. The system is managed by the Dean of Students and is also linked to the university's Public Safety unit. In this case, our student confined her message to the anonymous journaling project, which, by agreement, remained confidential and was not read until after the project was over. Hence, no one responded or offered her any help; nor did any of her professors notice anything amiss. Here we have professional staff in different offices and five professors passing each other like ships in the night while a student sinks in a slowly leaking rowboat.

Students also identified several academic pinch points regarding grading. In one case, a teacher's failure to turn in grades on time dramatically affected a student who had finished her undergraduate degree and had enrolled in graduate school at AU. When she attempted to register for graduate classes, she was surprised to be billed at the higher undergraduate tuition rate. She later learned through AU Central (a one-stop business service center to which I will return in the following pages) that a faculty member in one of her last undergraduate courses had not turned in their grades on time. From the university's perspective, she had not graduated. Once the faculty member entered the final course grade, the registrar issued her diploma and the Office of Student Accounts corrected her billing and issued a refund check. Months went by, and neither diploma nor refund appeared. After constant inquiries, she learned that both had been sent to the undergraduate residence hall where she no longer lived.

A staff member there eventually found the two documents and let the student know he had them. Students reported an alarming number of such unfortunate runarounds.

Incompletes – or more specifically, lack of communication about the rules surrounding Incompletes – produced stress for a number of students. A student may elect to take a grade of Incomplete in a course without fully understanding the implications of not completing the coursework on time. A student's advisor and the Office of Financial Aid can advise on those implications, but for this to happen, they have to know about it (see Chapter 2 for a more detailed case study). If the course load is too heavy, the advisor can review options, including reducing the number of courses the student selects in the future. If the Incomplete is in a required course or a prerequisite, the advisor can examine the availability of future course offerings that might delay the student's intended graduation date. The faculty member agreeing to the Incomplete may not know if the student is on probation and therefore ineligible to take an Incomplete. The relationship between student, faculty, advisor, and financial aid officer necessitates a level of coordination, swift assessment, and sharing of information to work in the student's best interest. As lines of communication are currently structured, such timely exchanges can prove challenging.

The students with whom we spoke understood that their school and academic department representatives, the Dean of Students, and the academic affairs vice provost all have different administrative obligations, expectations, and accountability. Their complaints were about poor coordination among those offices and individuals, leaving them spinning their wheels and duplicating requests, unclear as to who had authority over what. The fact that their issues crossed administrative divisions was not their concern. Their concern was that they spent too much time trying to resolve an issue only to find that the solution resided elsewhere or required the approval of more than one administrator. This is a structural issue that is difficult to resolve.

The students also indicated that they wanted one source for a holistic assessment of their academic progress. They observed, for instance, that students and faculty have access to different information on the AU student portal. They requested the ability to view the blocks of information side by side, or perhaps to toggle between faculty and student views.

Each school or college at AU had its own review committee to adjudicate violations of the academic integrity code, which delineates standards for plagiarism, cheating, falsification of academic information, proper attribution to sources, and the like. Students perceived, and staff verified, that the six schools serving undergraduates have different criteria and standards for violations. Recognizing the problem, the university has centralized adjudication of such matters and decision-making no longer resides in a school or college.

Finally, students questioned the university's late reappointment schedule for full-time contracted faculty, observing that delays caused exemplary teachers – and valuable faculty–student continuity – to be lost. This problem arises from the budget authorization process. At AU, as at many universities, funding for contracted faculty depends on the annual budget, enrollment numbers, and instructional demand in their area of expertise. While schools and colleges were promptly submitting their authorizations to hire contracted faculty, my office was holding off on approving the instructors' contracts until we were certain that funds would be available. In response to feedback from students, deans, and contracted faculty themselves, we reviewed the previous four years of funding and determined that, on an annual basis, at least 80 percent of the funds for contract faculty would be available from one year to the next. As a result, I permitted the deans to make earlier commitments to most contract faculty. This process does create some risk, should the funds not materialize. But waiting runs the risk of losing accomplished teachers who know the campus, the curriculum, and the students. Committing 80 percent of the previous year's allocation seemed a reasonable compromise that I readily agreed to implement.

Financial Pinch Points

The second-largest number of pinch points students identified involved financial interactions with the university, starting with financial aid. AU awards financial aid for an upcoming academic year in late June, a schedule that allows the Office of Financial Aid to assess each student's academic progress. But students observed that this schedule, set at the university's convenience, makes it difficult for them and their parents to arrange payment before the August 1 deadline. It also limits students' ability to enroll in their preferred courses, as many courses are already full by the time the financial aid information arrives. Students wanted to know why financial aid couldn't be announced earlier. At this point, the policy remains unchanged due to the information flow within the office and its need to ensure accurate financial information.

Other financial pinch points involving financial transactions already have solutions, at least partial ones, but students aren't necessarily aware of them. Students planning to study abroad, for instance, expressed concern about registering for courses in time to maintain federal financial aid eligibility. They need twelve to fifteen credit hours per term to maintain eligibility. However, they generally do not know the titles of their courses until they are admitted to the international college program, or, in some cases, until they arrive at the host college, which generally happens after course registration is closed. AU offers a partial solution, allowing students to register for generic placeholder study abroad courses, which safeguards financial aid as long as they remain in good academic standing. However, their transcript will not reflect their actual courses until the end of the term, when the international college submits the final grade. Students applying for scholarships, jobs, or internships while abroad want an accurate record of their coursework, as it can distinguish their applications from others. It seems that once students apply for study abroad, the link between their application and registration for generic courses could be made automatically, and AU's registrar could be notified as soon as the student has selected a course and could automatically amend the transcript. While technologically feasible, this remains a work in progress.

Students also cited stress produced by notices regarding the tuition payment due dates (August 1 for Fall Term, January 8 for Spring). As soon as the bill's due date passes, students and their families receive written notice of an overdue balance, shown in red, even if the university is expecting third-party payments from loans, VA benefits, 529 payments, outside scholarships, and the like, most of which typically land in students' accounts after the initial tuition due date. For this very reason, the university does not apply late fees and finance charges until approximately six weeks after the due date. But the immediate notification of an overdue payment still creates anxiety for students and their families. In response to student feedback, the Office of Student Accounts added a message to the website advising students to deduct expected third-party payments from the total amount due and pay only the difference. Before this change, the university received hundreds of inquiries each semester from students and parents worried that their external funding would not arrive in time. The simple act of adding a disclaimer to the website reduced the number of inquiries – and student stress – dramatically.

Other feedback concerned the Office of Financial Aid's practice of notifying students of either a new award or change to an existing one during the school year in an email that leaves out the specifics of, or reason for, the change. Students pointed out the uncertainty that the communication raises, the worry as to the expected amount of their financial aid, and the need on their part to seek additional information. As of this writing, this remains unresolved.

In yet another example of confusing communication practices, the Office of Student Accounts engaged a third-party provider to process student payments. Because that provider used the quaint salutation, "Dear Citizen" in its emails, many students deleted or dismissed them, suspecting, quite reasonably, that the message was phishing or spam. This remains unresolved because the third-party provider curiously claims it cannot change the salutation. Meanwhile, all campus offices have been asked to review their correspondence practices with students and their families. But even better communication will not resolve the problem of an overwhelming number of uncoordinated messages emanating from the institution, suggesting the need for a larger examination of existing processes, their interactions, and ways to streamline and integrate what are now independent activities.

In general, students reported confusion about the university's financial processes and how to access timely information. For instance, a student disagreeing with a financial aid package is entitled to appeal. But questions about the timing or status of an appeal must go to a professional in the Office of Financial Aid even though AU has an office meant to serve as a central, one-stop office for business practices (more on this shortly). No one outside the Office of Financial Aid is currently authorized to respond to such questions and the office guards such information carefully.

Students also cited concerns about tuition payment plans. The university requires students and their families to fill out an application to allow regular tuition payments throughout the term rather than a one-time payment of the full cost. Previously, the Office of Student Accounts did not confirm receipt of applications upon arrival, instead processing them in batches. This created uncertainty and anxiety as students had no way of knowing whether their applications had been received before the deadline. After learning of student and family concerns, the office now processes applications upon receipt, with a seven-business-day deadline, which has resolved this issue.

Financial transactions involve paperwork, and students reported difficulty accessing the required forms. One such document is the Internal Revenue Service's 1098T tax form, which the university files for every student enrolled. Each January, AU sends the form to all eligible students, but those who chose to receive it electronically ran into confusing glitches when they tried to download it, prompting hundreds of calls to the university. The problem turned out to be either a pop-up blocker or an outdated browser on students' computers. The fix was easy: the Office of Student Accounts provided additional instructions about the preferred browser and pop-up blocker, drastically reducing calls about this problem.

It is perhaps understandable that students had so many concerns about the various financial services offices, particularly the Office of Financial Aid, given that they so often deliver disappointing news. Not all students receive the amount of financial aid they had hoped for. The AU financial aid team is a skilled professional group, respected by their peers nationally. They expertly navigate federal regulations, financial requirements, lending laws, student record confidentiality, and university budget constraints in allocating awards. The feedback from students, however, makes clear that the office has room to grow in understanding the student perspective. The office continues to prioritize improving the way it communicates its decisions, aligning with other offices, and streamlining what appears to students as overly cumbersome administrative operations.

A final set of financial pinch points involve the actual costs of attending college. On top of tuition, room, board, and books, students find themselves burdened with additional and unexpected fees. Several academic departments with increasingly strained budgets have levied extra course fees to cover such essential costs as lab equipment or art supplies. Students pointed out that additional fees can deter students from taking those classes, potentially influencing career choices. Having paid substantial tuition bills, they were reluctant to pay again for classes they feel they should be entitled to take. Some have simply tapped out their financial resources and cannot afford the additional fees. By adding over $1 million to the budget and placing the funds in the relevant department accounts, AU has now been able to eliminate course-based fees, a decision recommended in the overall university budget and approved by the Board of Trustees.

Health insurance waivers also drew some consternation. All full-time students are automatically charged for health insurance, but receive regular reminders from the Health Center that the fee is waived if they are covered by another eligible plan. Not surprisingly, students sometimes miss these notices, with the result that many fail to file for the waiver. Even when they do request a waiver, the Office of Student Accounts can be slow to remove the charge from the account. The Health Center has now added messaging about the filing timeline and, during peak times, the Office of Student Accounts reviews the health insurance waiver process several times each week to remove the fee more promptly. This resolution required multiple meetings with the three relevant divisions (Health Center, Student Accounts, and AU Central) and a representative from the provost's office, and a willingness to coordinate and modify existing processes. They are now operational and working well.

Also, AU has contracted with an insurer to provide tuition refund insurance if students need to withdraw during the academic term. Such insurance is a wise investment, as there is always a risk of illness or some unanticipated reason to drop out and the loss of paid tuition can be financially devastating. But many students and their families complained about the cost of the insurance plan to which AU had subscribed. In response, beginning in Fall 2018 AU partnered with a new insurer to cover up to 100 percent of tuition charges not covered by the university's refund policy. The insurer created an AU-specific website to give students and families additional information about the elective program. So far, students and parents have approved of the new vendor.

Dining and Housing-Related Pinch Points

The quality of food and lodging has an enormous impact on students' experience of residential college life. This became clear to me after a focus group session in which students forcefully expressed their dissatisfaction with the variety and quality of dining options. Shortly afterward, we began to schedule regular meetings to receive student input on services and new meal plan options. Students successfully pushed to participate in reviewing bids and selecting the university's food vendor and their complaints have dropped significantly since.

For students who depend on meal plans for virtually all their meals, food quality, freshness, variety, attractiveness, and choice matter tremendously. One highly selective campus I recently visited had constructed a large and attractive dining hall in one of its new academic buildings that offered several meal stations comparable to a fast-casual restaurant marketplace. Meal stations, often run by well-known fast-food vendors, are quite common at universities. In this case, however, individual chefs at each station offer dining as good as or even better than local restaurants. At most of the stations, individual items are prepared hot and fresh, with the options changing daily. Gourmet salads are available and popular. Students, faculty, and staff all use the facility, the students paying with their meal plans, and faculty and staff paying market prices. The food is so good, and so sought after, that faculty and staff know to arrive for lunch just before classes break and crowds of eager students overwhelm the space.

The point is that high-quality dining options can enhance the entire campus community.

While students value quality, they (and their parents) are conscious of costs. Resident hall pricing varies according to the number of roommates, with singles costing most and triples least. Until recently, students living in a triple room on campus at AU would see the housing charge on their account listed as a "double" room. Even though they were being charged less than those living in double rooms, the statement made students wonder if their bill was accurate, sparking yet more calls to the university. Apparently, the computer system did not allow the description to be changed. As a workaround, the Office of Finance, Housing & Residential Life, in cooperation with IT, added a new line item listing a "triple discount," which eliminated the confusion and stopped the calls.

More static arose over charges assigned for damage to a residence hall or room. When Housing & Residential Life identifies a specific student as responsible for such damage, it places a charge on the student's account at the end of the semester. The charge is immediately marked as an overdue balance, blocking students from registering for future courses until it is paid. If Housing is unable to identify the culprit, the unit divides the repair bill among all residents on the floor. An internal review I conducted found that approximately 1,100 students, 32 percent of the total housing residents, received a bill for ten dollars or less for student-inflicted but unspecified damage on residence hall floors at the end of a single spring term.[3] One can imagine a student's (or parent's) reaction, after paying tuition, books, and room and board, to a bill for unspecified damage they did not cause and of which they were not even aware.

Small charges like this, often perceived by students or parents as unfair and petty, can generate significant and entirely unnecessary ill will. Resolving this issue required numerous meetings between the CFO, the provost, and the vice president for campus life. Eventually, AU added additional funds to the base operating account for the residence facilities. We expect this relatively modest increase in the university's expenses will be rewarded in the form of goodwill from students who are, after all, future alumni and prospective donors. Damages traceable to an individual student will continue to be billed accordingly, but the university now absorbs the cost of minor wear and tear.

Two Final Pinch Points

Let's return to the student's journal for insight into a final pinch point: the difficulty of accessing mental health services during a challenging time in a young adult's life. Students may need help, but either due to perceived stigma, inattentiveness to the onset of depression, or personal reasons may not reach out for assistance. A resident hall advisor, friends, roommates, or faculty may be conduits to connect a student in need of attention. I personally have offered to walk students over to the counseling center when they were reluctant to seek help. Nevertheless, as discussed in Chapter 2, the need for student mental health support is exceeding the capacity at many campuses. Many students have closely relied on their parents for emotional connection and support throughout their lives; some struggle to find that kind of support on campus.

> Today I am returning from an emergency trip back home. As you may be able to tell from my previous entries, my overall emotional health had been depleting as the weeks went by. On Thursday, I woke up feeling miserable and crying. I called my mom, told her everything I was feeling and asked if I could go back home. I had the most amazing weekend with my family, I felt like myself again. I didn't even want to leave my house because I was so happy doing that, just being home. I spoke with my parents and told them I was not happy at AU. That I couldn't really pinpoint where the problem was but that I was just not happy. I blamed it on the people, it felt like I could not connect with anyone here. I blamed it on the size of the school, maybe it was too small for me. After talking with them I realized that I need to find motivation to finish my semester out strong. I felt like this weekend had given me the energy and motivation necessary to come back and feel better. Sadly, as soon as I was dropped off at the bus station, I felt the same exact void and sadness that I had tried to escape with this trip.
>
> I spent half of my four-hour bus ride crying. The thought of my bus driving further and further away from home kept bringing tears to my eyes. I have never felt so lonely and so sad for such a long amount of time before. I got back to campus and started unpacking, pushing myself mentally to feel better. And then I got a text from one of my advisors at my previous institution and we ended up talking on the phone for nearly an hour. I vented and shared my frustration with her. I told her everything I was feeling. As the first child to attend college my parents were too struggling with how I was feeling. They've never dealt with something like this, because they never attended college. But talking to my advisor was different. She works with college students all the time and she understood exactly how I was feeling. And with her help I arrived at a very important conclusion: it is not AU's fault ... Since my first day here I have been trying to repeat my previous college experience, where I was highly involved and busy in organizations and student clubs. I keep comparing everything ... the experience, involvement, staff, students, everything side-by-side this whole time. And by doing so I haven't allowed AU to truly impress me or provide me with any type of satisfaction. Now that I realize this ... I have to allow this school and this experience to be a new chapter not a repetition of my previous chapter. If I don't give AU a chance, I am never going to be happy.

The despair evident in this journal excerpt reflects multiple failures across many different offices, individuals, and faculty at the university. A text message and call from the student's community college advisor helped her at a moment when she felt lost, lonely, and depressed. The community college advisor took the time to speak with her, showed empathy, listened, and provided needed guidance. We do not know if the timing of the text message was a coincidence or if her parents, concerned for their daughter, asked the advisor to reach out, but either way, it arrived at a critical time when both the university and the student were at risk of failure.

This series of journal excerpts reveal a self-aware student who knows how to reflect on her challenges and who had experienced previous academic success at a community college. Though initially denied admission to AU, she acquired the study skills at the community college to be academically successful. Now at her dream college, she felt drained and stressed by the university's lack of personal connection. As an administrator, I found it particularly painful to see someone who began AU with such excitement, energy, and enthusiasm ground down to such a low emotional point.

She was attending a university with multiple professional support staff for advising, career assistance, academic support, mental health counseling, and programs for first-generation and transfer students. She had regular contact with at least five different faculty members in her courses. But still, she got lost in a complex institution. Are there other students like her? Even the loss of one student is one too many. Her story, together with the array of pinch points highlighted by other students, reveals how students struggle to navigate the semi-independent offices of the university. So many different professionals and faculty have responsibility for students, yet no one is fully accountable.

While I do not know the student's identity, I did learn that, once the journals were submitted, the investigator who ran the journaling project followed up and helped guide her to the appropriate support services. I also understand that, partly through her own grit and determination, she had since turned the corner and was making progress at AU.

Even with mental health services available on campus, students may not take full advantage of the support. We can see this in another case, this time involving a first-year student with excellent high school grades and strong SAT scores, but a history of depressive symptoms. Upon arrival, he found his courses challenging, was uncertain about his performance, and struggled to see the relevance of his courses for the work he wanted to do – providing direct services to homeless families in the community in which he was raised. His academic uncertainty fed into his psychological symptoms, and soon he became more and more depressed. At one low point, he went to the counseling center to talk about his concerns, lack of interest in his studies, and feelings of sadness. When his in-take questionnaire indicated he was not in immediate crisis, he was asked to schedule an appointment two weeks in the future.

On the day of the appointment, an email informed him the appointment would have to be rescheduled; the counselor was out sick. Increasingly discouraged, unhappy with his courses, and feeling alone, he did not bother to follow up and reschedule. The downward spiral continued. He became despondent and eventually dropped out of the university.

People are complicated, resources are limited, and even in a comparatively well-resourced setting, students can find routine procedures overwhelming. To someone experiencing depression, even the task of scheduling a second appointment can prove daunting. Should the student have been handled differently and provided a priority interview with a different counselor instead of having his appointment canceled? The center has its policies and protocol. Were they appropriate in this case? Would a different set of protocols produce a different outcome?

Pinch points, like microaggressions, can be cumulative. Fairly or unfairly, they represent the university's modus operandi, its culture, and its sense of concern for details that influence a student's life. Too often, students experience a university through its limitations.

Technological Fixes

Pinch points are merely a symptom of deeper issues and problems in a university. To deal with them, we seek individuals with high levels of personal skills to intervene and also lean on the possibility of technological solutions. The former goes without saying, but the latter can ease at least some of the problems students identified. For example, students requested that administrators make greater use of mobile technology for forms, timesheets for work, and text messaging and social media platforms for engaging them and providing feedback. Today's students prefer these platforms to email, but they are used too sparingly in university academic or business exchanges. This cultural divide hampers communication. It is notable that, in the case of the transfer student's journal entry, it was a text message from her community college advisor that first caught her attention.

AU has not fully transitioned to a mobile-friendly mode of student services, but it has begun introducing tools that prioritize student needs. In 2008, in response to continual complaints about the lack of coordination among the Offices of Financial Aid, Student Accounts, and the Registrar (dubbed the Bermuda Triangle by students – once a document was caught between the three offices, it was believed lost forever), the administration created AU Central. It is intended to be a one-stop business office for student assistance in the areas of financial aid, student accounts, and registration; the first place students and their parents go with administrative or financial problems. The initial staff included thirteen professionals with each of the three functional units reassigning multiple positions to help staff the new office.

When AU Central opened in 2010, the volume of email and phone questions at the start of the term exceeded expectations and overwhelmed the staff. Response time lagged, creating exactly the kinds of complaints the office was intended to resolve. Further complicating matters was the fact that authority for certain decisions, particularly financial aid, still rested in the original offices. Moreover, despite its name, AU Central initially only handled issues related to the three offices, meaning that staff members could not help with questions about parking fees, ID cards, housing issues, or any number of queries related to campus life. Students began to see AU Central as a "first stop," not a "one-stop."

The situation has since improved. Students now have access to the National Student Clearinghouse, which provides enrollment verifications and degree clearance information. Should a student need a degree completion letter, AU Central can issue it. AU Central now also provides information for veterans. Every month, AU Central closes well over two thousand cases. Initially, the office tracked these queries using the iSupport ticketing system. More recently, it has switched to an application called Service Now, which all students and parents can access through the AU Central "Just Ask" screen. This system is intended to promote the self-service concept so familiar to Generation Z students by creating databases of the most commonly asked questions about all types of services across the university, not just those provided by AU Central.

Still, there are times when students seek personalized face-to-face interaction, so AU Central maintains a front desk of service advisors. Most university business offices, including AU Central, offer business hours of nine to five. If a student arrives at a university office at 5:05 pm, they likely find the doors locked and the lights off. It is not unusual for students to keep long hours, often late into the evening, and they frequently seek assistance at odd hours or when offices are closed. From a managerial perspective, this is a conundrum, in that staff have families and personal lives and student demand in the evening is unpredictable, making it difficult to justify keeping offices open late. As we look to the future, one can imagine the use of chatbots for frequently asked questions that might arise at any time. And, due to consistent demand, AU Central does keep later hours for the first two weeks of the term.

Beyond Pinch Points

During this multiyear assessment process, AU, like many other colleges and universities, encountered dissatisfaction and criticism from students of color, LGBTQIA students, students with religious identities, and conservative students, among others. Students of color, particularly Black students, identified and reported specific incidents of racial slurs, insensitivity, and marginalization in and out of class, leading some to increasingly feel a sense of racial animosity against their presence. These issues are not pinch points per se, but reflect embedded racist and discriminatory behavior that disillusions students about the college experience, derails them from reaching personal goals, and intensifies all other interactions, including pinch points.

The university's Office of Institutional Research and Assessment periodically surveys undergraduates to evaluate the overall campus climate. The findings reveal dramatic differences in a sense of belonging between Black and White students. Specifically, in the 2015 AU Campus Climate Survey, nearly 70 percent of White students responded affirmatively to the prompt, "I feel like part of the community at this institution." But only half as many Black students, 35 percent, agreed. Put another way, 65 percent of Black students felt themselves to be somehow apart from the AU community. In response to the prompt, "The university actively encourages a commitment to creating a campus community where everyone has a sense of belonging," we learned that nearly three-quarters of White students agreed, while just over half of Black students felt the same way.

In May 2017, a Black female student, the first person of color elected president of the AU student government association, became a victim of a hate crime on campus. The unknown perpetrator(s) dangled bananas from what looked like nooses all around campus, writing the Greek letters of the student's sorority as well as racially charged messages on the fruit in black marker. The incident disrupted campus operations and triggered unrest and protests. The targeted student leader handled the situation with remarkable bravery and led the campus through an intense and sustained dialogue on racial reckoning. But while the university benefitted from her leadership, the student herself was forced to shoulder the heavy burden of racial hate. The seriousness and gravity of the situation made national news and led to multiple investigations, including one by the FBI. This tragic incident, in the context of other previous incidents, further confirmed the racial prejudice lurking even at a special place like a university and cast a long shadow on AU.

Students of color can become a target of hate at any time. Black students at AU have often said to me that they did not come to the university to be victims and simultaneously teachers about racial issues to an ill-informed, majority-White student body and community. They find it painful to constantly endure such indignities, and exhausting to be asked to explain those indignities to others. Educating other students about their reality is an additional emotional burden they have rightfully been reluctant to carry.

Responding to calls to address the climate of racism on campus, AU has ongoing efforts to train faculty and staff and has hired more faculty of color, though it remains predominantly White. The university provided funding for a new, national, antiracism research center initially led by National Book Award winner Ibram X. Kendi and continues under new leadership since his departure. An ongoing, campus-wide initiative on "inclusive excellence" has enhanced the curriculum, improved teaching, influenced campus events, and strengthened interpersonal relationships. Every academic major now has a diversity course requirement, and all first-year students must take two 1.5-credit-hour courses that deal with multiculturalism.

And yet, this is just a start. Some students of color harbor a distrust of the university. Any single incident or pinch point that propagates individual or systemic racism can trigger a strong response. The tragic murder of George Floyd, recorded for the entire world to see, has brought calls for an antiracism movement involving deeper systemic changes. The university as an institution cannot stand apart from this historical moment.

With the increasingly mainstream presence of far-right ideology, AU's Jewish students have been also been targets of antisemitism. Swastikas have been placed in front of students' residence hall doors, and hate messages have been sent to both Jewish students and students of color. These are troubling times for students of different faiths, racial backgrounds, and gender identities who continue to experience microaggressions and overt acts of hate at AU.

At the same time, students who identify themselves as politically conservative describe specific incidents in which they claim to have been treated differently by their instructors, graded down based on their point of view, and told they are wrong on issues. They report that they have learned to pander to their professors to avoid being penalized in grading and that they avoid stating their true opinions. Despite these reports, all faculty members I have spoken with about these issues flatly deny that they treat any student differently because of their political opinions and preferences.

These are challenging times for all students as well as for those who teach, support, and manage the university, an institution that is a microcosm of the conflicts and prejudices of the larger society. This chapter has highlighted what we have learned at AU about the workings of some of our offices, policies, procedures, programs. and the experiences of students interacting with them. In seeking to uncover some of our internal problems we intentionally did not examine our successes, as we hear and trumpet these all the time. Our encounters revealed issues of communication, information flow, mismatched policies, inattentiveness, human errors, IT governance and technological limitations, lack of coordination, fragmentation across different functions, and lurking racism and discrimination, among other issues. While the particular pinch points will differ among peer colleges and universities, I doubt they will be dramatically different elsewhere. I am proud that at AU we are prepared to face our gremlins with the expectation of sustained improvement.

In the next chapter, I review the entire process of what we called Reinventing the Student Experience (RiSE), a four-year AU intervention, and the more systematic efforts we undertook to address the underlying issues evidenced by the multiple pinch points. In the last chapter, I wrestle with the current organizational form of nonprofit residential four-year colleges and universities and consider approaches that can foster a more holistic learning experience for today's and tomorrow's students.

Notes

1 Emery Bergmann, "My College Transition," October 13, 2017, accessed May 10, 2019, www.youtube.com/watch?v=oAUcoadqRlE&ab_channel=Emery Bergmann.

2 Peter Felten and Leo M. Lambert, *Relationship-Rich Education: How Human Connections Drive Success in College* (Baltimore: Johns Hopkins University Press, 2020), 42–49.

3 At that time, AU had a total of 3,480 beds in its residence halls. Some of the beds and rooms were allocated to residence hall staff, and a few to faculty.

CHAPTER 9

Reinventing the Student Experience: A Case Study

Many colleges and universities think of themselves as unique, even extraordinary, and American University (AU) is no exception. However, in many ways, it mirrors the challenges and struggles of other traditional American residential colleges and universities. It has many of the same departments, offices, functions, and services. It follows a common fifteen-week semester-based academic schedule, has similar academic regulations and procedures, including shared governance with faculty in academic matters. Its faculty members are involved in the various national academic associations and engage in both teaching and research. Several hold the honor of editing the most prestigious journals in their field. Its staff, like faculty, are active in their national associations. Its grounds and facilities are a source of pride. Its distinctive qualities reflect the emphasis placed on certain areas of study, particularly a balance of the liberal arts tradition with experiential professional programs.

Accredited by the Middle States Commission on Higher Education, AU is a doctorate-granting residential research institution – its Carnegie Classification is R-2, Doctoral Universities Higher Research Activity. The campus is situated on eighty acres in Northwest Washington, DC, near embassies, the National Cathedral, NBC (WRC-TV), the US Department of Homeland Security, restaurants, and shops. Public transportation links the campus to a wide range of activities and institutions in Washington and the region. The location in the nation's capital provides unique opportunities for both faculty and students. In the 2020–2021 academic year, the university served about fourteen thousand students, just over seven thousand of them undergraduates.[1] There are seven schools and colleges: Arts and Sciences, International Service, Public Affairs, Business, Communication, Education, and Law. Many of AU's programs are in the top tiers of national rankings, with an average student SAT (Scholastic Aptitude Test) score just under 1300.[2] Thanks to the faculty's well-established dedication to teaching and guiding undergraduate as well as graduate students, AU is known as a college-centered research university.

Historically, AU, a private nonprofit institution, has educated a predominantly White, economically affluent student body. In 2007, only 10 percent of AU's first-year students were eligible for Pell Grants. Only 3 percent represented the first generation in their family to attend college, and only 8 percent belonged to racial and ethnic groups historically underrepresented in higher education. Since 2008, AU has shifted the focus of its millions of dollars of financial aid awards from 80 percent based on merit to 80 percent based on need.[3] These efforts have diversified the student body: by 2015–2016, 19 percent of entering freshmen were Pell-eligible, 10 percent first-generation-in-college, and 35 percent members of underrepresented groups.[4] More recently, the annual Pell-eligible new student enrollment has ranged from 15 to 20 percent, with stable underrepresented minority enrolments. The university also adjusted its admissions criteria to encourage a wider pool of applicants and embraced test-optional admissions, allowing students to apply without consideration of their standardized test scores (although for external reporting purposes, all test scores are aggregated and published), created a series of selective undergraduate programs for high-achieving students, and cast a wider recruiting net to attract students from the south and west of the United States, as well as from around the world. The increase in AU's student diversity has been rapid and dramatic.

As the student body became more diverse in race, culture, geographic origin, family income, academic preparation, and prior experience, its academic caliber, based on grade point average and SAT scores, also rose. Not only were students entering with higher grade point averages, more college-level credits, and increasingly laudable cocurricular and personal experiences, but their drive to excel at AU seemed to intensify every year. Throughout the decade before the pandemic, 90 percent of the AU undergraduate class had completed at least one internship, over 60 percent had studied abroad for at least one semester, and 90 percent were employed and/or enrolled in graduate study within six months of graduation.

The pace of the changes brought new challenges, particularly for the university's student support network. In 2014, the Middle States Commission on Higher Education decennial accreditation review team recommended that "the University as a whole . . . should carefully consider how best to support the more diverse student body and ensure that its engagement in AU's special opportunities, sense of belonging, degree of satisfaction, and retention and graduation rates is carefully monitored and regularly assessed."[5] Students reported struggles with social acclimation and feelings of exclusion, depression, and anxiety, in addition to the more classic issues of homesickness, time management, and financial concerns. Although AU has managed to hold first-to-second-year retention rates steady at around 89 percent (this slipped 2 percent in 2019, but has since rebounded), efforts to further improve have been hampered by a myriad of issues, including those this book identifies as deeply embedded in its structure and culture and its fragmented student support system. One bright spot, however, is that AU has maintained a retention rate in the high 80s and low 90s for Pell-eligible students, an accomplishment in which the university takes great pride.

AU's leadership became convinced in 2015 that if the university were to be more responsive to its increasingly diverse student body, it would have to embrace a more holistic approach to student support. While it hosts a wide variety of student service and support programs, they were not smartly organized. Academic, financial, health, and psychosocial support came from different offices. Too often, procedures for coordinating and information-sharing between these offices were inefficient, cumbersome, or nonexistent. Wasting time responding to uncoordinated rules or inefficient systems is costly, disrespectful to individuals, and, with the dramatic expansion in technologies, no longer excusable. For students, the consequences of an uncoordinated system can be dire. Some students have been pushed away, never to return. Others have simply endured to earn the degree. I remember one bitter student at commencement who, instead of shaking the president's hand, put a penny in it, saying, "that is the last penny you will ever see from me."

It need not be this way.

In 2015 I sought support from the Andrew W. Mellon Foundation in New York to develop an effective, integrated approach to student support that could become a national model for addressing the academic, social, and financial challenges typically faced by today's students. The resulting $150,000 grant made the study possible, and it also drew significant credibility, respect, and engagement from key stakeholders on campus. Funds in hand, AU embarked upon what became known as the "Reinventing the Student Experience" project, or RiSE.[6] The funded initiative lasted eighteen months, through late Summer 2016. AU then continued RiSE without external support for an additional thirty months, until the end of my term as provost as the 2018 academic year closed.

With the support of the president, Neil Kerwin, I served as a catalyst for a project that involved the entire campus. Participation was voluntary, but the level of enthusiasm was extraordinary, driven by a commitment to improving the student experience. Those leading the process had heavy responsibilities in their primary jobs, nevertheless, they found time to think creatively about the structure and culture of the academy. They dug into ways that other industries had created a service culture and considered how such practices could be translated into higher education.

No area of the university was untouched in the four-year effort. In addition to me, the formal staffing included part-time assignments for one faculty member and one staff person. In keeping with typical university practice, however, we primarily operated through overlapping committees. These included a 22-person leadership steering committee (LSC), 29 members on different subcommittees, 60 student participants in an Innovation Lab, 70 student participants in focus groups and journaling projects with more joining at meetings and retreats, a class of 25 students who examined the IT systems most used by students, and another class that developed a student app for a smartphone. The first of two leadership retreats, each lasting a day and a half, drew 155 faculty and staff; the second 350. Fifty-nine faculty and staff participated in another RiSE retreat, and 250 faculty participated in a one-day conference examining RiSE. At one point, 19 senior academic leaders and faculty traveled by bus to Cleveland for daylong meetings at the Cleveland Clinic, and 2 external experts were identified for a daylong exploration of service innovation. The study also included focus groups for parents, faculty, and staff.

Study participants interviewed senior university staff members, reviewed data on retention and graduation rates, analyzed relevant administrative data, initiated an annual campus climate survey that included a review of other student surveys, reexamined findings from the National Survey of Student Engagement (NSSE), and implemented a formal AU research study on how two different advising models impacted student retention. RiSE evaluated existing staff positions, titles, and roles, compared AU to peer institutions for student outcomes and operations, and studied data gleaned from the retreats and workshops, including the "pinch points" discussed in Chapter 8. All told, this was a comprehensive effort that engaged the entire AU community.

RiSE 1.0

At the beginning of the project, we created a RiSE Research Task Force. In short order, this evolved into the campus LSC with all six university vice presidents, four deans, five vice provosts, four associate vice presidents, two

Faculty Senate-elected leaders, and myself – the provost. Support was provided by a RiSE administrative staff person and one faculty rapporteur to record the sessions. We established six subcommittees and invited individuals to serve based on their interests and knowledge. Three of these subcommittees focused on identifying useful models and best practices from which we could learn. One of these identified different organizational models within and outside of higher education; a second sought to identify leaders from outside education who could discuss ways their organizations had improved the stakeholder experience; and a third surveyed technological options that might improve service delivery. Two more subcommittees assembled and analyzed survey data and feedback initially from student, staff, faculty, and parent focus groups; second, from the 350 faculty and staff members who participated in the Fall 2015 retreat on RiSE initiatives; and, third, the ideas developed by 60 students in a Student Innovation Laboratory event in November 2015. A final subcommittee developed strategies to inform the campus community of RiSE's progress.

To expand opportunities for participation, in the summer of 2016 we instituted a weekly Design Lab to let faculty and staff explore innovative ideas to assist with the student experience. The Fall 2015 retreat was only the first of what became an annual staff and faculty gathering to discuss RiSE's progress and other academic matters. RiSE found its way into the classroom, with one Kogod Business School course, ITEC 350, Digital Leadership and Strategy, asking twenty-five students to write essays to the provost on "How to Improve AU's Information Systems." Participation and involvement ran deep and wide, from the Board of Trustees to first-year students.

Information from RiSE flowed up to administrators and out to the AU community and beyond through the LSC. The president, the other vice presidents, and I regularly briefed the AU Board of Trustees and its committees. Various participants periodically met with student groups about RiSE, and others gave presentations about it at national conferences. RiSE was discussed at regularly scheduled meetings with the deans, the Provost's Operational Council, Cabinet meetings, the President's Council, the Faculty Senate, and the Staff Senate. Once a year, RiSE was highlighted in the Provost's Annual Address to the campus community.

Our work produced several important insights, four of which I highlight here. First, during a RiSE workshop students unexpectedly began a conversation with the group regarding some of the administrative problems they were encountering on campus. This led to our initial exploration of the "pinch points" discussed in the previous chapter. This exchange between students, faculty, and staff, with most of the university decision-makers present, opened the door for greater insight into the severity of some of the challenges students faced, too many of which we were unaware. Second, the analysis of feedback from separate focus groups of students, faculty, staff, and parents suggested the university had room for improvement in areas beyond student services. These included topics such as communication, IT functionality, the general education curriculum, and bureaucratic operations. The third area of discovery involved the possibilities inherent in several new technology products and vendors, each of which offered some evidence of improved student retention and better information flow. The fourth was the most surprising – the realization that we had a lot to learn from highly successful organizations outside higher education with a reputation for customer, client, or patient satisfaction.

Two Exemplars

RiSE 1.0 looked outside higher education to two organizations famed for excellent service delivery. One was Wegmans Food Markets, a family-owned grocery chain founded in 1918 and based in Rochester, New York, with ninety-eight stores at the time of writing. Wegmans is frequently commended for its quality of service, customer experience, and worker satisfaction. It has been among *Fortune Magazine*'s "100 Best Companies to Work For" for twenty-one years, ranking second in 2018. With nearly forty-eight thousand employees, Wegmans spent $50 million on employee development in 2017 alone.[7] The RiSE team decided to learn more about how the company created an environment viewed so favorably by customers and employees.

The company's website emphasizes its core beliefs:

> At Wegmans, we believe that good people, working toward a common goal, can accomplish anything they set out to do. In this spirit, we set our goal to be the very best at serving the needs of our customers. Every action we take should be made with our customers in mind. We also believe that we can achieve our goal if we fulfill the needs of own people. To our CUSTOMERS and our PEOPLE we pledge our continuous improvement, and we make the commitment: Every Day You Get Our Best.[8]

On the same webpage, Wegmans listed its values as an employer:

> We **care** about the well-being and success of every person. **High standards** are a way of life. We pursue excellence in everything we do. We **make a difference** in every community we serve. We **respect** and listen to our people. We **empower** our people to make decisions that improve their work and benefit our customers and our company.[9]

Imagine a continuous succession of university presidents speaking these words about students and backing them up with actions year after year, generation after generation.

Mary Ellen Burris, senior vice president of consumer affairs for Wegmans, agreed to spend a day at AU, including an open session where she talked about the importance of worker satisfaction in driving a quality experience for customers. Wegmans' customers are loyal – even devoted. Their "fans" create hashtags to spread the word about the store's features. Before some store openings, customers have lined up overnight. Burris spoke of customers who regularly write about the joy they experience at the stores. The Wegmans leadership team has fostered a sense of caring about employees, customers, and the surrounding community that has carried across all of their stores. We considered this sense of collective mission, caring about their community, and dedication to excellence relevant "takeaways" for higher education.

The other organization AU examined in detail was the Cleveland Clinic.[10] While many health care providers have contacted the Clinic about its transformational approach, AU was the first university to do so. Universities and the health care industry have significant features in common. Hospitals, like universities, are filled with highly educated, independent-minded specialists. Within the hospital, doctors are in regular contact with patients. Too often, medical professionals have to deliver disappointing and disconcerting news; on other occasions, they save lives, assist with births, cure ailments, and can prolong the quality of life. During a patient's stay, the hospital temporarily becomes that person's total environment, spanning the range of services from nutrition, shelter, scheduling, testing, mobility, health care, medication, and spiritual support, to hygiene. A hospital, much like a university, is a complex organization with many units and divisions. Of course, students are not patients, but the similarities of the institutions and their challenges are notable.

The transformation of the Cleveland Clinic under the leadership of Dr. Delos "Toby" M. Cosgrove is often cited in discussions of best practices in the health care industry. At the start of his appointment, his motto was "Patients First," and he insists that "the single most successful move in transforming the patient experience at the Cleveland Clinic was to align the organization around Patients First."[11] The institution, in other words, moved from being physician-centric to patient-centric. In his book about the Clinic, *Service Fanatics* (2014), James Merlino writes, "One of health-care's challenges is that patient-centeredness can appear to be the responsibility of only the people who deal directly with patients. Nothing can be further from the truth. For hospitals to be successful, all clinical and nonclinical leaders must align around the patient. Failure will cause the patient experience messaging cascade to stop."[12] With a few minor word substitutions, Merlino's words apply to colleges and universities: all members of the university community need to align around the student. Our failure to do so yields an uncertain student experience, with some experiencing the best of the academy and others less so.

The important insight from both Wegmans and the Cleveland Clinic is that everyone within the organization is responsible for the experience of the customer, patient, or in our case, the student. *The experience is the sum of all interactions.* Everyone from the professor to the custodian is part of the student experience at the university, just as everyone from the doctor to the nutritionist is part of the patient's experience, and everyone from the baker to the cashier is part of the grocery shopper's experience. Everyone must share the same value of excellent and caring service.

At the Cleveland Clinic, the message of empathy, of caring about the patient experience, was front and center. Every employee was asked to participate in empathy training sessions. As one might imagine, doctors were skeptical about this top-down messaging, particularly given that it involved an abstract concept like empathy. With high demands on their time, doctors prioritize professional and technical matters within their respective specializations. They are less inclined to gravitate toward training initiatives in empathy. Like professors, doctors are an independent lot. The Cleveland Clinic, therefore, mandated that everyone at the Clinic, including doctors, participate in the training sessions. Afterward, doctors reported that spending more time actively listening to their patients, that is, being more empathetic, indeed had a significant positive impact on their treatment and health care outcomes.

Hospitals in the United States participate annually in a patient satisfaction survey required by the Centers for Medicare and Medicaid Services. This survey, the Hospital Consumer Assessment in Healthcare Providers and Systems (HCAHPS), provides a percentile rating on several indicators, including the hospital's overall performance, nurse communication, facility cleanliness, patient pain management, doctor communication, and discharge practice. At the Cleveland Clinic before the implementation of Dr. Cosgrove's initiative in 2008, the baseline score for overall performance was in the lowest quartile. By 2011, it had moved to the upper quartile, and by May 2014 to the ninety-second percentile for the second year running.[13] Similar outcomes were reported across the board. Nurse communication improved from 16 percent in 2008 to 79 percent by

2014.[14] Cleanliness ratings over the same period went from a low of 5 percent to 80 percent,[15] and pain management from 10 percent to 74 percent.[16] Other improvements reveal that the quality of doctor communication rose from 14 to 67 percent,[17] and satisfaction with discharge practices dramatically increased from 34 percent to 97 percent over the five years.[18] Obviously, there were lessons to be learned from the Cleveland Clinic.

On March 20, 2016, nineteen members of AU's RiSE LSC boarded a chartered bus from DC to Cleveland for a visit to the Clinic. We chose a bus ride to provide an opportunity for members from the many different university units on the LSC to communicate and bond, one of the trip's explicit goals. While everyone worked at the same university, each of the LSC members reported to a different unit or division. We hoped the experience might improve our relationship with one another and hopefully cascade into better policies, practices, and experiences for students. In addition to the LSC members participating in the visit, the Chair of the AU Board of Trustees accepted the invitation to join us.

Since AU was the first university to explore ways to translate the Cleveland Clinic's experience to higher education, the Clinic staff created a customized version of their usual briefing to address our interests and needs. The format revolved around consecutive back-to-back meetings from 8 a.m. to 4:30 p.m. We learned that to facilitate the principle that "every life deserves world-class care," the Clinic created several novel structures, including an Office of the Patient Experience, led by a chief experience officer (CXO) with a $9.2 million annual budget and a staff of 112. There is a director of service excellence, with employee training assistants, data analysts, and staff, allowing the Clinic to reach deep into the organization to hear from patients, nurses, and doctors.

Creating change at scale is difficult. At a hospital system with 67,500 caregivers, a caseload of 2.4 million patients who collectively make more than 10 million outpatient visits annually, and a 2019 operating revenue of $10.56 billion, the barriers to change are significant. By university standards, this is a very large enterprise.[19]

Beginning in 2008, Cosgrove undertook fundamental changes in both the structure and the culture of the Clinic. For example, instead of the traditional oversight structure – the department of medicine overseeing specialties and the department of surgery overseeing an array of surgical procedures – Cosgrove created multidisciplinary teams of medical colleagues working in collaboration on different organ systems. This new organization puts a physician in direct contact with the surgeon in the overall care relationship, something that previously would have been less likely to occur. Doctors, like faculty, are highly influential in their respective specializations and have significant oversight of their organizational domain. They resisted these changes, but Cosgrove persevered.

One of the early tasks was to have all hospital personnel recognize the limitations of the current system when it came to meeting patient needs. To foster a climate for change, Cosgrove and his deputy, James Merlino, the chief experience officer, first needed personnel to understand there was a serious problem. The Cleveland Clinic before Cosgrove's arrival was nationally recognized and its staff took great pride in affiliation with it, but the data from patients in the HCAHPS survey helped make the case that patients were not being served at the level of institutional expectations. Merlino referred to this as revealing "the burning platform" on which they were unwittingly standing.

Patient interviews identified areas where communication could be improved. For example, if a patient's discharge was delayed, someone needed to make sure that the appropriate parties were informed and that the patient was fed. Patients and family members alike needed to be notified if there was a delay in securing a private room. Cosgrove argued that a sense of empathy and concern for someone who is ill can contribute to a better experience in what, by its very nature, may be an unwelcome event. Being too cold, too warm, hungry, tired, in pain, or either needing or being unable to use the bathroom all leave lasting impressions on patients. Cosgrove required staff to do patient rounds every hour and ask five specific questions to ensure that patients felt cared for and attended to.

Understanding the patient experience required that Clinic employees cultivate greater empathy. To encourage that, the Clinic required every employee to participate in one half-day role-playing workshop spaced over a year to ensure that the groups stayed small – generally under ten people – with participants coming from different jobs and levels of seniority. Someone whose job might involve changing bed linens might end up assigned to a group with a nationally renowned surgeon. Cosgrove was committed to using the workshop structure to dismantle power inequities within the hospital's culture.

In each workshop, one member would role-play a patient while another would act out a hypothetical set of caregiving interactions. Following the exercise, the group would discuss ways to provide better, more empathic care. Trainers, who served as observers, talked about the little things that could make a big difference in staff-to-patient communication, such as the caregiver referring to the patient by their name, clearly informing the patient about what would happen, and telling them who else would be involved. The groups acted out how to enter a patient's room, including demeanor and facial expressions. Facilitators stressed that the most important thing was taking the time to listen to patients, to learn about their concerns or fears, and to hear what was particularly important to them. The trainers emphasized that a relationship of trust based on a caregiver's genuine interest in the patient was essential to creating the desired clinic–patient experience.

The Clinic also added new administrative procedures designed to improve the patient experience. An ombudsman position was created in what was labeled the Office of the Patient Experience, housed in the CEO's suite. Complaints are referred to that person, who, after listening, begins with an apology and then explores what the Clinic can do to rectify the situation. To foster increased workforce morale, caregiver awards for outstanding performance were instituted, with the annual Award for Excellence carrying a $25,000 cash prize. The organization began offering new opportunities for professional development to help employees be more empathetic, supportive, and well trained in the latest technologies.

After eight detailed forty-five-minute sessions with Clinic leadership, the AU team boarded the bus for the return home. Our assignment on the ride back was to consider how what we learned could be translated into higher education, specifically our institution. To facilitate this exchange, participants rotated seat partners during the bus ride. We stopped for dinner in Pittsburgh and debriefed in a private room, with one dean and the Chair of the AU Board of Trustees recording our initial ideas about how the Clinic's innovations might work at AU.

Once back at the university, we began thinking about ways to address AU's siloed nature and to encourage greater cooperation deeper in the organization. Inspired by the Clinic, we wanted to develop a culture of empathy, recognizing the challenges that students, parents, and our fellow employees experienced in trying to navigate the university. We developed messaging to promote the idea of "OneAU" to reiterate that every faculty and staff member is part of one larger mission around the student experience. This was routinely delivered in leadership speeches and general campus-wide communication. We hoped that "OneAU" would help faculty and staff see the importance of their actions for a student or parent's total experience. It was an attempt to bring all members of AU around to the powerful notion that every employee can engage and contribute to a quality, high-touch student experience.

Throughout RiSE, we had many conversations to identify ways that the university could better cultivate a *relationship-centered approach* to all it does. In conferences and workshops, each AU supervisor was asked to explore how to reward collaboration, stimulate further innovation, and foster a culture of continuous improvement. The "OneAU" message was further refined to underscore that, to be a great place for students, the university must also be a great place for employees. If an institution is to provide excellent service, faculty and staff need to feel empowered to accomplish their best work.

While "OneAU" was widely promoted on campus, the AU community did not embrace it in the way we had hoped. As trained specialists steeped in their own professional cultures, AU faculty and staff were not particularly adept in thinking about what it might be like to walk in the shoes of college students, the students' parents, or even of one another. Or perhaps faculty and staff alike viewed it as a slogan rather than an attempt at a culture change. Not until much later did evidence of any impact emerge.

RiSE 2.0

Although support from the Mellon Foundation concluded in 2016, the RiSE effort continued with in-house funding from AU. Growing out of what we had learned about the adjustment of first-year students, our first major initiative was to create new first-year seminar courses to help facilitate the transition to college and create a greater sense of belonging. The concept was not new: colleges and universities around the world offer various types of first-year experience courses. In fact, the University of South Carolina hosts a National Resource Center for the First-Year Experience and Students in Transition that serves as a clearinghouse to assist with this purpose. In addition to dispensing information students find valuable, these courses often provide them with an initial personal relationship with a faculty member or academic leader.

After some discussion, we decided to pilot two 1.5-credit-hour courses – one in the Fall Term and one in the Spring – each to run fifteen weeks with a class meeting once a week. The first would focus on the transition to college life, provide information on the various office functions and available support services, discuss psychosocial adjustment and multiculturalism, and facilitate students' ability to develop a personal relationship with an instructor (since class size would be under twenty students). The second would focus on identity, race, and culture, all salient issues for incoming students. To ensure consistency across class sections, the course content, assignments, and readings would be online, so that class time could be devoted to discussion and building relationships.

By summer 2016, my office had signed a contract with a faculty member interested in developing the first course, teaching it, and, using student feedback, to subsequently revise its content. The resulting course became known as AU Experience 1 (AUx1). Later that year, we awarded a second contract to a faculty member to develop AU Experience 2 (AUx2). Following the initial pilot classes, my office funded revisions based on student and faculty feedback, as well as a training manual and instructional guide to ensure consistency across the sections. Over time, the curriculum of AUx1 and AUx2 courses has continued to evolve and improve. The university owns the intellectual property, but from the start has considered sharing the materials with others.

AU began offering the pilot courses as options to incoming students in the 2017–2018 academic year. The courses were taught by skilled advisors, whom we called guides, trained in an integrated and coordinated approach to advising. To test the effectiveness of the approach, students were randomly assigned to either a professional, discipline-based advising model or the new integrated relationship-based advising model led by skilled professional guides. We were especially interested in the impact on retention, and in scaling up the approach. We found that, compared to students in the traditional advising groups, those in the guide-AUx model registered for the Spring Term at rates 1 percent higher than the control. Following the students over time, those in the experimental modules registered 4 percent higher for first-to-second-year retention, 7 percent higher in their second spring compared to the control group, and back to a 4 percent higher retention in their third year. Based on these initial findings, and with the support of the president and approval of the Board of Trustees, we implemented the program across the university in the 2018–2019 academic year. In the spring and summer of 2018, the university hired and trained twenty-five guides for the incoming Fall class.

In the spring of 2018, the university participated in the NSSE, which included the first-year students who were in the AUx pilot project. While the survey did not distinguish between students who had and had not participated in the pilot AUx courses, it did show that social integration and belongingness were salient factors in retention. Students who felt less engaged in the campus community were more likely to leave AU and not return for their second year of study. As to whether the institution provided opportunities to be involved socially, 66.5 percent of students who stayed into their second year at AU answered positively, while only

20 percent of those who eventually left AU did. Positive responses about the quality of interactions with other students came from 40 percent of those who left, compared to 73.5 percent for those who continued at AU. Only a third of those who left responded positively to a question about the university's support for "overall well-being (recreation, health care, counseling, etc.)," whereas those who stayed answered yes at nearly twice that rate. Questions about "using learning support services . . . encouraging contact among students of different backgrounds . . . [and] attending campus events and activities" revealed gaps of about 22 percent between affirmative responses from those who left and those who continued at AU.

Data more directly related to the guide model came from AU records. We knew that, before offering the AUx courses, 81.8 percent of full-time Black students registered for their second semester, as did 84.6 percent of Hispanic/Latinx students. In the first year of the required guide model with the AUx course, 98.5 percent of Black students and 95 percent of Hispanic/Latinx students registered for their second term. We had expected, and found, some attrition in first-to-second-year retention, with 91.1 percent of Black students and 85.5 percent of Hispanic/Latinx students returning and continuing their degree. The Black first-to-second-year retention rate exceeded that of White students, but the Hispanic/Latinx fell below it.

The university continued its support for the RiSE initiative through AUx and other initiatives. However, I remained unconvinced that the concept of everyone in the university being responsible for the student experience had successfully permeated deeply into the campus community. Units took care of their own issues, carefully protected their own resources, and, despite our efforts, the decentralized individualistic culture remained.

Despite this, I was surprised to learn that the assistant vice president of housing and dining programs had incorporated the integrated relationship-based advising model into a major two-year renovation of a first-year residence hall. Intrigued by the idea of better integrating student services across administrative units and concerned about the fragmented services first-year students were then experiencing, he decided to use funds from his own budget to integrate undergraduate academic affairs personnel, from a different division of the university, into the residence hall's first-floor office design, creating new office spaces matched to their needs. In one stroke, he provided ongoing direct and daily contact between academic affairs personnel, housing staff, and students in the residence hall. He also decided to build AUx classrooms on the first floor of the residence hall. The idea was entirely conceived and executed outside of the RiSE leadership team, and by an administrator I barely knew. The initiative was encouraging and indicated that someone listening, learning, and taking action for the broader good of the university and the best interests of the students could overcome entrenched silos and competition for resources.

All students applying for the Fall 2018 entering class were informed of the required AUx first-year sequence, taught by guides, with a student-to-guide ratio of 76:1. (The national student-to-advisor ratio is around 300:1.[20]) In addition to teaching, the guides serve as the student's primary point of contact for accessing university services. Every student would see the guide in a small class of twenty or fewer students at least once a week, as well as during office hours, regular advising meetings, and informal conversation. We envisioned that students would quickly identify with their guide and develop the sense of belonging at the institution that is so crucial to college success. The guides could assist in managing problems, or promptly link students to the professional who could best assist them. In practice, guides reached out to the incoming students during the summer even before they arrived on campus.

The model is expensive, requiring that the university hire and train twenty-five full-time guides. But evidence from the pilot helped justify the expense. At a private university, increased student satisfaction, retention, and, hopefully, eventual graduation extends the overall value for students. Further, by retaining students, the university keeps tuition that otherwise would be lost, savings that are cumulative over each year that students remain enrolled. With only a modest increase in instructional costs to cover the additional retained students, the university would be doing the right thing for the students, avoiding disruption and uncertainty in their lives, and simultaneously achieving its financial goals.

Amid these major changes to the first-year curriculum, our LSC meetings continued to surface ideas for even more sweeping academic change. Students had been regularly complaining about AU's General Education Program, which served as a broad introduction to the liberal arts. Many students saw the curriculum as a set of requirements to get out of the way so they could take the courses they really wanted. The dean of the College of Arts & Sciences argued that RiSE should extend its reach into the center of the undergraduate curriculum and revisit our General Education program. In response, we formed a faculty committee to review and eventually revise the program. What emerged was a new Core Curriculum built on the concept of "Habits of Mind." Over the first two years, students would be expected to take courses that covered five habits of the mind – creativity and aesthetic sensibility, cultural interpretation, ethical reasoning, natural-scientific inquiry, and sociohistorical understanding.

It has been said that changing a General Education program is as hard as moving a graveyard. Curriculum revisions have downstream effects on the faculty as well as on departmental resources. This is particularly the case for units that compete for resources and, eventually, faculty lines, based on enrollment. If a unit's introductory courses are no longer required, enrollment numbers for those courses will drop, and students will miss exposure to the field. Without the initial exposure of an introductory course, a department may struggle to recruit students to major in the field. And when majors drop, overall course enrollments drop, which may lead to significant consequences for a department's budget and faculty allocation. Changing the structure and course requirements, therefore, pits departments against one another.

At AU, heated discussions across the different schools, colleges, and departments within them centered on the transition from a General Education program to a new Core Curriculum. The leaders of the Core Curriculum planning committee held open meetings with faculty, gave presentations to different schools and colleges, and participated in many conversations with deans, faculty, and students. The committee also held preliminary discussions with the Faculty Senate, which would need to approve such a major change.

Eventually, after considerable discussion among faculty over two years and a full review by a subcommittee of the Faculty Senate, the proposal was ready for a vote by the full Senate in mid-2017. To my astonishment, the new Core Curriculum and all its requirements were unanimously approved, and we were able to introduce it in the 2018–2019 academic year along with the AUx initiative. It is unusual for faculty to approve anything unanimously, let alone a new sweeping core curriculum.

Under the new Core Curriculum, first-year students take five courses each semester, including one, Complex Problems, specifically designed to reflect how college-level intellectual work differs from high school classes. It is taught by a faculty member with expertise in a field with challenging questions that have no easy right or wrong answers. The course is designed intentionally to push students, who may be familiar with studying for the right answer on a test, to explore intellectual questions from different points of view. The professor, an expert resource, encourages students to fully examine a challenging issue from multiple perspectives. The course emphasizes analytical and reasoning skills rather than specific answers to prepared questions. With a maximum class size of twenty students, the university needed ninety-six faculty instructors each year to teach Complex Problems. To our delight, more faculty volunteered to teach a course on a complex problem of their own interest than there were sections available.

In addition to Complex Problems and AUx1 and AUx2, first-year students take Foundations Courses, which include Written Communication & Information Literacy I and Quantitative Literacy I. For their remaining courses, students can select options in their intended major or other interests.

In Years Two and Three, students draw heavily on the courses in the Habits of Mind track. They also enroll in such integrative courses as Written Communication & Information Literacy II, Quantitative Literacy II, and a new Diversity and Equity requirement. In Years Three and Four, students focus on their major (or majors), study abroad, and internships. As I mentioned earlier, before the pandemic most AU students completed at least one fifteen-week internship – often more than one – and 60 percent spent at least one full term studying abroad. These activities are often concentrated in the third year. Finally, in Year Four, students are required to complete an integrative capstone project.

A final phase of RiSE 2.0 involved the LSC's recognition that, if the university were to become more responsive to its students, it would also have to be more supportive of its workers. The RiSE initiative inspired a discussion between the Office of Human Resources and the various AU administrative units about existing processes and policies. As a result, HR reorganized itself, created a variety of more flexible hiring and onboarding practices, and, with considerable input from the community, completely revised the periodic performance review process for all university employees other than faculty.

RiSE 3.0

RiSE 2.0 remains a work in progress. Implementing, coordinating, and assessing so many changes in structure and support systems at the same time has strained the capacity of many at AU. New personnel, no matter how skilled, need time to learn to work together. During the full rollout of the AUx courses to all students, it became clear that more faculty and students wanted greater involvement and voice in shaping the content of the courses, particularly around issues of race. There were bumps in the road with so many campus-wide changes, but the leadership stayed steady and did not waver from the implementation efforts.

The guides, meanwhile, are carrying out an entirely new role as the central point of first-year student relationships, but they lack a fully integrated dataset that reflects all the experiences of the students they are guiding. There is currently no system in place for sharing the full range of student information with the guide, primarily due to issues of confidentiality and areas of specialization. To assist the guides, the university introduced a new constituent relationship management system (CRM) called "Advise." It is intended to provide more coordinated student support, early alerts, enhanced student access to resources, and data analytics for more informed academic decisions. It is a step in the right direction, but obtaining this information in a timely and manageable way remains more aspiration than reality, as does the vision of having essential data available for guides and students on their mobile devices.

As we look to the future, it is clear that we need to invest conceptual work and planning efforts beyond the first-year students. In Year Two, students still remain vulnerable to dropping out of school. If students are to graduate, we also need to reconsider their experiences in the final two years of study. And this is to say nothing of rethinking the graduate experience.

After a decade as provost, I have returned to the faculty and handed over the goal of a more student-centered university to new leadership. In all probability, a RiSE 3.0 will begin evaluating the current efforts and adjust accordingly – a phase every bit as important as planning new initiatives.

However, in March 2020 the appearance of the novel coronavirus disrupted the university in fundamental ways, displacing previous efforts at student-centeredness. Like so many other universities, AU closed that month. Faculty and students were evacuated from campus, and all education immediately transitioned online, with both students and faculty working from their private residences. Some staff considered essential for core operations and public safety remained, but most of the other operations, including the library, were closed.

In response to the initial disruption, AU returned student payments for unused room and board. The university's expenses also increased, given the immediate surge in technological demand and online instructional support to faculty. The unanticipated costs swiftly added to a shortfall in the range of $140 million. Spending reductions were necessary to sustain a balanced budget, but layoffs were kept to a minimum.

How AU will bridge the issues of an infrastructure that has expanded incrementally over the years, high levels of fragmentation among semi-autonomous units, and a stressed student population, remains a work in progress. The campus faces multiple jeopardies inflicted by the novel coronavirus, notably the health of the community, the economic hit to family budgets, lost university revenue, and the additional expenses required to deliver the program – all taking place in a context of glaring evidence of racial injustice and calls for structural reform. To its credit, the university had been cautious about spending and accumulated some reserves over the years to assist during difficult times, reserves that have now been tapped.

Only time will tell if AU can further reimagine the student experience and fully shift from a professional-centric to a more student-centered support system. The challenges of rethinking and redistributing the delivery of services across the institution remain fundamental. They are reflected in the structural lag between students' needs and expectations and the university's administrative operations. The global pandemic may have left AU in uncharted territory, but if it has learned anything from its study of the Cleveland Clinic and Wegmans, it's that even further commitment to empathy and to the stakeholder experience is the way to bridge the gap and close the structural lag between university and student.

Notes

1 American University, Office of Institutional Research and Assessment, *Academic Data Reference Book 2020–2021*, 51st ed. (Washington, DC: American University, 2021), 13–14, table 1-1, accessed June 9, 2021, www .american.edu/provost/oira/upload/2020-21-academic-data-reference-book.pdf.

2 American University, Office of Institutional Research and Assessment, *Academic Data Reference*, 47, table 2-2.

3 "Next: A Culture of Innovation," American University, accessed June 9, 2021, www.american.edu/next/#agile.

4 "Culture of Innovation," American University.

5 Eric F. Spina et al., *Report to the Faculty, Administration, Trustees, and Students of American University, Washington, District of Columbia, by the Evaluation Team Representing the Middle States Commission on Higher Education* (Philadelphia: Middle States Commission on Higher Education, 2014), 6, www.american.edu/middlestates/upload/2014-eval-team-report-american-uni versity-a.pdf.

6 To assist me in recalling and accurately recounting the actions taken at AU during my time as provost, I have drawn upon the following documents that I helped prepare or oversaw: (1) The 2015 American University Proposal to the Andrew W. Mellon Foundation, "Restructuring Student Support for Student Success: Developing a National Model"; (2) "Reinventing the Student Experience: A Case Study" by faculty member Kelly Joyner, who participated in the project, prepared under contract to AU in 2016; (3) "The June 10, 2016 RiSE Findings to Date" by Kelly Joyner, prepared under

contract to AU; and (4) "The Report to the Andrew W. Mellon Foundation" by American University, August 31, 2016.

7 Justin Bariso, "How a Family-Owned Supermarket Chain Became One of the Best Places to Work in America," *Inc.*, March 13, 2017, accessed May 14, 2020, www.inc.com/justin-bariso/how-a-family-owned-supermarket-chain -became-one-of-the-best-places-to-work-in-am.html.

8 "Company Overview," Wegmans, accessed May 20, 2019, www.wegmans .com/about-us/company-overview.html.

9 Wegmans, "Company Overview."

10 For more information about the Cleveland Clinic, see James Merlino's *Service Fanatics: How to Build Superior Patient Experience the Cleveland Clinic Way* (New York: McGraw-Hill Education, 2015), James I. Merlino and Ananth Raman's "Health Care's Service Fanatics," *Harvard Business Review*, May 2013, and Toby Cosgrove's *The Cleveland Clinic Way: Lessons in Excellence from One of the World's Leading Health Care Organizations* (New York: McGraw-Hill Education, 2014).

11 Merlino, *Service Fanatics*, 15.

12 Merlino, *Service Fanatics*, 43.

13 Merlino, *Service Fanatics*, 222, figure 13.1.

14 Merlino, *Service Fanatics*, 222, figure 13.2.

15 Merlino, *Service Fanatics*, 223, figure 13.3.

16 Merlino, *Service Fanatics*, 223, figure 13.4.

17 Merlino, *Service Fanatics*, 224, figure 13.5.

18 Merlino, *Service Fanatics*, 224, figure 13.6.

19 Cleveland Clinic, *2019 Year-End Facts + Figures*, December 2019, accessed April 6, 2020, https://my.clevelandclinic.org/-/scassets/files/org/about/who -we-are/cleveland-clinic-facts-and-figures-2019.ashx?la=en.

20 Rich Robbins, "Advisor Load," *NACADA Clearinghouse of Academic Advising Resources*, November 5, 2012, accessed May 20, 2019, www.nacada.ksu.edu /Resources/Clearinghouse/View-Articles/Advisor-Load.aspx.

CHAPTER 10

Administratively Aligned: A Blueprint for a More Supportive and Holistic Learning Experience

The American Council on Education's 1937 report – *The Student Personnel Point of View* (discussed in Chapters 1 and 5) – spoke of the "obligation to consider the student as a whole."[1] More than an option, obligation entails responsibility and a sense of duty. More than eight decades later, a confluence of student expectations, world events, and technological breakthroughs forces us to wrestle with that obligation and decide if this is the moment to finally create the oft-discussed student-centered university.

The phrase conjures a vision of a residential university that engages the whole person, one where thriving and engaged students learn to become well-educated graduates, appropriately curious and capable of interacting with a diverse, increasingly polarized, and swiftly changing society. Their academic experience would reach beyond career achievement to explore aesthetic appreciation, civic responsibility, global connectedness, self-awareness, personal growth, and social development. Such a university would approach students holistically, listening to their experiences and providing information and services in a manner that is respectful, empathetic, efficient, and appropriately tailored to their needs. Its service systems and information flow would be matched to the changing student population and reflect their use of technology and preferred forms of communication. Its administrative operations might lag at times but, with routine feedback from students and others, they would evolve to keep up with expectations of current and future cohorts of students. At such an institution, all members of the community would share a commitment to student success and well-being. They would recognize that all interactions, both inside and outside the classroom, are of consequence.

Contrasted with that vision, the experiences at American University (AU) and elsewhere recounted in this book suggest the academic and administrative realities that many students actually encounter are too frequently discrepant. As we have seen, the siloing of administrative units too often means university faculty and staff can become oblivious to the challenges students face in areas outside their own domain. Even when they are aware, they are often unable to help students solve problems that bridge bureaucratic divides.

A few years ago, AU set out to address those challenges and identified strategies to create a more holistic and attentive educational experience. Based on our efforts and successful initiatives elsewhere, I believe that a determined college or university leadership team can undertake a range of interventions that are responsive to today's students, meritorious in their own right, and that will ultimately move the university toward a holistic, student-centered approach. It will be necessary to tackle current structural barriers, inefficiencies, redundancies, turf battles, and entrenched cultures with a multiyear commitment to reform, including support from boards of overseers, as the effort will likely reach beyond the duration of a single campus presidency. The goal is to overcome institutional barriers that are impeding student success.

In the previous chapters, I identified the various challenges that a new generation of students face, both before, during, and following a pandemic (whenever that arrives), along with their preferred forms of societal and organizational interaction. Along with this analysis, I explored the historical development of the college and university setting and the complexity of that structure, its voracity to retain traditions and practices, its internal priorities and reward structure, and its diffusion of power and authority – all of which make it exceedingly difficult to enact change. Throughout the book, I not only identified these challenges, but pointed out realistic institutional options or solutions designed to improve student success and well-being – and mitigate the inverse. From among these many issues, I have selected three broad categories of institutional improvement for student success, each with five steps, that collectively will lead to a more holistic and student-centered institution. Summarized in Table 10.1, they are: (1) transforming the undergraduate experience, (2) creating new pathways to build a holistic approach to student success, and (3) enhancing university climate and culture. Some of these steps have been tested on American campuses, while others are best practices drawn from outside higher education. This list is not exhaustive, but rather intended to foster increased dialogue among academic leaders serious about reimagining their college or university in light of the seismic changes underway in America and around the globe.

Table 10.1 *Administratively aligned: a blueprint for a more supportive and holistic learning experience chapter guide*

I. Transforming the Undergraduate Experience

1. Establish a Relationship-Centered Culture for All Students
2. Prioritize High-Impact Learning Experiences
3. Institute a Comprehensive Individual Student Academic Plan
4. Ensure Quality Health Care and Campus-Wide Engagement for Mental Health Support
5. Improve Student Retention and Graduation

II. Creating New Pathways to Build a Holistic Approach to Student Success

6. Identify Pinch Points, Listen to Students, and Eliminate Chafing
7. Integrate Student Services with a Case Management System and a Digital Strategy
8. Diminish Silos to Focus on Student Success While Preserving Decentralized Operations
9. Enhance Faculty Awareness and Responsibility for the Student Experience
10. Create a Culture of Continuous Academic Innovation and Student Well-Being

III. Enhancing University Climate and Culture

11. Build a More Diverse and Culturally Competent Faculty
12. Support a More Representative Curriculum and Institutional Messaging
13. Prioritize Financial Aid to the Most Vulnerable
14. Modify Facilities to Promote Public Health
15. Maintain Vigilance for Cost Containment

I. Transforming the Undergraduate Experience

The coronavirus pandemic has made clear that the residential college experience is a unique, concentrated, and intense encounter at a pivotal moment in students' lives, one that is not easily replaced at a distance. It provides the opportunity to intensify the life of the mind while enriching one's personal character, cornerstones for future experiences. Below are five ways to enrich that encounter.

1)   *Establish a Relationship-Centered Culture for All Students*

Sociologists Daniel Chambliss and Christopher Takacs emphasize the importance of students building personal relationships with peers, faculty, and staff as soon as possible to ensure a successful transition from high school to college.[2] Student attrition is heavily weighted to the first year of college, then the second; hence the importance of a quick adjustment to college life.[3] Personal ties to others help students develop a sense of being welcomed, of belonging. Such early connections are particularly important for those in the first generation of their families to attend college. An Elon University survey of 4,006 US bachelor's and graduate degree-holders found that the cultivation of personal relationships was key for respondents who had found their undergraduate university experience "very reward-ing." Of particular significance was a relationship with an adult mentor, which for a majority began during the first year of college.[4]

Findings from the 2020 National Survey of Student Engagement (NSSE) revealed the significance that first-year students place on relationships they develop at the university. Students were asked to what extent advisors "actively listened to [their] concerns," "respected [their] identity and cul-ture," and "cared about [their] well-being."[5] First-year students reporting higher scores on these measures indicated they expected to return for the second year, while those with lower scores were unsure or not intending to return.[6] Building respectful relations with students can be a salient factor in their retention and success. The NSSE investigators concluded that "a trusting and respectful rapport with an advisor is essential for new students adjusting to and navigating a complex institution."[7]

In their volume *Relationship-Rich Education: How Human Connections Drive Success in College*, historian Peter Felten and Elon University president emeritus Leo M. Lambert stress the importance of helping students make deep and lasting friendships with faculty, staff, and other students. They note that "decades of research demonstrate that peer-to-peer, student-faculty, and student-staff relationships are the foundation for learning, belonging and achieving in college."[8] They add that these connections are particularly influential for underrepresented students.

A university can build a more intentionally relationship-centered culture in many ways.[9] As soon as students enroll for their first term, and even before they arrive on campus, for example, the enrollment management team can use social media to encourage peer connections. During the summer before classes begin, advisors and financial aid officers can reach out to prospective students and, where appropriate, their parents, to help forge relationships.

Once the student arrives on campus, social events with food and entertainment can facilitate peer interactions among first-year students and students further along in their academic careers. Experienced students can inform the new entrants about the support available and act as positive role models. Evidence from AU surveys reveals significant differences in the sense of belonging across racial groups, with Black students in particular feeling less connected to the campus. Receptions for new students who belong to constituencies underrepresented on campus – Black or Hispanic/Latinx students, for example – that include both upper-level students and faculty who identify with that constituency would foster dialogue and provide role models early in the academic year. Many colleges and universities already do these sorts of activities routinely. Others may want to consider them.

Small, discussion-based courses during the first college term provide additional opportunities to enhance personal relationships. Even modest faculty gestures that may seem obvious, such as using students' names in class or asking how they are doing, can help students feel welcome. Involving faculty members known for teaching excellence in first-year courses is another way to ensure a strong start for new students. Psychologist Mary C. Murphy and her colleagues found that furthering students' sense of "belongingness" and "fit" in their settings increases degree persistence.[10] One way to do this is through exercises in the first-year writing class that encourage students to write about their experiences of belonging.

Efforts in building a greater sense of affiliation are an important ingredient in retaining students. One method that Murphy et al. explored was to have students read a collection of essays by a diverse group of successful third- and fourth-year students about their transition to college and how they overcame challenges. First-year students were then asked to write about their own experiences along the same lines. In a final step, the first-year students prepared a letter of support to a fictional prospective student anxious about their capacity for success at the university. Such approaches provide an opportunity for students to express their fears, hear how others have overcome obstacles, and advise still others.[11]

At AU, in addition to AUx1 and AUx2 courses, we created a required first-year discussion-based course called Complex Problems (discussed in Chapter 9). Taught in classes of twenty students or fewer, the course exposes students to the kind of learning and critical thinking expected in college. The course is taught by gifted instructors teaching a subject they enjoy, assisted by a third- or fourth-year college student who is available to first-year students for conversation outside the class that can further enrich the course.

While it is important to create a sense of belonging from the very start of the college experience, fostering a relationship-centered culture should not be limited to the first year. There must be an ongoing effort to personalize the residential setting as a place to learn, grow, make friends, and connect to mentors who will guide and advise students throughout the entirety of this formative experience.

2) Prioritize High-Impact Learning Experiences

In 2008, George D. Kuh identified a series of high-impact learning experiences: first-year seminars; common intellectual experiences; learning communities; writing-intensive courses; collaborative assignments and projects; undergraduate research; diversity, global, service, and community-based learning; internships; and capstone courses and projects.[12] He urged universities to include at least two of these student-centered learning experiences in their undergraduate offerings. Other high-impact learning activities include honors programs, intensive summer boot camps, intellectual competitions, peer tutoring, experiential learning, innovation and design labs, and study abroad, to name a few. Today, many institutions offer most or all of these options. But in an era of financial challenges, maintaining or even expanding these initiatives will require a concerted effort to highlight the educational benefits students derive from them.

Some universities have explored ways to enhance student learning by improving classroom pedagogy. One approach that stands out is Cornell University's Active Learning Initiative, an approach used across the university that helps students develop problem-solving skills useful for the course they are taking and generalizable to others. Some disciplines have added online supplemental material that runs concurrently with a required introductory course. Other subject areas aim to foster a multidisciplinary approach, for example, by exploring the public policy implications of basic scientific or analytic questions. The introductory social science courses at Cornell employ interactive and participatory classroom techniques and often use in-class polling, small group exercises, or assignments that require immersion in the community. Cornell has adapted the Active Learning approach to almost every undergraduate department and documented its positive impact on student acquisition of course content.[13]

3) Institute a Comprehensive Individual Student Academic Plan

Developing a formal written academic plan with an advisor can help students customize their learning experience and focus on their future. Since 2010, AU's highly selective Frederick Douglass Distinguished Scholars (FDDS) program for exceptionally talented students has employed this approach. Each student identifies learning goals, personal development aspirations, and career ambitions, a process that helps clarify the pathways and resources needed for success. Developing and revising the draft plan, which integrates curricular and cocurricular components such as career or academic areas of interest, relevant courses, social activities and clubs, internships, volunteer opportunities, and strategies for personal growth, takes time and self-reflection. Students share the draft with program faculty, staff, and selected peers for feedback. Periodically, they inventory their existing skills and possibilities for growth, and at least once a semester reexamine the plan, make adjustments, amend it if they find new areas of interest, and discuss it with selected mentors.

The plans serve as cornerstones for the entire four-year experience. In their senior year, FDDS students undertake a formal, self-reflective review of their learning pathways and personal growth, and present it to a faculty and staff audience. Several of these sessions have been among the most rewarding and moving experiences of my academic career.

4) Ensure Quality Health Care and Campus-Wide Engagement for Mental Health Support

An investigative report by the *Washington Post* on college and university health care services raised serious questions about their quality and range.[14] It found instances of inadequate medical care, misdiagnoses, poor supervision, and insufficient oversight at campus health centers imperiling students' lives. The exposé set off alarm bells among parents concerned about the care their children receive on campus.

Even before students arrive, campuses need to be transparent with students and their families about the physical and mental health services provided and the availability of 24/7 support on or off campus, or via telemedicine. Universities need to make health insurance requirements and billing procedures for health visits – essential information for setting expectations – clear to students and their parents, and particularly important for students with special medical needs.

Campus leaders need to ensure that the health care center is adequately funded, has appropriately skilled staff, including oversight by a qualified professional, and can serve the anticipated volume of students. If not managed well, health care services can become an area of risk to students and a potential liability to the university. Parents expect and trust the campus to take care of their children.

Concerns over students' mental health and vulnerability have prompted many campuses to expand the number of counselors for those seeking help (see Chapters 2 and 5). In some institutions, demand has exceeded supply. Students have asked not only for more counselors, but for counselors who reflect their own diversity. In addition to clinical counseling, colleges and universities have developed an array of programs to help students reduce stress. For example, Vanderbilt University offers students a coordinator to help them navigate the support services available at the university or, if necessary, off campus.[15] Other campuses have sought to provide stress reduction and mental health advice early in the academic experience, often as part of the orientation program. Florida State University, for example, has developed the Student Resilience Project to provide students techniques for coping with anxieties and stressors.[16]

Universities are also turning to private companies for help for their students. Companies like Kognito Solutions offer virtual simulations for college students around mental health issues and suicide prevention to foster greater awareness of signs of psychological distress and provide guidance on what peers can do to help friends or roommates. Grit Digital Health uses student-friendly tools on a smartphone to assist with mental health support, well-being, and strategies for building social connections for students who feel lonely. The Jed Foundation advises colleges and universities about early intervention practices to promote mental health and prevent self-harm.[17]

Some campuses have developed courses or modules on stress reduction, health maintenance, and mental health; a few require these courses for all students. Others have enlisted student peers to provide support and build resilience. Still others make use of internet-based health screenings and twenty-four-hour online crisis intervention and treatment services. In 2021, a survey of 1,685 faculty at 12 different colleges and universities was conducted by Boston University School of Public Health, the Healthy Minds Network, and the Mary Christie Foundation. It found that faculty were concerned about the state of student mental health and its deterioration and that most faculty (80 percent) reported at least one conversation with students regarding mental health. Nearly two-thirds of faculty indicated they are "comfortable having conversations with students about their mental health." And, nearly three-quarters seek additional professional training on the subject, with 61 percent indicating such training should be mandatory.[18] What is most disturbing in the study is that a quarter of the faculty believed that the institution "is hostile or somewhat hostile toward students of color," with disproportionately negative responses about the treatment of students of color reported by faculty of color.[19]

The point is that campus counselors are not the exclusive solution. Mental health support and a healthy campus climate promoting inclusiveness require that all members of the community be sensitively engaged in helping college students through challenges they may be facing.

5) *Improve Student Retention and Graduation*

Student success must remain foremost in the mind of every employee in the academy. All campus interactions are part of the student experience, and every interaction can be of consequence. With the national graduation rate after six years of study at nonprofit residential colleges hovering just above the 60 percent range, every permanent withdrawal from the university is a loss that should be avoided.

The Bill & Melinda Gates, Kresge, and Lumina Foundations have funded strategies to improve student retention and graduation rates nationwide, from community colleges to research universities, particularly for underrepresented groups.[20] Ithaka S+R has established a national network of colleges and universities that represent best practices in student retention. Their case studies highlight strategies to improve student outcomes along with several reports and self-assessment approaches to help campuses retain their students.[21] EAB, an educational consulting organization, uses a blend of technology and intervention strategies to assist colleges and universities with student retention. It maintains a rich catalog of promising practices tried around the country.[22] Many of the major national collegiate professional organizations have also zeroed in on this issue. Collectively, these and other organizations are identifying innovative models and best practices to make the four-year residential college more welcoming, inclusive, and responsive to undergraduates.

Georgia State University (GSU) has developed numerous effective interventions for retaining students, including the use of predictive analytics, as I discussed in Chapter 7. GSU also offers a chatbot, developed with artificial intelligence, that can respond at any hour to student questions submitted via text message. The approach has increased by

20 percent the number of admitted students who actually arrive at the start of college.[23] Other campuses use constituent relationship management (CRM) software to map the learner life cycle and develop advisor-driven personal communications with large numbers of students (see Chapter 8).

For the most part, the solutions discussed thus far do not require re-imagining aspects of the structure and culture of the university. I explore that next frontier in improving student success and well-being in the following section.

II. Creating New Pathways to Build a Holistic Approach to Student Success

This section explores responses to structural and organizational impediments, introduces best practices from outside higher education, and suggests strategies to maximize campus-wide prioritization of student success. Campuses around the nation are constantly developing new ways to enhance the student experience, but institutions of higher education are not the only sources of innovation. Academic leaders should look beyond the university for ideas that may be transferable. I present a few of them here.

6) Identify Pinch Points, Listen to Students, and Eliminate Chafing

It is easy for administrators to underestimate the problems students encounter in routine interactions across the campus. The sheer numbers of those interactions and their dispersion across so many offices make it difficult for senior administrators to know what actually takes place between students and the units servicing them and gain an overarching view of all campus operations including their interactions with students. Yet even seemingly small "pinch points" – interactions that aggravate, frustrate, and create uncertainty for students – add up over time, much like microaggressions, and can be of consequence. Enough of them can send students the message that the institution does not care about them. For Generation Z students accustomed to accessing personalized services through smartphone technologies, the layers of institutional bureaucracy can be particularly discordant and add to the impression of institutional indifference. Identifying pinch points and ameliorating them is necessary if the student experience is to be improved (see Chapter 8).

Listening to students involves actively engaging them in a format comfortable for them. Some students are eager to provide feedback about their experiences; others are more reluctant. Campus personnel need to develop different listening approaches to better assess campus operations and services.

Some options include: weekly journaling projects about the campus experience, regular dialogue in first-year experience seminars, scheduling meetings, workshops, focus groups, point of service assessments, campus climate surveys, using social media and text messages, dialogue with student government representatives, conduct faculty and staff rounds in student spaces, sponsor meals with small groups of students, identity group meetings, feedback from "secret shoppers" (students or others providing feedback on assigned encounters), exit interviews with students who have decided to leave or transfer before earning their degree, meetings with direct service providers about the problems they observe, review student course evaluations, and findings from the NSSE. Only by asking, listening, and probing will administrators understand what students regularly encounter and be able to make the changes that tell students they are in a place that cares about them.

Conversations with parents, faculty, and staff are also essential. One approach I found useful was to invite a dozen leaders across a range of different student services to lunch. The "cost" of the free lunch was a presentation about two complicated student incidents they had to manage. The incidents could involve multiple administrative units, stuck cases, or system issues difficult to resolve. They provided insight into the intertwined nature of student encounters and were riveting for all in the room. The discussion gave a granular sense of what staff members have to manage and how certain administrative structures increase the difficulty of their tasks. Better administrative policies, practices, and systems help staff as well as students.

The task here is to better understand where institutional practices, services, and policies are inadvertently chafing students, or are inattentive, ineffective, redundant, or imprecise. Once the pinch points are documented, efforts can be undertaken to correct or improve the administrative practices that are interfering with a quality student experience.

7)   Integrate Student Services with a Case Management System and a Digital Strategy

There are a variety of strategies to provide a more integrated delivery of student services. The NASPA and Entangled Solutions report discussed in Chapter 5 points to a series of targeted student services in which greater integration would improve student success. Reinforcing a theme of this book, it points out that "there is a growing base of evidence demonstrating that a range of student support services . . . can positively impact student achievement outcomes."[24] Yet accomplishing this integration remains a challenge for most universities. One integration strategy universities have explored is placing the different student databases into a "data lake" for selective use by different personnel. However, there remains the issue of pertinent but confidential information, to which staff have restricted access.

Other campuses facing bureaucratic hurdles across core administrative services have turned to a one-stop center to ease student access to information and services. In response to the trudging from office to office in search of answers that students had dubbed the "Miami Shuffle," the University of Miami established a one-stop center with a virtual self-service portal and an in-house service facility to help reduce student frustrations. A CRM system provides students more personal and customized responses (see Chapter 7). One-stop centers are a step toward better communication and relationships, but they do not address the larger issues of the fragmented organization of administrative and direct services.

Community colleges may be at the forefront of efforts to develop more integrative student services. For example, Achieving the Dream, a network representing over 277 community colleges, created a toolkit to help colleges redesign student services. It emphasizes "the need for colleges to redefine the way they understand, design, integrate with academics, and deliver services that are critical for the success of every student."[25] The organization provides a wide range of research, training, and support services, including activities to "envision the ideal student experience, develop a prioritized action plan to address core issues, [and] improve operational workflows and internal communication."[26] It seeks to "create the structure and culture to support continuous improvement."[27] Other community colleges and smaller four-year colleges and universities, such as St. John Fisher College, Lynn University, and Central Arizona College, have identified the integration of support systems as a way to promote student success.

However, none of these approaches provides students with someone who has the authority and information to provide an integrated response to their needs. It is the missing link to the integration of student services. To create such a position and not violate federal, state, or local confidentiality laws would involve a job description requiring access to all pertinent student information across the four essential domains including academic progress, social interactions, health (both physical and mental), and financial information. Armed with such a job description, the college or university is now in a position to create a case management system.

A case management system, common in other service sectors such as health care, mental health, medicine, law, and government, is a "collaborative process of assessment, planning ... coordination, evaluation, and advocacy for options and services to meet an individual's ... needs."[28] Such a role can serve as the hub through which specialized professional spokes connect to address all aspects of a student's academic, cocurricular, financial, health, and social interactions. Case managers in colleges or universities could potentially alter the current fragmented situation and foster a more administratively aligned system. Case management is a systems approach to a structural problem. Its delay in arriving at colleges and universities is possibly due to individual specialists at universities seeing it as a threat to the control that they hold. Nevertheless, if implemented properly, it provides one person with the information and authority to provide or access timely support to students. It also provides a level of accountability that currently is absent.

To be effective, the case manager would need to be familiar with and connected to the different specialists on campus and work in consultation with students. The case manager would also need to have a manageable caseload, actionable information about the student, risk identification software, and the authority to connect and at times intervene across divisions. Early intervention and preventive care for a student facing academic or other risks would potentially avoid more serious negative consequences later.

A successful case management system in higher education would not end with the case manager. It also would provide students with agency and timely information, built around what the student needs and when they need it. Armed with information on their overall progress, students can, with the assistance of their case manager, choose to access the services they need.

A case management system represents more than the coordination of services. Coordination assumes that individual units will retain their control over existing information, but, as we have seen, siloed data structures limit the university's ability to make sense of the student's overall experience. In a case managed system, considerable effort goes into the design of the data elements, the selected flow of information from the service specialists, and the manner of data presentation, providing the case manager and student with actionable intelligence. Making that information available to a case manager requires participation, engagement, and support among the specialized units serving students and IT systems designers.

Case managers would need an information dashboard that links to a customized profile of the student, updates progress from specialists, and issues an alert from any of the specialists or instructors should something go awry. The cooperation of the array of professionals with whom students are in contact would be essential in order to provide timely information to the case manager. Equally essential would be the dissemination of pertinent information from the case manager to the service provider. In such an integrated data system, students would also receive feedback on their smartphones, including lists of people to see (imagine pop-up pictures of the key contacts, their available times to meet, and the ability to schedule meetings) or notices of relevant information.

The difficulty of developing such a digital strategy for student support should not be underestimated. It would be a mistake to jump to software solutions without implementing the necessary organizational redesign. Careful thought is required, for example, about what information a case manager would actually need. Too much information could overload the case manager, but timely and action-oriented data is essential. The flow of information would need to be smartly designed and thoughtfully integrated, a task with which artificial intelligence could assist.

While business applications focus on what management needs, a university case managed system would need to begin with a customized assessment of which supports students need to maximize their potential. In a word, a university or college case management system would be student-centric. Therefore, the digital strategy might start with a student entering a personal academic plan, including milestones, into the system, along with coursework, choice of major, internship, athletic, cocurricular, and career plans. The plans could be modified and updated with links to tools to help manage time, set milestones and deadlines, clarify priorities, and record accomplishments (see I.3 above). Such a system would enable students, together with the case manager, to create a customized learning and support team of relevant faculty, staff, peers, and other professionals. A student dashboard, with images of the core support network, would permit sending or receiving alerts, flags, or messages at a touch of an icon.

The case manager's dashboard would include access to the student's dashboard, academic plan, and key information on academic progress, including any early warnings, behavioral incidents, illness or excessive stress reports, changes in financial aid circumstances, and student-self reports. It could also be available on smartphones.

The previously mentioned comprehensive learner record (CLR) standard can be a useful academic record along with learning relationship management (LRM) software. The LRM system brings together many of the fragmented pieces of information crucial to student success. These programs vary depending on who designs them, but according to an analysis by Wainhouse Research, they all have the features I outlined in Chapter 7.[29]

Case managers, armed with information from different sectors, would develop insights into university operations along with their holistic view of the student. Inevitably, they would notice delays in services, backlogs, or inefficiencies, information valuable to university decision-makers, as discussed below. To lead a process of continuous improvement, managers could convene meetings with service colleagues to discuss ways to improve work, collegiality, and student support, a concept from Japan called *kaizen*. A final case management system, of course, will never be achieved, as feedback from the process will lead continuously to further efficiencies and improvements.

There may be existing members from academic affairs, student affairs, financial aid officers, and advisors who, with additional professional development, might be viable candidates for transfer to the role of case manager. It will take time for the approach to cultivate support across campus and time to develop a digital strategy with the necessary flow of information. However, the creation of a case managed system and the accompanying digital strategy could prove transformative in the alignment of student support services that engages a student-centric and holistic approach.

8) *Diminish Silos to Focus on Student Success While Preserving Decentralized Operations*

In developing a digitally enhanced case management system, the university will have created a role for individuals with the information and responsibility for the overall student experience. But what about all the other offices and personnel pivotal to the smooth functioning of the university and, ultimately, student life? Change starts from the top; the president's institutional priorities and messaging are essential if all members of the community are to recognize their role in student success, even when they may be tangentially involved with students.

Hospitals, often very large and highly decentralized organizations, can face similar management challenges as colleges and universities. The Cleveland Clinic, discussed in Chapter 9, developed strategies that may prove successful in the university setting. To improve the patient experience, it emphasized the central importance of examining every hospital encounter from the patient's point of view. The Clinic's president created several new positions within the executive office, led by a chief experience officer with the responsibility to gain an overview and positively influence the way patients are treated at the Clinic. This included all direct encounters as well as how the separate professional divisions interact and align with one another around patient care. The messaging from the president, backed by an enhanced role among central management, also reiterated respect for the historic culture of unit authority, professional judgment, and decentralization.

Applying its approach at residential colleges and universities could begin with two new positions in the president's office: a university experience officer (UXO) reporting directly to the president to ensure that all units work together on university-wide goals, and an ombudsperson with the authority to intervene across campus units to resolve or mediate student or parent problems.

I envision the UXO as a cabinet-level position whose purpose would be to ensure a broader student-centric, integrated, and university-wide perspective. As the university is currently configured, and given its internal distribution of power, this would not be an easy assignment. University units long ago found ways to institutionalize their activities, processes, and procedures and develop mechanisms to ensure their relative independence. A UXO insensitive to these power dynamics and to the fact that the various vice presidents are accountable to the president – not to a UXO – might swiftly be undermined. Both diplomatic skills and the president's full and explicit support would be essential. A fundamental task would be to expand the perspective of university cabinet members beyond their distinct administrative assignments and obligations to the wider view of how their decisions and processes connect to other university units and, in turn, how these choices and activities potentially impact students. Achieving this would translate a president's message into an actionable agenda designed to encourage units to work more seamlessly together to achieve the common purpose of student well-being and success.

In the context of the university's well-documented history of vacillating between centralization and decentralization, the UXO is neither intended to foster greater centralization nor to exert greater control from the top. Rather, the role would be one of facilitation, to align campus units and administrative structures with clear institutional priorities. This is a fine line to implement, but an important distinction – more than coordination but less than central decision-making. One path to that balance might be to add to annual performance evaluations for each division and office, one that contained assessments of its relationship with and support of at least the three administrative units allied most closely to it. Each of those units, in turn, would provide feedback on the specific integrative and collaborative efforts they carried out with the other units. Each participating administrative program and division would amass data about the perception of service provision across offices and then share the findings with the

UXO. Feedback from case managers, discussed in the previous pathway, would provide an additional perspective on inter-unit operations and relationships around direct student services.

Armed with these findings, the UXO could inform the president and cabinet about how the units are functioning and highlight sectors doing well and those experiencing challenges. Problems arising from differences between the administrators' self-perception and the aggregate data, including student feedback, would necessitate some intervention and plan for improvement. For example, the UXO might find that decisions in marketing appear comically dated or culturally insensitive from the perspective of different students, or that study abroad staff are not adequately communicating with faculty experts capable of enriching the international experience. Or, via an ombudsperson, the UXO might learn of excessive undocumented student work hours occurring in a university laboratory but tolerated by international students hesitant to speak up for fear of deportation. Other gaps in services, redundancies, and inefficiencies would likely emerge. The UXO could explore ways to improve individual choices or decisions that might previously have been made in isolation or kept silent, but could, within a broader set of considerations, be addressed to enhance the collective community.

Many campuses already have an ombudsperson. For those currently without one, the role would help resolve the all-too-frequent situations in which student cases get stuck between multiple divisions or remain unresolved in one. As I have discussed throughout this book, students and parents are often caught in a bureaucratic web wherein staff either feel they lack the authority, or actually do lack it, to resolve an issue (see Maurice's story in Chapter 1). Having a representative of the president available to assist is one possible solution. The ombudsperson provides a central place for those with complaints to go and possibly find a swift resolution. Not all complaints can be resolved to the complainants' satisfaction. But, as we learned from the Cleveland Clinic, the fact that a representative of the head of the organization listens carefully and is thoughtful and professional when handling complaints can go a long way toward communicating concerns about how the institution is carrying out its responsibilities.

The ombudsperson would also continuously provide the UXO with data about potential problem areas and pinch points where complaints are frequent, where conflicts exist across units, where units may be understaffed, or where individuals lack the necessary training and fail to perform at the expected level. With the president's support, the UXO could then work with the appropriate vice president to intervene. Depending on the problem, the solution might involve allocating additional staff, adopting different management approaches, offering further professional development, or revising policies. If the situation involves a specific personnel matter, a formal HR performance review could potentially result in probation or, in certain situations, eventual termination.

The Cleveland Clinic's experience shows that influencing the collective performance of an institution is a long-term agenda that requires persistence and determination. Employing another strategy from the Clinic, the UXO might introduce required faculty and staff training sessions and workshops for all employees, independent of rank or stature. The Clinic's theme in its training sessions was empathy. A college or university would select its own unifying theme, but empathy is not a bad choice. Being more empathetic to the experiences of other colleagues, students, and their families could go a long way toward improving the campus experience.

The UXO could also bring campus leaders together to regularly visit different units, similar to doctors' and nurses' rounds in hospitals. Often, faculty and staff know university leadership only from public presentations and emails. By making rounds, administrative leaders could build closer alliances with faculty and staff, learn about internal issues, and increase opportunities for faculty and staff exchanges outside of formal meetings.

Taking the campus to its next level of attentiveness to students not only involves improving services for students and their families, but also improving the experience of the employees providing the services. If the overall work environment lacks civility, collegiality, and a sense of shared purpose, it is difficult for workers to give the kind of support today's students expect and need. A healthy workplace where employees have fair remuneration, benefits, support, respect, sense of community, shared purpose, and a voice is more likely to produce the sort of culture that delivers quality services. Part of the UXO's responsibility is to encourage this kind of workplace culture. One way to do this might be to suggest units offer cash "spot awards" to individuals who have undertaken collaborative activities outside of their daily responsibility, along with a major annual cash award. On one campus, an annual "Silo Buster" award went to a notably collaborative staff member. Even without a UXO model, at a minimum, university leadership must set and communicate overall institutional goals for which every employee is accountable. Poor performance in achieving institutional goals, even while meeting unit goals, could factor into decisions on compensation, promotion, and even termination.

9)   Enhance Faculty Awareness and Responsibility for the Student Experience

Thus far, much of the discussion of ways to promote a more holistic approach to university operations has skirted the role of faculty. While it is very difficult to change the well-ensconced faculty structure and culture, there are ways to work within it to enhance the student experience. The faculty senate, in particular, can play a role in building support and nurturing campus-wide investment in change. The key change is to shatter the barrier between the owners of the cognitive domain of the student experience – the faculty – and the perceived owners of all other personal growth experiences – the professional staff. It is in the spirit of shared faculty governance to break that barrier.

Awareness and Accountability

One potential pathway for creating change is to establish a standing subcommittee of the faculty senate focused on the overall university-wide student experience. A subcommittee on the student experience would receive data collected from students, faculty, and staff (including appropriate information from the UXO and case managers) regarding pinch points, campus climate surveys, NSSE findings, information from focus groups, and ongoing case studies. Faculty could be involved in survey design, interviews, and data review and analyses, if they chose. The director of the campus office of institutional research could serve as an ex officio member. The subcommittee could invite feedback from administrators across the campus.

The involvement of faculty members could lead to recommendations to enhance the overall student experience. For example, faculty senators could hear case studies highlighting the effectiveness of early intervention when a student is performing poorly in class. Armed with this information, the provost, in cooperation with the faculty senate, could require (yes, *require*) all faculty to provide at least one assessment of each student's academic performance by the third week of class and submit an early warning notice for those having difficulties. Instructors would immediately flag struggling students for additional support. While the administration could implement this policy on its own, the involvement of the faculty senate would help ensure faculty buy-in. This role requires skills the faculty already possess: gathering and analyzing information to lead to recommendations. Faculty members' greater awareness of the student experience will likely promote their support for changes needed in the management of services.

Explicit Linkage across Academic and Student Support Domains
Establishing a more coordinated relationship between the academic and student service domains may require rethinking reporting lines within the university. Across the nation, the office of student affairs (OSA) may report to either the president or the provost. A structure in which the OSA is a separate and distinct unit from the office of academic affairs reinforces the historic bifurcation between faculty and staff who serve students. Formally connecting an OSA with the office of academic affairs is a necessary step toward enhancing a holistic student perspective. For OSAs that currently report to the president, this does not necessarily mean exclusion from the president's cabinet. The president might still choose to invite the head of the OSA to cabinet meetings, but the reporting line would have shifted to the chief academic officer.

For university staff professionals currently working in separate units within the OSA, this would mean more than just a change in managerial hierarchy. The move to the office of academic affairs would signal that the two major organizational components of a student's life will be more integrated under overarching educational goals. Full accountability for smoother operations across and within units would become the provost's ultimate responsibility.

As should be clear by now, a realignment of organizational reporting without a change in day-to-day procedures and operations will have little effect on students' experiences. The point is to create an administrative form that fosters real connectivity, alignment, and convergence while respecting the professional skills of those who work in student affairs and related services.

Flexibility for Greater Faculty Engagement
Centering the student experience has other potential implications for faculty and their current activities. Some of these changes are already afoot in the ways faculty are hired and retained. In recent years, some universities have expanded the number of full-time contract faculty as an alternative to either committing to permanent, tenure-track positions or using PhD-level part-time adjunct faculty to teach courses on an ad hoc basis. Part-time adjunct faculty paid by the course cannot (and are not expected to) provide the long-term continuity and important student mentoring relationships identified in item I.1 above. Nevertheless, there remains a role for part-time faculty with full-time or nearly full-time positions outside of academia. They can bring insights from industry, government, health care, business, nongovernmental organizations, research centers,

and start-ups into the classroom. Their viewpoints and experiences can amplify faculty expertise with real-world insights and provide an invaluable perspective for student learning. But the inappropriate, even exploitive use of part-time faculty hopefully will fade as the newer category of full-time teaching faculty emerges on numerous campuses.

Universities recruit contractual, full-time faculty primarily for their instructional and advising responsibilities. Their compensation is often considerably less than that of research-active and tenure-track faculty, and their course load is generally greater. Contract length can vary, usually beginning with a one-year renewable contract offering full benefits. Multiyear contracts are available for experienced instructors in areas of high instructional demand. These can stretch to five years or more and are customarily renewable.

Contractual teaching faculty can provide sustained guidance to students, earn rewards based on performance reviews, and begin building a career. Some campuses, recognizing the importance of such instructors to the university's operations, have developed a career path for instructional faculty, including a promotion ladder based on performance and service. For example, the twenty-four-campus Pennsylvania State University System has instituted a three-tiered promotion system complete with recognition and financial compensation increments paralleling that of tenure-track faculty.[30] AU includes full-time contractual faculty in almost all aspects of academic governance except tenure reviews. Nearly half of the Faculty Senate at AU are contractual faculty, and many of them have emerged as campus leaders, including serving as chair of the faculty senate and as an ex officio member of the Board of Trustees.

With this structure already emerging, we can imagine new and expanded opportunities for either tenured or contractual full-time faculty, including explicit initiatives to integrate the curricular and cocurricular components of the student experience. Full-time faculty, either tenured or contractual, could conceivably become more engaged in student development in exchange for a reduction in classroom instruction. At campuses around the country, some faculty members have volunteered to live in the residence halls and are available to mentor undergraduate students. Faculty might sponsor mini-courses on civic engagement, community service, ethical standards, the reliability of information sources, or democratic processes. They could hold noncredit sessions in spaces frequented by students, or offer cocurricular classes for those interested. Of course, teaching loads need to be adjusted to accommodate these new responsibilities, but the point is to provide the faculty greater flexibility and a wider range of options that link faculty more organically to the student experience. Their success in building a deeper rapport with students, making more time to listen to students' troubles and fears (see item I.4 above), can be a pivotal component in a student's success. The opportunity for such interaction and involvement in the life of the student – with clearly established boundaries – would be a goal at a thriving student-centered university.

Tenured faculty remain an essential part of the university. To ensure that the number of contractual faculty does not reduce the aggregate number of tenured faculty, universities could set an overall base percentage of tenure-track positions to preserve a sustained research and teaching mission.

Faculty members possess a wide variety of skills and pass through phases in their careers. Some are very good administrators, some spectacular teachers and mentors, others brilliant scholars. Some possess the full array of skills. Presumably, some would thrive in a role that drew on their strengths for the holistic development of students. This is not to suggest that faculty would assume the duties of student affairs staff. It is professional staff who will be on call when students are at physical risk in the middle of the night, or on the front lines for a crisis, a hate incident, a conflict, a protest, or popular social events. But there are opportunities to design a more immersive role for faculty as intellectual mentors, which could enrich a student's "world view, attitudes, and values, cultivation of moral and ethical standards; and preparation for global citizenship in a diverse nation and world."[31]

While the divide between faculty in academic affairs and staff in student affairs may seem impossibly wide, there are promising examples from campuses that have begun to bridge it. For example, a senior tenured faculty member at AU with expertise in race, culture, and identity decided to retire. As a reflection of the university's respect for her and her skills as a student mentor, the student affairs office invited her to return to campus in a staff leadership role. As an emerita faculty member, she proved enormously helpful in educating students outside the classroom. It was not unusual to find her in long conversations with students about issues of justice, equity, truth, and morality. In the opposite direction, AU has a leader in student affairs with expertise in international relations who holds a dual appointment as a member of the faculty and periodically teaches. All AU first-year student guides have dual appointments. Such experiences could serve as models for the changes in faculty-staff roles that will be necessary to build a more holistic university.

Models exist of student-centered programs where faculty and staff are collectively engaged in a holistic educational experience. Since 1988, the cohort approach of the Meyerhoff Program at the University of Maryland, Baltimore County (UMBC) (highlighted in Chapter 2) has proven what a program designed with faculty and staff engagement can achieve. The successful approach involves distinguished faculty, supported by trained professional staff, engaging in the full spectrum of students' personal and professional development. The education of the whole person at the UMBC program is a national model that demonstrates the impact of an integrated faculty and support staff collaborating for student success.[32]

As I have emphasized throughout this volume, campuses emulate one another. Those with high status, where future faculty members receive their doctoral training, often serve as role models for other institutions. Any campus can expand its faculty roles and responsibilities, but when those in the Association of American Universities (AAU) or otherwise ranked in the top tier broaden faculty roles and responsibilities, others will follow. The journey to an ever more coordinated and holistic student-centered institution has already begun – it just needs further definition, role models, leadership, and refinement.

10) Create a Culture of Continuous Academic Innovation and Student Well-Being

Organizations always have room for improvement. For a college or university, success is never final. Students' perspectives change along with the changing broader circumstances in which they are raised. To build the capacity for continuous evolution, several universities have created design labs under various names and in different forms. For example, Georgetown University has established "The Red House" to promote and encourage innovation within a traditional Jesuit university founded more than 250 years ago. One of its strategies is to "re-bundle" aspects of what makes a leading research university successful and to shed features that are barriers to an increasingly diverse student body.[33] Types of design labs might range from an individual faculty member freed up to explore and eventually introduce innovative practices to the campus, to a specific unit with a budget and staff charged with developing and testing prototypes for future institutionalization.

A design or innovation lab is one strategy to help foster and normalize internal expectations about a culture of sustained, continuous, and planned organizational change. At scale, perhaps no other institution can match Arizona State University (ASU)'s efforts to promote a spirit of innovation. In direct defiance of the traditionally staid culture of higher education, ASU has fostered and institutionalized rapid change and innovation. Through the Office of Applied Innovation, ASU brings together an interdisciplinary team that explores innovative ideas and conducts research that leads to the swift design and implementation of new initiatives. The president, Michael M. Crow, has fostered a culture at ASU that provides the freedom to take risks.[34] In 2021, ASU established the Taskforce on Higher Education and Opportunity with the intent of enriching 2.5 million students by linking resources and capabilities across thirty-seven different educational institutions.[35] The TomorrowTalks bring ASU students in direct contact with some of the nation's leading innovators and changemakers.[36] The Office of Applied Innovation's Student Design Studio provides opportunities for students to work closely with designers as well as have time to develop their own entrepreneurial projects.[37] ASU has also fostered university–corporate partnerships labeled Innovation Zones. It created the Starbucks College Achievement Plan, providing full-time Starbucks employees access to full tuition coverage for the campus's online programs. In 2021, *US News and World Report* ranked ASU as the most innovative campus in the nation.[38] It has built the concept of continuous improvement and change into the structure of the university.

Of course, it is important to maintain balance and perspective, particularly in matters of institutional change. Well-intentioned efforts at student-centeredness and enriching the learning experience sometimes can be watered down to superficial entertainment, a way of pacifying or pampering students with little actual benefit to their development. Also, implementing changes without sensitivity to the setting will likely engender hostility from key stakeholders. Rather than recommending an abrupt or radical transformation, I am suggesting that university leaders work patiently and within the framework of shared governance. Involving campus leaders with vision and determination can enhance the university's ability to accomplish change and better serve its student body. Institutional recalibration must be ongoing.

III.   Enhancing University Climate and Culture

A positive campus climate and culture requires that faculty and staff feel respected and appreciated. A university community that feels good about itself makes students feel welcomed and part of that community. With student diversity increasing, the university experience needs to be recalibrated to better match their educational interests and need for support. This section discusses five ways to do that.

11)   Build a More Diverse and Culturally Competent Faculty

As American campuses welcome students from a wider range of backgrounds, these students increasingly complain about the limited number of faculty who reflect their identity. Colleges and universities have made modest gains in diversifying their faculty, but the gap between faculty and student demographics remains significant.[39] As they have done for nearly half a century, students of color have continuously advocated for more faculty members from underrepresented groups. In response, some administrators and faculty cite challenges in hiring faculty of color – a limited pipeline of candidates and a marketplace where other universities are competing for the same individuals. At the same time, many candidates of color report that, while they often make a shortlist and are invited for interviews, they are too often passed over in the final selection. Search committees can become mired in discussions of the candidate's "fit" with departmental culture. Intentionally or not, "fit" becomes a way of excluding qualified minority candidates.[40]

Educating faculty search committees about unconscious bias in hiring is one way to begin to break this cycle. Many universities already require diversity training for all faculty. Some also provide training for each faculty search committee at the start of the process, with input as the pool of candidates narrows. In the two years of faculty searches since this training began at AU, over 40 percent of the new tenured or tenure-track faculty hired were underrepresented minority candidates. Closing this gap is an important aspect of becoming a more student-centered and inclusive campus.

Another approach that has helped universities build a more student-centered and welcoming campus environment is a commitment to "inclusive excellence," an academic community where all, independent of abilities, health conditions, gender, age, sexual preference or identity, race, ethnicity, socioeconomic status, religion, national origin, or position, are respected and supported. It asks those in positions of power and influence to think more deeply about how their interactions support or hinder the success of individuals from underrepresented groups. While inclusive excellence embraces the academy's expectations of distinguished performance and accomplishment, it also develops and nurtures the multiple pathways for faculty, staff, and students of different backgrounds to achieve at these high levels, and thus broaden the intellectual reach of a pluralistic community. Traditional forms of discourse, academic venues, presentation styles, research design, and creative direction can be broadened, depending on the field or professional area, to become more welcoming of ideas and topics reflective of the perspectives of historically excluded groups. Customization of student career pathways, recognition of different learning styles, and appreciation of cultural differences can lead to more successful experiences and individual achievement. More than a concept, inclusive excellence entails regular training and professional development for the entire academic community.[41]

12) Support a More Representative Curriculum and Institutional Messaging

A by-now familiar student complaint is that many course readings are dominated by "old White guys." On many campuses, students perceive an imbalance in the arts and humanities between a dominant Western emphasis and a limited number of courses focused on the Global South. Inclusion goes beyond enrolling a diverse student body to intentionally incorporating courses that reflect the contributions of artists and scholars from around the world. Students want to hear other points of view and other voices.

Some of this is easy to achieve. Important works by women and underrepresented scholars, for instance, can easily be added to the syllabus. The same goes for readings and insights that originate from the Global South. As the faculty adds new members from diverse backgrounds, whose identities are more aligned with the students they serve, wider perspectives will likely emerge in the coursework. The curriculum is the province of the faculty, who guide students through ideas and perspectives, and with this responsibility, it is incumbent upon faculty to ensure that material in the curriculum remains current and vital.

Courses that engage faculty and students in matters of meaning, purpose, ethics, justice, character, aesthetics, truth, wisdom, values, civility, and civic engagement are all part of the learning and growth necessary for a more holistic education. With the raging polarization and acceptance of misinformation evident in today's America, students need more than casual conversations in residence halls to learn to assess the reliability of information, wrestle with ambiguity, and address intolerance and extremism. These issues necessitate deliberate attention in the curriculum.

Derek Bok, president of Harvard for more than twenty years, writes about infusing the college curriculum with "higher standards of ethical behavior and personal responsibility."[42] He argues that

> colleges share a responsibility to do what they can to help students build their character. College, after all, fills the lives of undergraduates during a period of years in which they have an unusual capacity for growth in personal responsibility and habits of self-control while living in an environment that offers them exceptional opportunities to discover, clarify, and apply the values they wish to live by.[43]

Fostering deeper critical thinking and reflection about students' societal roles and responsibilities can be an integral part of a holistic student-centered university's curriculum. As highlighted in item II.9 above universities can facilitate this educational exposure by making certain elective courses required or embedding relevant content in them, encouraging the development of new courses or mini-courses, and connecting cocurricular activities with faculty-guided reflection and analysis. While such courses may at first glance appear to be peripheral to training for a specific career, this kind of exposure broadens thinking, helps build the educated citizenry key to a modern democracy, and provides insights into values and perspectives instrumental in a college graduate's subsequent career.

A national student survey examining the most salient factors in the college experience by the Huron Consulting Group reaffirms the importance of connecting personal growth and character development with traditional coursework. "In defining success on students' terms," they report that "survey respondents felt most rewarded when their institutions helped them holistically – through intellectual development, personal growth, and sense of fit on campus."[44] Curricular choices that provide an enriched learning experience and the engagement of faculty beyond the classroom are integral to fostering the personal and professional growth of the college student.

Of course, critical thinking might not be focused solely on the world beyond the campus. Students are keenly aware of the names of buildings, monuments, statues, or programs on the campus. They note to whom the paintings or photographs that line university walls or passageways pay tribute. They are concerned about the sources of large gifts as well as directed investments in the campus endowment. Individuals or companies who have been found guilty of crimes, who have had a legacy of racist actions, and whose lifework contradicts the core values of the institution, but whose names or images remain visible on campus, are precisely why students question their college or university's commitment to its stated values. These issues tie into students' sense of belonging and identification with their school and merit the attention of campus leaders.

13)   Prioritize Financial Aid to the Most Vulnerable

Each year residential campuses across the country compete with one another to build their entering class, typically by offering discounts in the form of scholarships. In the 2020–2021 academic year, the average discount rate at private nonprofit universities was 53.9 percent.[45] The amount of financial aid, including federal support and loans, varies based on internal calculations, but it draws from a finite set of resources. Universities weigh multiple issues when they assemble financial aid packages. In the past, they have supported affluent students on the argument that their academic credentials would not only enhance the university's reputation, but increase its overall graduation rate. To build a class, some campuses provide merit scholarships from their own funds to students they want to attract but who may not be eligible for federal financial aid and, at times, also may be in a position to pay. Academic credentials and test scores may be the determining factor in bringing these students to campus.

Student talent, however, takes many forms. Evidence from AU suggests that low-income students who receive 100 percent of their calculated financial need are as likely to graduate in four years as other students. If the funding is less than their need, they may struggle to earn their degree or leave without a college degree at all, exhausted by the financial struggle. At the same time, AU has found that financially secure students may enroll because of the incentive of a scholarship but, after realizing the financial benefits and simultaneously strengthening their academic portfolio, transfer to another higher-ranked institution after a year or two. There is an argument to be made that colleges and universities should make every effort to meet 100 percent of the calculated need for admissible students but targeted to the most financially needy.

Once these students are admitted, universities have to find ways to support their success. According to the Pew Research Center, poverty among students nearly doubled from 1996 to 2016.[46] In a more recent study of first-year college students, researchers found 19 percent of the sample were food-insecure and just over a quarter "were at risk of food insecurity."[47] Even students with jobs can find themselves short of money to buy food. When forced to choose between tuition and food, students who see education as their ticket to a better life may decide to put tuition first. Inadequate nutrition can negatively influence academic performance and behavior. Hungry students have to manage the daily discomfort as well as the indignity of being food-insecure in a setting surrounded by food. In response, many universities have established food pantries. They can also encourage needy, eligible students to apply for federal Supplemental Nutritional Assistance (SNAP).

14) Modify Facilities to Promote Public Health

The novel coronavirus is not the first pathogen to hit campuses, nor will it be the last. Public health considerations undoubtedly will influence future renovations to campus facilities, such as designs that increase touch-free entrances or remove entry doors altogether, like the open-access bathrooms found in airports. Restrooms may be redesigned for hygiene, ensuring a safe distance between occupants, lids that cover commodes when flushed, and touchless faucets, soap, and paper towel dispensers. Airflow in classrooms and student spaces should be frequently refreshed and filtered to reduce or eliminate the flow of pathogens. Interior passageways can be designed or redesigned to direct the flow of people and increase the distances between them. One can imagine the expanded use of sound-dampening interior modular classrooms with movable partitions to adjust for class size. Surrounding communities may expect universities to maintain quarantine facilities for students who become ill, even if those spaces (hopefully) remain vacant.

Collectively, these and other changes will help communicate to students that their health and safety are paramount. Financing will need to come from multiple sources, including the university's facility renewal funds, donors, federal or state resources, or new construction bonds.

15) Maintain Vigilance for Cost Containment

No higher education topic has captured public attention more than the cost of college and the resulting increase in student debt. The numerous existing proposals to help reduce the debt involve greater expenditures from either the state or federal government, whether to reduce tuition costs or to partially or wholly forgive college debt. Greater financial relief to those least able to afford college would be particularly effective. But while such plans would reduce the financial burden to the undergraduate, they would not necessarily reduce the cost of higher education; they would just shift the source of payment.

Some ideas to reduce education's actual cost center around reusable courseware, either created by faculty members or produced by educational companies. It would increase faculty productivity by "packaging" course material for use by larger audiences, an approach familiar to many large public universities. Cost savings can come from increasing the ratio of students taught per faculty member and compensation per course taught, but this approach may have already reached its zenith. While technology may wring out further savings, there are limits to online learning's ability to achieve the multifaceted learning experience students seek in a residential setting. Unfortunately, there are no magic bullets to cut costs in the labor-intensive industry of residential colleges and universities.

Another strategy to use faculty time more efficiently is hybrid instruction, a combination of in-person and online teaching. Instructors can prepare asynchronous course material in advance, allowing students to examine it outside of class time. The prepared material would then be available for use in future classes, freeing up time for more personalized instruction, mentorship, student guidance, and the numerous student-centered activities I have proposed in other sections of this chapter.

An approach attractive to adult students involves more flexible online learning modules, bundled course clusters, competency packages, or certificates that, over time, may accumulate to a college degree. Colleges and universities with a strong brand might offer such programs to augment revenue while retaining the more expensive residential program aimed at students who enter college directly or soon after high school.

For university presidents, keeping expenditures in check is a constant challenge. At some point, the rising sticker price will make college unattainable except for the wealthy and those receiving substantial tuition subsidies. According to the Integrated Postsecondary Education Data System (IPEDS), the increase in expenses for student services stands out among the rising expenses at public and private universities.[48] I have shown how often the components of student and administrative services are uncoordinated and inefficiently managed. This is an area where savings and improvements in the student experience can be combined.

Many of the organizational improvements I have suggested will initially add costs, just as they would in other industries. Over time, however, greater efficiency and improving service operations can also produce cost savings. Other justifications for spending on administrative improvements include enhancing a college's or university's image, its competitiveness for new students, and its ability to retain existing students. An increase in student retention may be one of the most significant revenue enhancements a president can pursue. A university that seeks not only to retain its current students, but to ensure they thrive in an enriched learning experience, derives many benefits, including a potential increase in the number of future alumni donors.

Universities can save money by clarifying responsibilities, coordinating communication and data sharing, using technology in an appropriate and targeted manner, and assigning accountability for student outcomes. In the updated university systems I described in this chapter, designated faculty, staff, and case managers would all know more about individual students and their academic and social progress, facilitating the early intervention that is critical to avoiding more intensive and expensive crisis support. If universities could better confront and manage student stresses, anxieties, and fears earlier in the experience, fewer students would require emergency mental health counseling services. Perhaps fewer would eventually leave the university. The same goes for academic performance: providing timely support for a student performing poorly in a class could avert the threat of failure.

Cost containment is a real issue that merits the attention of university leadership, but a university president does not need to choose between improved quality and leaving things as they are. Building a better system comes with costs, but eventually, it can reduce wasteful expenses and lost revenue.

Conclusion

Society benefits from an educated and well-trained citizenry. Well-prepared college graduates help fuel a growing economy. They are critical thinkers who approach sources of information with appropriate skepticism, who can distinguish fact from fantasy. They value research and scientific inquiry, bring aesthetic appreciation to the world around them, and are respectful of different traditions and cultures. They can provide leadership on multifaceted topics, have an historical perspective, and generate responses to problems that are matched to the complexity of the problems themselves. A democratic society depends on the goodwill and thoughtful judgment of its citizens to sustain its sense of justice, democratic values, and even its sense of morality. Societal, political, economic, public health, and environmental challenges have never been greater, demanding educated citizens up to the challenge.

Colleges and universities in the United States remain among the best in the world. An American college degree carries a certain cachet almost anywhere. Faculty research and scholarship remain pathbreaking, contributing to global prestige and brand identity. Today, American higher education is no longer available only to the wealthy and privileged. It successfully reaches and includes wider and more diverse populations, expanding these remarkable opportunities to wider segments of society. But it can do better.

These ten chapters have traced how the American residential nonprofit college or university has evolved over the last one hundred years, and how choices, influences, constraints, and priorities during that period have shaped the current student experience. I have emphasized how university structure, culture, and system functions lag behind the needs and expectations of the students the university seeks to serve and cause sufficient discomfort to negatively influence educational outcomes for too many.

The novel coronavirus disrupted life worldwide, including at the university. The initial response of residential colleges and universities was to keep the community safe, to continue teaching, and to manage costs and expenses. The next phase, and the emphasis of this book, is how the academy will reach beyond the multiple crises of 2020 and 2021 to become more streamlined, assertively align administrative functions, and be more responsive to the experiences and expectations of its students. The disruption provides an opportunity for universities to confront some of the administrative gremlins that have frustrated the campus community for too long: the complexity of decision-making because of the distribution and dilution of power, the culture of specialization and professional territoriality among both faculty and administrative staff, the influences and rewards for faculty that shape priorities and use of time, the isomorphic replication of services and structures, and the limits of technology as a solution to administrative and human dynamic problems.

I have provided examples of what can be accomplished now and in the future, drawing on experiences both within the university and on models of constituent-centric service delivery that have taken hold beyond the campus. The suggestions in this book are intended not as prescriptions but rather as springboards for others with original suggestions and ideas to test and assess them for their contributions to the goal of the student-centered university.

I hope I have awakened academic leaders to the challenges they face, scholars to the areas in need of further research and examination, and the broader public to the needed investments in higher education to ensure that residential colleges and universities maximize student success and well-being. I remain optimistic about our ability to manage change in such a complicated, entrenched, politicized, and fragmented environment, optimistic as well that there is enthusiasm in the academy for better aligning its operations with an increasingly diverse student body and the challenges of contemporary citizenship.

Notes

1 American Council on Education, *The Student Personnel Point of View* (Washington, DC: American Council on Education, 1937), 1.
2 Daniel F. Chambliss and Christopher G. Takacs, *How College Works* (Cambridge, MA: Harvard University Press, 2014), 3–6.
3 Vincent Tinto, *Completing College: Rethinking Institutional Action* (Chicago: University of Chicago Press, 2012), 3.
4 Peter Felten and Leo M. Lambert, *The Importance of Mentors and Peers in the Undergraduate Experience: Survey of College Graduates* (Elon, NC: Elon University, 2018), 18, accessed November 12, 2019, www.elon.edu/u/elon-poll/wp-content/uploads/sites/819/2019/02/Elon-Poll-Report-082218.pdf.
5 "The LRCs of Advising: Listening, Respecting, and Caring," National Survey of Student Engagement, accessed December 14, 2020, https://nsse.indiana.edu/research/annual-results/advising/index.html.
6 "The Relationship of Advising LRC with Intentions to Persist," National Survey of Student Engagement, accessed December 14, 2020, https://nsse.indiana.edu/research/annual-results/advising/lrc-fy.html.
7 National Survey of Student Engagement, "LRCs of Advising."
8 Peter Felten and Leo M. Lambert, *Relationship-Rich Education: How Human Connections Drive Success in College* (Baltimore: Johns Hopkins University Press, 2020), 5.
9 See Lisa M. Nunn, *College Belonging: How First-Year and First-Generation Students Navigate Campus Life* (New Brunswick, NJ: Rutgers University Press, 2021).
10 Mary C. Murphy et al., "A Customized Belonging Intervention Improves Retention of Socially Disadvantaged Students at a Broad-Access University," *Science Advances* 6, no. 29 (July 2020): 1, accessed July 20, 2020, doi.org/10.1126/sciadv.aba4677.
11 Murphy et al., "Customized Belonging Intervention," 5.
12 See George D. Kuh, *High-Impact Educational Practices: What They Are, Who Has Access to Them, and Why They Matter* (Washington, DC: Association of American Colleges and Universities, 2008).
13 "University-Wide Active Learning Initiative," Cornell University, Office of the Provost, accessed November 3, 2020, https://provost.cornell.edu/leadership/vp-academic-innovation/active-learning-initiative/.
14 Jenn Abelson et al., "At College Health Centers, Students Battle Misdiagnoses and Inaccessible Care," *Washington Post*, July 13, 2020, accessed July 14,

2020, www.washingtonpost.com/investigations/2020/07/13/college-health-centers-problems/?arc404=true.

15 Ted Mitchell and Suzanne Ortega, "Mental Health Challenges Require Urgent Response," *Inside Higher Ed*, October 29, 2019, accessed October 30, 2019, www.insidehighered.com/views/2019/10/29/students-mental-health-shouldnt-be-responsibility-campus-counseling-centers-alone.

16 Kara Irby, "FSU Fully Launches Student Resilience Project," *Florida State University News*, September 28, 2018, 3:00 p.m. EDT, accessed May 20, 2021, https://news.fsu.edu/news/university-news/2018/09/28/fsu-fully-launches-student-resilience-project-2/.

17 John MacPhee, "Promoting Student Mental Health in Difficult Days," *Inside Higher Ed*, May 29, 2020, accessed May 29, 2020, www.insidehighered.com/views/2020/05/29/advice-promoting-student-mental-health-during-pandemic-opinion.

18 Sarah Ketchen Lipson et al., *The Role of Faculty in Student Mental Health* (Boston: Boston University, Mary Christie Foundation, and Healthy Minds Network, 2021), 3, accessed May 29, 2021, https://marychristieinstitute.org/wp-content/uploads/2021/04/The-Role-of-Faculty-in-Student-Mental-Health.pdf.

19 Lipson et al., *Role of Faculty*, 15. Lipson et al.'s findings reveal that 57.9 percent of Hispanic or Latinx faculty, 38.5 percent of Black faculty, and 24 percent of Asian or Asian American faculty believe that their institution is hostile or somewhat hostile to students of color.

20 "Postsecondary Success," Bill & Melinda Gates Foundation, accessed May 20, 2021, www.gatesfoundation.org/our-work/programs/us-program/postsecondary-success; "Our Strategies: We Invest in These Focus Areas," Kresge Foundation, accessed December 1, 2021, https://kresge.org/our-work/education/#our-strategies; "Areas of Work," Lumina Foundation, accessed December 1, 2021, www.luminafoundation.org/our-work/areas-of-focus/.

21 "Student Success," Ithaka S+R, accessed May 20, 2021, https://sr.ithaka.org/our-work/student-success/.

22 "EAB Helps You Support and Graduate More Students," EAB, accessed May 20, 2021, https://eab.com/colleges-and-universities/student-success/.

23 "Reduction of Summer Melt," Georgia State University, accessed April 30, 2021, https://success.gsu.edu/initiatives/reduction-of-summer-melt/.

24 NASPA: Student Affairs Administrators in Higher Education and Entangled Solutions, *Accelerating the Growth of Institutional Success Services: Working Together to Scale and Sustain Integrated Advising and Holistic Student Support* (working paper, NASPA: Student Affairs Administrators in Higher Education and Entangled Solutions, Washington, DC, 2019), 10.

25 Achieving the Dream, *Holistic Student Supports Redesign: A Toolkit for Redesigning Advising and Student Services to Effectively Support Every Student, Version 3.0* (Silver Spring, MD: Achieving the Dream, 2018), 3, accessed November 12, 2019, www.achievingthedream.org/sites/default/files/resources/atd_hss_redesign_toolkit_2018.pdf.

26 "Holistic Student Supports," Achieving the Dream, accessed November 3, 2020, www.achievingthedream.org/services-supports/holistic-student-supports.

27 Achieving the Dream, "Holistic Student Supports."

28 "What Is a Case Manager?," Case Management Society of America, accessed May 20, 2021, https://cmsa.org/who-we-are/what-is-a-case-manager/.

29 Alan D. Greenberg, *Learning Relationship Management: Ending the Expectation of Average While Getting Back to Basics* (Duxbury, MA: Wainhouse Research, 2016), 12–13.

30 Alina Tugend, "How Penn State Improved Conditions for Adjuncts," *Chronicle of Higher Education,* October 30, 2019, www.chronicle.com/article/how-penn-state-improved-conditions-for-adjuncts/.

31 Matthew J. Mayhew et al., *How College Affects Students, Vol. 3: 21st Century Evidence That Higher Education Works* (San Francisco: Jossey-Bass, 2016), 159.

32 See Freeman A. Hrabowski III with Philip J. Rous and Peter H. Henderson, *The Empowered University: Shared Leadership, Culture Change, and Academic Success* (Baltimore: Johns Hopkins University Press, 2019).

33 Cathy N. Davidson, *The New Education: How to Revolutionize the University to Prepare Students for a World in Flux* (New York: Basic Books, 2017), 230.

34 "Office of Applied Innovation," Arizona State University, Office of Applied Innovation, accessed May 29, 2021, https://appliedinnovation.asu.edu/.

35 Anusha Natarajan, "ASU Partners with 37 Organizations to Support Higher Education Goals," *State Press,* March 29, 2021, 8:34 p.m. MST, accessed May 29, 2021, www.statepress.com/article/2021/03/spcommunity-asu-joins-community-taskforce.

36 Emma Greguska, "New ASU Student Engagement Initiative Hopes for a Better Tomorrow," *ASU News,* February 23, 2021, accessed May 29, 2021, https://news.asu.edu/20210223-solutions-new-asu-student-engagement-initiative-hopes-better-tomorrow.

37 "Student Design Studio," Arizona State University, Office of Applied Innovation, accessed May 29, 2021, https://appliedinnovation.asu.edu/?q=student-design-studio.

38 Emma Greguska, "ASU Ranked No. 1 in Innovation for the 6th Year by US News and World Report," *ASU News,* September 13, 2020, accessed May 20, 2021, https://news.asu.edu/20200913-asu-news-us-news-world-report-no-1-innovation-sixth-year.

39 "Full-Time Faculty in Degree-Granting Postsecondary Institutions, by Race/Ethnicity, Sex, and Academic Rank: Fall 2015, Fall 2017, and Fall 2018," table 315.20, National Center for Educational Statistics, accessed November 2, 2020, https://nces.ed.gov/programs/digest/d19/tables/dt19_315.20.asp.

40 Damani K. White-Lewis, "The Facade of Fit in Faculty Search Processes," *Journal of Higher Education* 91, no. 6 (2020): 834, 850–851, accessed May 19, 2021, doi.org/10.1080/00221546.2020.1775058.

41 See Damon A. Williams, Joseph B. Berger, and Shederick A. McClendon, *Toward a Model of Inclusive Excellence and Change in Postsecondary Institutions*

(Washington, DC: Association of American Colleges and Universities, 2005), accessed June 22, 2020, www.researchgate.net/publication/238500335 _Toward_a_Model_of_Inclusive_Excellence_and_Change_in_Post-Secondary _Institutions.

42 Derek Bok, *Higher Expectations: Can Colleges Teach Students What They Need to Know in the 21st Century?* (Princeton, NJ: Princeton University Press, 2020), 58.

43 Bok, *Higher Expectations*, 58.

44 Rosemaria Martinelli, Joselyn Zivin, and Laura Yaeger, *Understanding What Matters Most in the Higher Education Experience: The Perspective of Recent College Graduates* (Washington, DC: Huron Consulting Group, 2019), 2, accessed November 12, 2019, www.ecampusnews.com/files/2019/04 /Huron_Student_RecentGradReport_eCampusMedia.pdf.

45 Emma Whitford, "Tuition Discount Rates Reach New High," *Inside Higher Ed*, May 20, 2021, accessed May 29, 2021, www.insidehighered.com/news /2021/05/20/private-colleges-cut-539-tuition-sticker-price-freshmen-average.

46 Richard Fry and Anthony Cilluffo, "A Rising Share of Undergraduates Are from Poor Families, Especially at Less Selective Colleges," *Pew Research Center*, May 22, 2019, accessed July 17, 2019, www.pewsocialtrends.org /2019/05/22/a-rising-share-of-undergraduates-are-from-poor-families-especially- at-less-selective-colleges/.

47 Aseel El Zein et al., "Prevalence and Correlates of Food Insecurity among US College Students: A Multi-Institutional Study," abstract, *BMC Public Health* 19, no. 660 (2019): 1, accessed May 16, 2021, doi.org/10.1186/s12889–019- 6943-6.

48 Peter L. Hinrichs, "Trends in Expenditures by US Colleges and Universities, 1987–2013," *Economic Commentary, Federal Reserve Bank of Cleveland*, September 14, 2016, accessed April 23, 2019, www.clevelandfed.org/news room-and-events/publications/economic-commentary/2016-economic-com mentaries/ec-201610-trends-in-expenditures-by-us-colleges-and-universities .aspx.

References

Abelson, Jenn, Nicole Dungca, Meryl Kornfield, and Andrew Ba Tran. "At College Health Centers, Students Battle Misdiagnoses and Inaccessible Care." *Washington Post*, July 13, 2020. Accessed July 14, 2020. www .washingtonpost.com/investigations/2020/07/13/college-health-centers-prob lems/?arc404=true.

ABET. "At a Glance." Accessed February 19, 2021. www.abet.org/about-abet/at -a-glance/.

Abbott, Andrew. *Chaos of Disciplines*. Chicago: University of Chicago Press, 2001.

Achieving the Dream. "Holistic Student Supports." Accessed November 3, 2020. www.achievingthedream.org/services-supports/holistic-student-supports.

Holistic Student Supports Redesign: A Toolkit for Redesigning Advising and Student Services to Effectively Support Every Student, Version 3.0. Silver Spring, MD: Achieving the Dream, 2018. Accessed November 12, 2019. www.achievingthedream.org/sites/default/files/resources/atd_hss_redesign _toolkit_2018.pdf.

American Association of University Professors. "1940 Statement of Principles on Academic Freedom and Tenure with 1970 Interpretive Comments." In *Policy Documents and Reports*, 11th ed., 13–19. Baltimore: Johns Hopkins University Press, 2015.

"Data Snapshot: Contingent Faculty in US Higher Ed." October 11, 2018. Accessed August 13, 2019. www.aaup.org/news/data-snapshot-contingent -faculty-us-higher-ed#.YLhJWn1Kjb9.

"Shared Governance." Accessed March 4, 2021. www.aaup.org/our-programs/ shared-governance.

American College Health Association. "A Brief History of ACHA." Accessed March 18, 2021. www.acha.org/ACHA/About/History/Brief_History /ACHA/About/Brief_History.aspx.

American College Health Association – National College Health Assessment II: Reference Group Data Report – Fall 2018. Silver Spring, MD: American College Health Association, 2018. Accessed August 20, 2019. www.acha .org/documents/ncha/NCHA-II_Fall_2018_Reference_Group_Data_Report .pdf.

American College Health Association – National College Health Assessment II: Reference Group Data Report – Spring 2019. Silver Spring, MD: American

College Health Association, 2019. Accessed December 16, 2020. www.acha
.org/documents/ncha/NCHA-II_SPRING_2019_II_SPRING_2019_US_
REFERENCE_GROUP_DATA_REPORT.pdf.

*American College Health Association – National College Health Assessment II:
Reference Group Executive Summary – Fall 2018.* Silver Spring, MD:
American College Health Association, 2018. Accessed August 20, 2019.
www.acha.org/documents/ncha/NCHA-II_Fall_2018_Reference_Group
_Executive_Summary.pdf.

American College Personnel Association. "The History of ACPA." Accessed
March 8, 2021. www.myacpa.org/history.

"Who We Are." Accessed March 8, 2021. www.myacpa.org/who-we-are.

American Council on Education. *The Student Personnel Point of View.*
Washington, DC: American Council on Education, 1937.

American University. "Next: A Culture of Innovation." Accessed June 9, 2021.
www.american.edu/next/#agile.

American University, Office of Institutional Research and Assessment. *Academic
Data Reference Book 2020–2021,* 51st ed. Washington, DC: American
University, 2021. Accessed June 9, 2021. www.american.edu/provost/oira
/upload/2020-21-academic-data-reference-book.pdf.

Arizona State University, Office of Applied Innovation. "Office of Applied
Innovation." Accessed May 29, 2021. https://appliedinnovation.asu.edu/.

"Student Design Studio." Accessed May 29, 2021. https://appliedinnovation
.asu.edu/?q=student-design-studio.

Association on Higher Education and Disability. "Home Page." Accessed
November 4, 2019. www.ahead.org/home.

Astin, Alexander W. *Four Critical Years: Effects of College on Beliefs, Attitudes, and
Knowledge.* San Francisco: Jossey-Bass, 1977.

Astin, Alexander W., and Leticia Oseguera. "Pre-College and Institutional
Influences on Degree Attainment." In *College Student Retention: Formula
for Student Success,* 2nd ed., edited by Alan Seidman, 119–146. Lanham,
MD: Rowman & Littlefield Publishers, 2012.

Asurion. "Americans Check Their Phones 96 Times a Day." Press release,
November 21, 2019. Accessed June 5, 2020. www.asurion.com/about
/press-releases/americans-check-their-phones-96-times-a-day/.

Baldridge, J. Victor. *Power and Conflict in the University: Research in the Sociology
of Complex Organizations.* New York: John Wiley & Sons, 1971.

Bangert, Dave. "Purdue Reverses Cuts to African American, Women's Studies,
among Others, on Eve of Creating Diversity Task Force." *Lafayette Journal
& Courier,* last modified August 6, 2020, 3:22 p.m. EDT. Accessed October
19, 2020. www.jconline.com/story/news/2020/08/06/purdue-reverses-cuts
-african-american-womens-studies-among-others-eve-creating-diversity-task-
force/3307231001/.

Barbato, Carole A., Laura L. Davis, and Mark F. Seeman. *This We Know:
A Chronology of the Shootings at Kent State, May 1970.* Kent, OH: Kent
State University Press, 2012.

Bariso, Justin. "How a Family-Owned Supermarket Chain Became One of the Best Places to Work in America." *Inc.*, March 13, 2017. Accessed May 14, 2020. www.inc.com/justin-bariso/how-a-family-owned-supermarket-chain -became-one-of-the-best-places-to-work-in-am.html.

Barton, Dorothy. "Edwin Emery Slosson: A Chemist of the West." *Journal of Chemical Education* 19, no. 1 (January 1942): 17–20. Accessed July 12, 2019. doi.org/10.1021/ed019p17.

Bashaw, Carolyn Terry. *"Stalwart Women": A Historical Analysis of Deans of Women in the South.* New York: Teachers College Press, 1999.

Bauer-Wolf, Jeremy. "2 Decades of Abuse, 177 Victims, No Action." *Inside Higher Ed*, May 20, 2019. Accessed March 24, 2020. www.insidehighered .com/news/2019/05/20/former-ohio-state-doctor-abused-nearly-200-young-men-no-consequences-decades.

Bean, John P., and Shevawn Bogdan Eaton. "A Psychological Model of College Student Retention." In *Reworking the Student Departure Puzzle*, edited by John M. Braxton, 48–61. Nashville, TN: Vanderbilt University Press, 2000.

Bergmann, Emery. "My College Transition." October 13, 2017. Accessed May 10, 2019. www.youtube.com/watch?v=oAUcoadqRlE&ab_channel =EmeryBergmann.

Berman, Bruce, Brenda Lee, Kaitlyn Ferguson, et al. *Report of Independent Investigation: Allegations of Sexual Misconduct against Robert E. Anderson.* Washington, DC: Wilmer Cutler Pickering Hale and Dorr LLP, 2021. Accessed May 12, 2021. https://regents.umich.edu/files/meetings/01-01 /WH_Anderson_Report.pdf.

Bill & Melinda Gates Foundation. "Postsecondary Success." Accessed May 20, 2021. www.gatesfoundation.org/our-work/programs/us-program/postsecondary -success.

Birnbaum, Robert. *How Colleges Work: The Cybernetics of Academic Organization and Leadership.* San Francisco: Jossey-Bass, 1988.

Blinder, Alan. "University of Michigan will Pay $490 Million to Settle Abuse Cases," *The New York Times*, January 19, 2022, updated January 20, 2022, accessed January 25, 2022, www.nytimes.com/2022/01/19/sports/ncaafoot ball/michigan-abuse-settlement-robert-anderson.html.

Bohrer, Jeff. "New Ways of Documenting Student Success: Comprehensive Learner Records." *EvoLLLution*, February 24, 2021. Accessed May 17, 2021. https://evolllution.com/programming/applied-and-experiential-learning /new-ways-of-documenting-student-success-comprehensive-learner-records/.

Bok, Derek. *Higher Expectations: Can Colleges Teach Students What They Need to Know in the 21st Century?* Princeton, NJ: Princeton University Press, 2020.

Bowen, William G., and Eugene M. Tobin. *Locus of Authority: The Evolution of Faculty Roles in the Governance of Higher Education.* Princeton, NJ: Princeton University Press, 2015.

Burke, Lilah. "University of Akron to Cut 6 Colleges." *Inside Higher Ed*, May 6, 2020. Accessed September 15, 2020. www.insidehighered.com/quicktakes /2020/05/06/university-akron-cut-6-colleges.

Burke, Michelle, Amelia Parnell, Alexis Wesaw, and Kevin Kruger. *Predictive Analysis of Student Data: A Focus on Engagement and Behavior.* Washington, DC: NASPA: Student Affairs Administrators in Higher Education, 2017. www.naspa.org/images/uploads/main/PREDICTIVE_FULL_4-7-17 _DOWNLOAD.pdf

Burnette, Angela, and Julia Dempewolf. "Clarity Instead of Confusion; Available Solutions under the HIPAA Privacy Rule and FERPA to Prevent Student Violence." *Health Care Law Monthly* 2014, no. 3 (March 2014): 2–13. Accessed June 6, 2021. www.alston.com/-/media/files/insights/publications /2014/04/clarity-instead-of-confusion-available-solutions-u/files/march2014 _health-care-law-monthly-article/fileattachment/march2014_health-care-law -monthly-article.pdf

Carter, Laura Stephenson. "Cold Comfort." *Dartmouth Medicine*, Winter 2006. Accessed May 11, 2020. https://dartmed.dartmouth.edu/winter06/html/cold _comfort.php.

Case Management Society of America. "What Is a Case Manager?" Accessed May 20, 2021. https://cmsa.org/who-we-are/what-is-a-case-manager/.

Center for Collegiate Mental Health. *2015 Annual Report.* January 2016. 2. Accessed April 24, 2019. http://sites.psu.edu/ccmh/files/2017/10/2015 _CCMH_Report_1–18-2015-yq3vik.pdf.

Centers for Disease Control and Prevention. "1918 Pandemic (H1N1 Virus)." Last modified March 20, 2019. Accessed May 11, 2020. www.cdc.gov/flu /pandemic-resources/1918-pandemic-h1n1.html.

Certis, Hannah. "The Emergence of Esther Lloyd-Jones." *Journal of Student Affairs Research and Practice* 51, no. 3 (2014): 259–269. Accessed March 11, 2021. doi.org/10.1515/jsarp-2014-0027.

Chambliss, Daniel F., and Christopher G. Takacs. *How College Works.* Cambridge, MA: Harvard University Press, 2014.

Chen, Renee Rui, Carol Xiaojuan Ou, Wei Wang, Zhuo Peng, and Robert M. Davison. "Moving Beyond the Direct Impact of Using CRM Systems on Frontline Employees' Service Performance: The Mediating Role of Adaptive Behaviour," *Information Systems Journal* 30, no. 3 (May 2020): 458–491. Accessed March 29, 2021. doi.org/10.1111/isj.12265.

Christensen, Clayton M., and Henry J. Eyring. *The Innovative University: Changing the DNA of Higher Education from the Inside Out.* San Francisco: Jossey-Bass, 2011.

Civitas Learning. "Measuring Supplemental Instruction Direct Impact on Persistence." Accessed December 2, 2019. https://media.civitaslearning .com/wp-content/uploads/sites/3/2020/02/Civitas_Learning_University_ Missouri_Kansas_City_CASE_STUDY_Impact.pdf?_ga=2.248917319.1 528597137.1586787617-1303241950.1580755375.

"One Quarter of Current College Students Believe It Will Be Difficult to Graduate; Cite Anxiety, Non-academic Responsibilities as Top Barriers to Completion." Press release, July 12, 2018. Accessed April 23, 2019. www .civitaslearning.com/press/one-quarter-of-current-college-students-believe-it-will-be-difficult-to-graduate-cite-anxiety-non-academic-responsibilities-as-top-barriers-to-completion/.

Cleveland Clinic. *2019 Year-End Facts + Figures.* December 2019. Accessed April 6, 2020. https://my.clevelandclinic.org/-/scassets/files/org/about/who-we-are/cleveland-clinic-facts-and-figures-2019.ashx?la=en.

Cohen, Michael D., James G. March, and Johan P. Olsen. "A Garbage Can Model of Organizational Choice." *Administrative Science Quarterly* 17, no. 1 (March 1972): 1–25.

Coley, Chrissy, Tim Coley, and Katie Lynch-Holmes. *Retention and Student Success: Implementing Strategies That Make a Difference.* Fairfax, VA: Ellucian, 2016. www.ellucian.com/assets/en/white-paper/whitepaper-retention-and-student-success.pdf.

Cornell University, Office of the Provost. "University-Wide Active Learning Initiative." Accessed November 3, 2020. https://provost.cornell.edu/leadership/vp-academic-innovation/active-learning-initiative/.

Cosgrove, Toby. *The Cleveland Clinic Way: Lessons in Excellence from One of the World's Leading Health Care Organizations.* New York: McGraw-Hill Education, 2014.

Cox, Geoffrey M. *Theorizing the Resilience of American Higher Education: How Colleges and Universities Adapt to Changing Social and Economic Conditions.* New York: Routledge, 2019.

Crist, Carolyn. "Mental Health Diagnoses Rising among US College Students." *Reuters*, November 1, 2018, 2:33 p.m. Accessed October 21, 2020. www.reuters.com/article/us-health-mental-college/mental-health-diagnoses-rising-among-u-s-college-students-idUSKCN1N65U8.

Curti, Merle, Richard H. Shryock, Thomas C. Cochran, and Fred Harvey Harrington. *An American History.* New York: Harper & Brothers, 1950.

Davidson, Cathy N. *The New Education: How to Revolutionize the University to Prepare Students for a World in Flux.* New York: Basic Books, 2017.

Delgado, Richard, and Jean Stefancic. *Critical Race Theory: An Introduction.* New York: New York University Press, 2001. Accessed October 12, 2020. https://uniteyouthdublin.files.wordpress.com/2015/01/richard_delgado_jean_stefancic_critical_race_thbookfi-org-1.pdf.

Deloitte. *Global Mobile Consumer Survey, US Edition.* 2018. Accessed October 30, 2019. www2.deloitte.com/content/dam/Deloitte/us/Documents/technology-media-telecommunications/us-tmt-global-mobile-consumer-survey-extended-deck-2018.pdf.

Dilley, Patrick. "20th Century Postsecondary Practices and Policies to Control Gay Students." *Review of Higher Education* 25, no. 4 (Summer 2002): 409–431. Accessed March 18, 2021. doi.org/10.1353/rhe.2002.0018.

DiMaggio, Paul J., and Walter W. Powell. "The Iron Cage Revisited: Institutional Isomorphism and Collective Rationality in Organizational Fields." *American Sociological Review* 48, no. 2 (April 1983): 147–160.

Dolan, Kerry A. "Forbes' 35th Annual World's Billionaires List: Facts and Figures 2021." *Forbes*, April 6, 2021, 6:00 a.m. EDT. Accessed April 8,

2021. www.forbes.com/sites/kerryadolan/2021/04/06/forbes-35th-annual -worlds-billionaires-list-facts-and-figures-2021/?sh=6cdc6bad5e58.

EAB. "EAB Helps You Support and Graduate More Students." Accessed May 20, 2021. https://eab.com/colleges-and-universities/student-success/.

Eisenberg, Daniel, and Sarah Ketchen Lipson. *The Healthy Minds Study: 2018–2019 Data Report.* Ann Arbor, MI: Healthy Minds Network, 2019. Accessed March 19, 2021. https://healthymindsnetwork.org/wp-content /uploads/2019/09/HMS_national-2018-19.pdf.

El Zein, Aseel, Karla P. Shelnutt, Sarah Colby, Melissa J. Vilaro, Wenjun Zhou, Geoffrey Greene, Melissa D. Olfert, Kristin Riggsbee, Jesse Stabile Morrell, and Anne E. Mathews. "Prevalence and Correlates of Food Insecurity among US College Students: A Multi-institutional Study." Abstract. *BMC Public Health* 19, no. 660 (2019): 1–12. Accessed May 16, 2021. doi.org/10.1186/ s12889-019-6943-6.

Ellis, Lindsay. "Thought Control: When Politicians Probe Teaching." *Chronicle of Higher Education*, March 5, 2021.

Euben, Donna R. "Termination & Discipline (2004)." Presentation at the 14th Annual Legal Issues in Higher Education Conference, University of Vermont, Burlington, VT, October 24, 2004, 4–6. Accessed May 14, 2021. www.aaup.org/file/Termination_Discipline_2004.pdf.

Felten, Peter, *Relationship-Rich Education: How Human Connections Drive Success in College.* Baltimore: Johns Hopkins University Press, 2020.

Felten, Peter, John N. Gardner, Charles C. Schroeder, Leo M. Lambert, and Betsy O. Barefoot. *The Undergraduate Experience: Focusing Institutions on What Matters Most.* San Francisco: Jossey-Bass, 2016.

Felten, Peter, and Leo M. Lambert. *The Importance of Mentors and Peers in the Undergraduate Experience: Survey of College Graduates.* Elon, NC: Elon University, 2018. Accessed November 12, 2019. www.elon.edu/u/elon -poll/wp-content/uploads/sites/819/2019/02/Elon-Poll-Report-082218.pdf.

Flaherty, Colleen. "Tracking Attacks on Scholars' Speech." *Inside Higher Ed,* August 31, 2021. Accessed September 24, 2021. www.insidehighered.com /news/2021/08/31/fire-launches-new-database-tracking-attacks-speech.

Flexner, Abraham. "The Usefulness of Useless Knowledge." *Harper's Magazine,* June/November 1939, 544.

Foster, Carly, and Peter Francis. "A Systematic Review on the Deployment and Effectiveness of Data Analytics in Higher Education to Improve Student Outcomes." *Assessment & Evaluation in Higher Education* 45, no. 6 (2020): 822–841. Accessed June 2, 2021. doi.org/10.1080/02602938.2019.1696945.

FoundSF. "Patient No More: 1977 Occupation of Federal Offices in San Francisco." Accessed May 7, 2021. www.foundsf.org/index.php?title =Patient_No_More:_1977_Occupation_of_Federal_Offices_in_San_Francisco.

Freeland, Richard M. *Academia's Golden Age: Universities in Massachusetts, 1945–1970.* New York: Oxford University Press, 1992.

Transforming the Urban University: Northeastern, 1996–2006. Philadelphia: University of Pennsylvania Press, 2019.

Frumkin, Peter, and Joseph Galaskiewicz. "Institutional Isomorphism and Public Sector Organizations." *Journal of Public Administration Research and Theory* 14, no. 3 (July 2004): 283–307.

Fry, Richard, and Anthony Cilluffo. "A Rising Share of Undergraduates Are from Poor Families, Especially at Less Selective Colleges." *Pew Research Center*, May 22, 2019. Accessed July 17, 2019. www.pewsocialtrends.org/2019/05 /22/a-rising-share-of-undergraduates-are-from-poor-families-especially-at-less-selective-colleges/.

Gable, Rachel. *The Hidden Curriculum: First Generation Students at Legacy Universities*. Princeton, NJ: Princeton University Press, 2021.

Gagliardi, Jonathan S. "The Analytics Revolution in Higher Education." In *The Analytics Revolution in Higher Education: Big Data, Organizational Learning, and Student Success*, edited by Jonathan S. Gagliardi, Amelia Parnell, and Julia Carpenter-Hubin, 1–14. Sterling, VA: Stylus, 2018.

Gale. *Research Centers Directory*, 50th ed. Farmington Hills, MI: Gale Research, 2021. Accessed April 29, 2021. www.cengage.com/search/productOverview .do?N=197+4294904996&Ntk=P_EPI&Ntt=10090591251987922422201811092045537 58&Ntx=mode%2Bmatchallpartial.

Gallagher, Chris W. *College Made Whole: Integrative Learning for a Divided World*. Baltimore: Johns Hopkins University Press, 2019.

Gangone, Lynn M. "The National Association for Women in Education: An Enduring Legacy." *NASPA Journal about Women in Higher Education* 1, no. 1 (2009): 3–24. Accessed June 5, 2021. https://doi-org.proxyau.wrlc.org/10 .2202/1940-7890.1002.

Geiger, Roger L. *To Advance Knowledge: The Growth of American Research Universities, 1900–1940*. New York: Routledge, 2017. Accessed April 14, 2021. https://books.google.com/books?id=0803DwAAQBAJ&source=gbs _book_other_versions.

———. *American Higher Education since World War II: A History*. Princeton, NJ: Princeton University Press, 2019.

Georgia State University. "Reduction of Summer Melt." Accessed April 30, 2021. https://success.gsu.edu/initiatives/reduction-of-summer-melt/.

Gerber, Larry G. *The Rise and Decline of Faculty Governance: Professionalization and the Modern American University*. Baltimore: Johns Hopkins University Press, 2014.

Gerda, Janice Joyce. "A History of the Conferences of Deans of Women, 1903–1922." PhD diss., Bowling Green State University, 2004. Accessed January 13, 2020. http://rave.ohiolink.edu/etdc/view?acc_num=bgsu1100290629.

Girchenko, Tetiana, Yana Ovsiannikova, and Liudmyla Girchenko. "CRM System as a Keystone of Successful Business Activity." In *Knowledge, Economy, Society: Management in the Face of Contemporary Challenges and Dilemmas*, edited by Andrzej Jaki and Bogusz Mikuła, 251–261. Cracow: Foundation of the Cracow University of Economics, 2017. Accessed March 18, 2021. https://cfm.uek.krakow.pl/media/files/36/ff/MANAGEMENT _%20CFM%202017.pdf.

Godwin, Glen J. and William T. Markham. "First Encounters of the Bureaucratic Kind: Early Freshman Experiences with a Campus Bureaucracy." *Journal of Higher Education* 67, no. 6 (November–December 1996): 660–691. Accessed October 7, 2020. doi.org/10.2307/2943816.

Goodloe, Abbe Carter. "Undergraduate Life at Wellesley." In *Portraits of the American University, 1890–1910*, edited by James C. Stone and Donald P. DeNevi, 311–334. San Francisco: Jossey-Bass, 1971.

Graham, Hugh Davis, and Nancy Diamond. *The Rise of American Research Universities: Elites and Challengers in the Postwar Era.* Baltimore: Johns Hopkins University Press, 1997.

Graham, Patricia Albjerg. "Expansion and Exclusion: A History of Women in American Higher Education." *Signs* 3, no. 4 (Summer 1978): 759–773. Accessed May 3, 2021. www.jstor.org/stable/3173112.

Greenberg, Alan D. *Learning Relationship Management: Ending the Expectation of Average While Getting Back to Basics.* Duxbury, MA: Wainhouse Research, 2016.

Greguska, Emma. "ASU Ranked No. 1 in Innovation for the 6th Year by US News and World Report." *ASU News*, September 13, 2020. Accessed May 20, 2021. https://news.asu.edu/20200913-asu-news-us-news-world-report-no-1-innovation-sixth-year.

"New ASU Student Engagement Initiative Hopes for a Better Tomorrow." *ASU News*, February 23, 2021. Accessed May 29, 2021. https://news.asu.edu/20210223-solutions-new-asu-student-engagement-initiative-hopes-better-tomorrow.

Groves, Robert. "Student-Centered." *The Provost's Blog*, March 15, 2017. Accessed April 23, 2019. https://blog.provost.georgetown.edu/student-centered/.

Gumbel, Andrew. *Won't Lose This Dream: How an Upstart University Rewrote the Rules of a Broken System.* New York: The New Press, 2020.

Halkias, Maria. "A One-of-A-Kind, No Checkout Sam's Club Is About to Open on Lower Greenville in Dallas." *Dallas Morning News*, October 28, 2018, 11:00 p.m. CDT. Accessed April 23, 2019. www.dallasnews.com/business/retail/2018/10/29/a-one-of-a-kind-no-checkout-sam-s-club-is-about-to-open-on-lower-greenville-in-dallas/.

Hammer, Michael, and James Champy. *Reengineering the Corporation: A Manifesto for Business Revolution.* New York: HarperBusiness, 1993.

Hanks, Megan. "UMBC Leads Nation in Producing African-American Undergraduates Who Pursue MD-PhDs." *UMBC News*, January 2, 2018. Accessed August 22, 2019. https://news.umbc.edu/umbc-leads-nation-in-producing-african-american-undergraduates-who-pursue-m-d-ph-d-s/.

Harvard Crimson. "1919 Record-Breaking Year for American Colleges." December 6, 1919. Accessed May 11, 2020. www.thecrimson.com/article/1919/12/6/1919-record-breaking-year-for-american-colleges/.

Hedegaard, Holly, Sally Curtin, and Margaret Warner. *Suicide Rates in the United States Continue to Increase.* NCHS Data Brief no. 309. Hyattsville, MD:

National Center for Health Statistics, 2018. Accessed July 31, 2019. www
.cdc.gov/nchs/products/databriefs/db309.htm.

Hefling, Kimberly. "The 'Moneyball' Solution for Higher Education." *Politico*,
January 16, 2019, 5:04 a.m. EST. Accessed June 17, 2020. www.politico
.com/agenda/story/2019/01/16/tracking-student-data-graduation-000868/.

Hendrickson, Robert M., Jason E. Lane, James T. Harris, and Richard H.
Dorman. *Academic Leadership and Governance of Higher Education:
A Guide for Trustees, Leaders, and Aspiring Leaders of Two- and Four-Year
Institutions*. Sterling, VA: Stylus, 2013.

Henretta, James A., Eric Hinderaker, Robert O. Self, and Rebecca Edwards. *America:
A Concise History, Vol. 2: Since 1865*. 6th ed. Boston: Bedford/St. Martin's, 2015.

Hevel, Michael S. "Toward a History of Student Affairs: A Synthesis of Research,
1996–2015." *Journal of College Student Development* 57, no. 7 (October
2016): 844–862. Accessed June 5, 2021. doi.org/10.1353/csd.2016.0082.

Hinrichs, Peter L. "Trends in Expenditures by US Colleges and Universities,
1987–2013." *Economic Commentary, Federal Reserve Bank of Cleveland*,
September 14, 2016. Accessed April 23, 2019. www.clevelandfed.org/en
/newsroom-and-events/publications/economic-commentary/2016-economic-com
mentaries/ec-201610-trends-in-expenditures-by-us-colleges-and-universities.aspx.

Hirt, Suzanne. "'Shame and Blame': Are College COVID-19 Cases the
Fault of Campuses Full of Reckless Partiers? Experts, Students Say No."
Augusta Chronicle, August 31, 2020, 10:12 a.m. EDT. Accessed September
4, 2020. www.augustachronicle.com/story/news/2020/08/31/shame-and
-blame-are-college-covid-19-cases-fault-of-campuses-full-of-reckless-partiers
-experts-stude/114786366/.

History.com Editors. "Kerner Commission Report Released." History.com.
Accessed June 12, 2020. www.history.com/this-day-in-history/kerner-com
mission-report-released.

Hrabowski III, Freeman A. With Philip J. Rous and Peter H. Henderson. *The
Empowered University: Shared Leadership, Culture Change, and Academic
Success*. Baltimore: Johns Hopkins University Press, 2019.

Hussar, Bill, Jijun Zhang, Sarah Hein, Ke Wang, Ashley Roberts, Jiashan Cui,
Mary Smith, Farrah Bullock Mann, Amy Barmer, and Rita Dilig.
"Characteristics of Postsecondary Faculty." In *The Condition of Education
2020*, 150–153. Washington, DC: National Center for Education Statistics,
2020. Accessed June 2, 2021. https://nces.ed.gov/pubs2020/2020144.pdf.

Iansiti, Marco, and Karim R. Lakhani. "The Truth about Blockchain." *Harvard
Business Review*, January–February 2017. Accessed March 29, 2021. https://
hbr.org/2017/01/the-truth-about-blockchain.

Ikenberry, Stanley O., and Renee C. Friedman. *Beyond Academic Departments:
The Story of Institutes and Centers*. San Francisco: Jossey-Bass, 1972.

Irby, Kara. "FSU Fully Launches Student Resilience Project." *Florida State
University News*, September 28, 2018, 3:00 p.m. EDT. Accessed May 20,
2021. https://news.fsu.edu/news/university-news/2018/09/28/fsu-fully
-launches-student-resilience-project-2/.

Ithaka S+R. "Student Success." Accessed May 20, 2021. https://sr.ithaka.org/our-work/student-success/.

Jack, Anthony Abraham. *The Privileged Poor: How Elite Colleges Are Failing Disadvantaged Students*. Cambridge, MA: Harvard University Press, 2019.

Jacobs, Jerry A. *In Defense of Disciplines: Interdisciplinarity and Specialization in the Research University*. Chicago: University of Chicago Press, 2013.

Johnson, Mathew B. "Social Class and Cultural (Re)production in Higher Education: An Ethnographic Look at the Culture of Student Affairs Offices." PhD diss., Brandeis University, 2002. Accessed April 4, 2021. https://search.proquest.com/docview/305343824?pq-origsite=primo.

Johnston, Susan Whealler. "Sharing Governance." *Trusteeship*, Summer 2018.

Kelderman, Eric. "Iowa Ideologues: Tenure under Siege." *Chronicle of Higher Education*, March 5, 2021.

Kendall, Nancy, Denise Goerisch, Esther C. Kim, Franklin Vernon, and Matthew Wolfgram. "The True Costs of Student Fees." In *The True Costs of College*, 91–122. Cham, Switzerland: Palgrave Macmillan, 2020.

Kirp, David. *The College Dropout Scandal*. New York: Oxford University Press, 2019.

Klein, Arthur Jay. *Survey of Land-Grant Colleges and Universities*. Vol. 1. Washington, DC: United States Government Printing Office, 1930.

Kraft, David P. "One Hundred Years of College Mental Health." *Journal of American College Health* 59, no. 6 (June 2011): 477–481. Accessed March 18, 2021. doi.org/10.1080/07448481.2011.569964.

Kresge Foundation. "Our Strategies: We Invest in These Focus Areas." Accessed December 1, 2021. https://kresge.org/our-work/education/#our-strategies.

Kuh, George D. *High-Impact Educational Practices: What They Are, Who Has Access to Them, and Why They Matter*. Washington, DC: Association of American Colleges and Universities, 2008.

Kuh, George D., Jillian Kinzie, Jennifer A. Buckley, Brian K. Bridges, and John C. Hayek. *What Matters to Student Success: A Review of the Literature; Commissioned Report for the National Symposium on Postsecondary Student Success: Spearheading a Dialog on Student Success*. Washington, DC: National Postsecondary Education Cooperative, 2006. https://nces.ed.gov/npec/pdf/Kuh_Team_Report.pdf.

Lederman, Doug. "COVID-19's Forceful Financial Hit: A Survey of Business Officers." *Inside Higher Ed*, July 10, 2020. Accessed September 4, 2020. www.insidehighered.com/news/survey/covid-19s-forceful-financial-hit-survey-business-officers.

"Pandemic-Fueled Confidence for College Presidents." *Inside Higher Ed*, March 22, 2021. Accessed April 8, 2021. www.insidehighered.com/news/survey/survey-shows-college-presidents-emerging-covid-19-more-confident-their-institutions-can.

Lee, Phillip. "The Curious Life of In Loco Parentis at American Universities." *Higher Education in Review* 8 (Spring 2011): 65–90. Accessed May 3, 2021. https://papers.ssrn.com/sol3/papers.cfm?abstract_id=1967912.

LeViness, Peter, Carolyn Bershad, Kim Gorman, Lynn Braun, and Trish Murray. *The Association for University and College Counseling Center Directors Annual Survey 2018*. Indianapolis: Association for University and College Counseling Center Directors, 2019. Accessed March 18, 2021. www.aucccd.org/assets/documents/Survey/2018%20aucccd%20survey-public-revised.pdf.

Lipson, Sarah Ketchen, Amber Talaski, Nina Cesare, Marjorie Malpiede, and Dana Humphrey. *The Role of Faculty in Student Mental Health*. Boston: Boston University, Mary Christie Foundation, and Healthy Minds Network, 2021. Accessed May 29, 2021. https://marychristieinstitute.org/wp-content/uploads/2021/04/The-Role-of-Faculty-in-Student-Mental-Health.pdf.

Lipson, Sarah Ketchen, Julia Raifman, Sara Abelson, and Sari L. Reisner. "Gender Minority Mental Health in the US: Results of a National Survey of College Campuses." *American Journal of Preventive Medicine* 57, no. 3 (September 2019): 293–301.

Lombardi, John V. *How Universities Work*. Baltimore: Johns Hopkins University Press, 2013.

Lorenzetti, Jennifer Patterson. "The Power of Predictive Analytics for Student Retention." *Academic Briefing*, June 14, 2017. www.academicbriefing.com/marketing/retention/analytics-student-retention/.

Lumina Foundation. "Areas of Work." Accessed December 1, 2021. www.luminafoundation.org/our-work/areas-of-focus/.

MacPhee, John. "Promoting Student Mental Health in Difficult Days." *Inside Higher Ed*, May 29, 2020. Accessed May 29, 2020. www.insidehighered.com/views/2020/05/29/advice-promoting-student-mental-health-during-pandemic-opinion.

MacTaggart, Terrence. "Nontraditional Presidents: A New Wave of Enterprise Leadership." *Trusteeship*, Summer 2018, 12.

Madaus, Joseph W. "The History of Disability Services in Higher Education." *New Directions for Higher Education* 2011, no. 154 (Summer 2011): 5–15.

Maese, Rick. "Ohio State Team Doctor Sexually Abused 177 Students over Decades, Report Finds." *Washington Post*, May 17, 2019, 7:27 p.m. EDT. Accessed March 24, 2020. www.washingtonpost.com/sports/2019/05/17/ohio-state-team-doctor-sexually-abused-students-over-decades-report-finds/.

Maloney, Edward J., and Joshua Kim. "15 Fall Scenarios." *Inside Higher Ed*, April 22, 2020. Accessed May 29, 2020. www.insidehighered.com/digital-learning/blogs/learning-innovation/15-fall-scenarios.

Marcinkevage, Carrie Hancock. "Critical Success Factors of Constituent Relationship Management (CRM) Strategy in a Higher Education Institution." PhD diss., Pennsylvania State University, 2020. Accessed March 28, 2021. https://etda.libraries.psu.edu/files/final_submissions/20995.

Marterer, Aaron Charles. "Enterprise Resource Planning in Higher Education: A Comparative Case Study." PhD diss., University of North Florida, 2008. Accessed March 25, 2021. https://digitalcommons.unf.edu/etd/360/.

Martin, James, and James E. Samels. "First among Equals: The Current Roles of the Chief Academic Officer." In *First among Equals: The Role of the Chief Academic Officer*, edited by James Martin and James E. Samels, 3–20. Baltimore: Johns Hopkins University Press, 1997.

Martinelli, Rosemaria, Joselyn Zivin, and Laura Yaeger. *Understanding What Matters Most in the Higher Education Experience: The Perspective of Recent College Graduates.* Washington, DC: Huron Consulting Group, 2019. Accessed November 12, 2019. www.ecampusnews.com/files/2019/04/Huron_Student_RecentGradReport_eCampusMedia.pdf.

Mayhew, Matthew J., Alyssa N. Rockenbach, Nicholas A. Bowman, Tricia A. Seifert, and Gregory C. Wolniak. With Ernest T. Pascarella and Patrick T. Terenzini. *How College Affects Students, Vol. 3: 21st Century Evidence That Higher Education Works.* San Francisco: Jossey-Bass, 2016.

McBride, David R., Sarah Van Orman, Chris Wera, and Victor Leino. *ACHA Benchmarking Committee Report: 2010 Survey on the Utilization of Student Health Services.* Silver Spring, MD: American College Health Association, 2010. Accessed March 19, 2021. www.acha.org/documents/resources/survey_data/benchmarking/ACHA_Benchmarking_Report_2010_Utilization_Survey.pdf.

McCallion, Gail. *History of the Clery Act: Fact Sheet.* Washington, DC: Congressional Research Service, 2014. Accessed March 24, 2021. https://crsreports.congress.gov/product/pdf/R/R43759.

McCoy, Dorian L., and Dirk J. Rodricks. "Critical Race Theory in Higher Education: 20 Years of Theoretical and Research Innovations." *ASHE Higher Education Report* 41, no. 3 (April 2015): 1–117.

Merlino, James. *Service Fanatics: How to Build Superior Patient Experience the Cleveland Clinic Way.* New York: McGraw-Hill Education, 2015.

Merlino, James I., and Ananth Raman. "Health Care's Service Fanatics." *Harvard Business Review*, May 2013.

Mintzberg, Henry. "The Adhocracy." In *The Structuring of Organizations: A Synthesis of the Research*, 431–467. Englewood Cliffs, NJ: Prentice-Hall, 1979.

Mitchell, Brian C., and W. Joseph King. *How to Run a College: A Practical Guide for Trustees, Faculty, Administrators, and Policymakers.* Baltimore: Johns Hopkins University Press, 2018.

Mitchell, Ted, and Suzanne Ortega. "Mental Health Challenges Require Urgent Response." *Inside Higher Ed*, October 29, 2019. Accessed October 30, 2019. www.insidehighered.com/views/2019/10/29/students-mental-health-shouldnt-be-responsibility-campus-counseling-centers-alone.

MLK Day Committee. "Diversity in Student Life." In *Michigan's Story: The History of Race at U-M.* Digitized library exhibit, Ann Arbor: University of Michigan Library, 2018. Accessed June 12, 2020. www.lib.umich.edu/online-exhibits/exhibits/show/history-of-race-at-um/diversity-in-student-life/activism.

Mommsen, Wolfgang J. "Max Weber in America." *American Scholar* 69, no. 3 (Summer 2000): 103–109. Accessed April 24, 2021. www.jstor.org/stable/41213044.

Munro Prescott, Heather. "Student Bodies, Past and Present." *Journal of American College Health* 59, no. 6 (2011): 464–469.

Murphy, Mary C., Maithreyi Gopalan, Evelyn R. Carter, Katherine T. U. Emerson, Bette L. Bottoms, and Gregory M. Walton. "A Customized Belonging Intervention Improves Retention of Socially Disadvantaged Students at a Broad-Access University." *Science Advances* 6, no. 29 (July 2020): 1–7. Accessed July 20, 2020. doi.org/10.1126/sciadv.aba4677.

NASPA: Student Affairs Administrators in Higher Education. "About NASPA." Accessed March 8, 2021. www.naspa.org/about.

"Graduate Program Directory." Accessed September 28, 2020. http://apps .naspa.org/gradprograms/srchres.cfm.

NASPA: Student Affairs Administrators in Higher Education and Entangled Solutions. *Accelerating the Growth of Institutional Success Services: Working Together to Scale and Sustain Integrated Advising and Holistic Student Support.* Working paper, NASPA: Student Affairs Administrators in Higher Education and Entangled Solutions, Washington, DC, 2019.

Natarajan, Anusha. "ASU Partners with 37 Organizations to Support Higher Education Goals." *State Press*, March 29, 2021, 8:34 p.m. MST. Accessed May 29, 2021. www.statepress.com/article/2021/03/spcommunity-asu -joins-community-taskforce.

National Association of College and University Business Officers. "Private Colleges Now Use Nearly Half of Tuition Revenue for Financial Aid." *Press release*, May 9, 2019. Accessed March 22, 2020. www.nacubo.org /Press-Releases/2019/Private-Colleges-Now-Use-Nearly-Half-of-Tuition- Revenue-For-Financial-Aid.

"Welcome to the NACUBO Product Center." Accessed May 10, 2019. https:// products.nacubo.org.

National Association of Student Affairs Professionals. "History." Accessed April 2, 2021. www.nasap.net/about/history/.

National Center for Education Statistics. *Factors That Influence Student College Choice.* November 2018. Accessed May 16, 2019. https://nces.ed.gov /pubs2019/2019119.pdf.

"Full-Time Faculty in Degree-Granting Postsecondary Institutions, by Race/ Ethnicity, Sex, and Academic Rank: Fall 2015, Fall 2017, and Fall 2018." Table 315.20. Accessed November 2, 2020. https://nces.ed.gov/programs /digest/d19/tables/dt19_315.20.asp.

"Graduation Rate from First Institution Attended for First-Time, Full-Time Bachelor's Degree-Seeking Students at 4-Year Postsecondary Institutions, by Race/Ethnicity, Time to Completion, Sex, Control of Institution, and Acceptance Rate: Selected Cohort Entry Years, 1996 through 2011." Table 326.10. Accessed January 21, 2020. https://nces.ed.gov/programs /digest/d18/tables/dt18_326.10.asp.

"Graduation Rate from First Institution Attended for First-Time, Full-Time Bachelor's Degree-Seeking Students at 4-Year Postsecondary Institutions, by Race/Ethnicity, Time to Completion, Sex, Control of Institution, and

Percentage of Applications Accepted: Selected Cohort Entry Years, 1996 through 2013." Table 326.10. Accessed April 11, 2021. https://nces.ed.gov /programs/digest/d20/tables/dt20_326.10.asp.

"List of 2018 Digest Tables." Tables 301.20, 302.10, 302.20, and 302.60. Accessed August 20, 2019. https://nces.ed.gov/programs/digest/2018menu _tables.asp.

"Number and Percentage Distribution of Students Enrolled in Postsecondary Institutions, by Level, Disability Status, and Selected Student Characteristics: 2003–04 and 2007–08." Table 240. Accessed April 7, 2021. https://nces.ed.gov/programs/digest/d10/tables/dt10_240.asp.

"Number and Percentage Distribution of Students Enrolled in Postsecondary Institutions, by Level, Disability Status, and Selected Student Characteristics: 2015–16." Table 311.10. Accessed April 7, 2021. https:// nces.ed.gov/programs/digest/d19/tables/dt19_311.10.asp.

"Protecting the Privacy of Student Education Records." Accessed May 6, 2019. https://nces.ed.gov/pubs97/web/97859.asp.

"Total Undergraduate Fall Enrollment in Degree-Granting Postsecondary Institutions, by Attendance Status, Sex of Student, and Control and Level of Institution: Selected Years, 1970 through 2028." Table 303.70. Accessed January 21, 2020. https://nces.ed.gov/programs/digest/d18/tables/dt18_303 .70.asp.

National Center for Science and Engineering Statistics, National Science Foundation. *Doctorate Recipients from US Universities: 2018: Data Tables and Resources*. Special report NSF 20-301. Alexandria, VA: National Center for Science and Engineering Statistics, National Science Foundation, 2019. Accessed March 5, 2020. https://ncses.nsf.gov/pubs/nsf20301/downloads.

National Survey of Student Engagement. "The LRCs of Advising: Listening, Respecting, and Caring." Accessed December 14, 2020. https://nsse .indiana.edu/research/annual-results/advising/index.html.

"The Relationship of Advising LRC with Intentions to Persist." Accessed December 14, 2020. https://nsse.indiana.edu/research/annual-results/advis ing/lrc-fy.html.

Netburn, Deborah. "Q&A: Google Claims 'Quantum Supremacy.' What Could That Mean for the Future of Computing?" *Los Angeles Times*, October 23, 2019, 6:47 p.m. PST. Accessed October 28, 2019. www.latimes.com/sci ence/story/2019-10-23/quantum-supremacy-google-computers.

Newnham, Nicole, and James LeBrecht, dirs. *Crip Camp: A Disability Revolution*. Los Angeles: Higher Ground Productions, 2020. www.netflix.com/title /81001496.

Nunn, Lisa M. *College Belonging: How First-Year and First-Generation Students Navigate Campus Life*. New Brunswick, NJ: Rutgers University Press, 2021.

Oberlin College & Conservatory. "Oberlin History." Accessed May 6, 2021. www.oberlin.edu/about-oberlin/oberlin-history.

Ohio History Central. "Antioch College." Accessed May 6, 2021. https:// ohiohistorycentral.org/w/Antioch_College.

Owen-Smith, Jason. *Research Universities and the Public Good: Discovery for an Uncertain Future*. Stanford, CA: Stanford Business Books, 2018.

Paley, Amit R. "The Secret Court of 1920." *Harvard Crimson*, November 21, 2002. Accessed April 3, 2021. www.thecrimson.com/article/2002/11/21/the-secret-court-of-1920-at/.

Parker, Patsy. "The Historical Role of Women in Higher Education." *Administrative Issues Journal* 5, no. 1 (Spring 2015): 3–14. Accessed May 3, 2021. doi.org/10.5929/2015.5.1.1.

Patel, Vimal. "Are Students Socially Connected? Check Their Dining-Hall-Swipe Data." *Chronicle of Higher Education*, April 26, 2019.

Patrizio, Andy. "IDC: Expect 175 Zettabytes of Data Worldwide by 2025." *Network World*, December 3, 2018, 2:30 a.m. PST. Accessed April 25, 2021. www.networkworld.com/article/3325397/idc-expect-175-zettabytes-of-data-worldwide-by-2025.html.

Pavey, Frank D., William Nelson Cromwell, and Philippe Bunau-Varilla. *The Story of Panama: Hearings on the Rainey Resolution before the Committee on Foreign Affairs of the House of Representatives*. Washington, DC: United States Government Printing Office, 1913. Accessed August 26, 2019. https://books.google.com/books?id=1IY-AAAAYAAJ.

Pew Research Center. "Mobile Fact Sheet." April 7, 2021. Accessed June 2, 2021. www.pewresearch.org/internet/fact-sheet/mobile/.

Pignolet, Jennifer. "University of Akron Trustees Vote to Eliminate 178 Positions; Faculty Yell 'Protect Our Students!'" *Akron Beacon Journal*, July 15, 2020, 2:44 p.m. EDT. Accessed October 30, 2020. www.beaconjournal.com/story/news/local/2020/07/15/university-of-akron-trustees-vote-to-eliminate-178-positions-faculty-yell-ldquoprotect-our-studentsr/113365458/.

Pomerantz, Jeffrey. "C-Level Reporting Lines." *EDUCAUSE Review*, April 5, 2018. Accessed April 25, 2021. https://er.educause.edu/blogs/2018/4/c-level-reporting-lines.

Powell, Cammille. "Bridging the Gaps: Connecting Student Services to Promote Student Success." *EdSurge*, April 4, 2018. Accessed August 22, 2019. www.edsurge.com/news/2018-04-04-bridging-the-gaps-connecting-student-services-to-promote-student-success.

Purdue Student Government. *PSG COVID-19 Student Survey Report*. July 1, 2020. Accessed September 4, 2020. https://static1.squarespace.com/static/5980ddo5d482e9f36b9d9160/t/5efdb3140227f53a11f1fo1c/1593684758580/PSG+COVID-19+Student+Survey+Report.pdf.

Radesky, Jenny, and Randy Kulman. "My Kids Are on Screens All Day: Is That Okay?" *ADDitude Magazine*, last modified January 21, 2022. Accessed June 5, 2020. www.additudemag.com/screen-time-limits-during-pandemic/.

Ramanathan, Kumaresan. "QC101: Quantum Computing & Quantum Physics for Beginners." *Udemy* (website). Accessed October 28, 2019. www.udemy.com/course/qc101-introduction-to-quantum-computing-quantum-physics-for-beginners/.

Reich, Justin. "Ed-Tech Mania Is Back." *Chronicle of Higher Education.* September 14, 2020. www.chronicle.com/article/ed-tech-mania-is-back.

Renick, Timothy M. "How to Best Harness Student-Success Technology." *Chronicle of Higher Education,* July 1, 2018. www.chronicle.com/article /how-to-best-harness-student-success-technology/.

"Predictive Analytics, Academic Advising, Early Alerts, and Student Success." In *Big Data on Campus: Data Analytics and Decision Making in Higher Education,* edited by Karen L. Webber and Henry Y. Zheng, 177–197. Baltimore: Johns Hopkins University Press, 2020.

Riley, Matilda White, Robert L. Kahn, and Anne Foner, eds. *Age and Structural Lag: Society's Failure to Provide Meaningful Opportunities in Work, Family, and Leisure.* New York: John H. Wiley & Sons, 1994.

Robbins, Rich. "Advisor Load." *NACADA Clearinghouse of Academic Advising Resources,* November 5, 2012. Accessed May 20, 2019. www.nacada.ksu .edu/Resources/Clearinghouse/View-Articles/Advisor-Load.aspx.

Schneider, Mark, and Lu Michelle Yin. *The High Cost of Low Graduation Rates: How Much Does Dropping Out of College Really Cost?* Washington, DC: American Institutes for Research, 2011. Accessed October 30, 2019. https:// files.eric.ed.gov/fulltext/ED523102.pdf.

Schroeder, Ray. "Emergence of Blockchain." *Inside Higher Ed,* June 5, 2019. Accessed July 17, 2019. www.insidehighered.com/digital-learning/blogs /online-trending-now/emergence-blockchain.

Schwartz, Robert. *Deans of Men and the Shaping of Modern College Culture.* New York: Palgrave Macmillan, 2010.

"Reconceptualizing the Leadership Roles of Women in Higher Education: A Brief History on the Importance of Deans of Women." *Journal of Higher Education* 68, no. 5 (September–October 1997): 502–522. Accessed March 31, 2021. doi.org/10.2307/2959944.

"The Rise and Demise of Deans of Men." *Review of Higher Education* 26, no. 2 (Winter 2003): 217–239.

Section 504 of the Rehabilitation Act of 1973, 29 U.S.C. § 794 (1973).

Seemiller, Corey, and Meghan Grace. *Generation Z Goes to College.* San Francisco: Jossey-Bass, 2016.

Seidman, Alan. "Taking Action: A Retention Formula and Model for Student Success." In *College Student Retention: Formula for Student Success,* 2nd ed., edited by Alan Seidman, 267–284. Lanham, MD: Rowman & Littlefield Publishers, 2012.

Seidman, Alan. ed. *College Student Retention: Formula for Student Success.* 2nd ed. Lanham, MD: Rowman & Littlefield Publishers, 2012.

Shaw, Kenneth A. *The Intentional Leader.* Syracuse, NY: Syracuse University Press, 2005.

Snyder, Thomas D., ed. *120 Years of American Education: A Statistical Portrait.* Washington, DC: National Center for Educational Statistics, 1993. Accessed May 6, 2021. https://nces.ed.gov/pubs93/93442.pdf.

Snyder, Thomas D., Cristobal de Brey, and Sally A. Dillow. *Digest of Education Statistics 2017*. Washington, DC: National Center for Education Statistics, 2019.

Spina, Eric F., Amar Dev Amar, David N. Rahni, Marin Clarkberg, Richard I. Resch, Jeffrey L. Gray, Gloria Grant Roberson, Paula Hooper Mayhew, and Ronald J. Paprocki. *Report to the Faculty, Administration, Trustees, and Students of American University, Washington, District of Columbia, by the Evaluation Team Representing the Middle States Commission on Higher Education*. Philadelphia: Middle States Commission on Higher Education, 2014. www.american.edu/middlestates/upload/2014-eval-team-report-ameri can-university-a.pdf.

Staley, David J. *Alternative Universities: Speculative Design for Innovation in Higher Education*. Baltimore: Johns Hopkins University Press, 2019.

Stevens, Mitchell L., Cynthia Miller-Idriss, and Seteney Shami. *Seeing the World: How US Universities Make Knowledge in a Global Era*. Princeton, NJ: Princeton University Press, 2018.

St. John, Edward P., Alberto F. Cabrera, Amaury Nora, and Eric H. Asker. "Economic Influences on Persistence Reconsidered: How Can Finance Research Inform the Reconceptualization of Persistence Models?" In *Reworking the Student Departure Puzzle*, edited by John M. Braxton, 29–47. Nashville, TN: Vanderbilt University Press, 2000.

Stone, James C., and Donald P. DeNevi, eds. *Portraits of the American University, 1890–1910*. San Francisco: Jossey-Bass, 1971.

Strom, Ralph J. *The Disabled College Veteran of World War II*. Washington, DC: American Council on Education, 1950. Accessed November 5, 2019. https://hdl.handle.net/2027/uc1.b4237151.

Thelin, John R. *A History of American Higher Education*, 2nd ed. Baltimore: Johns Hopkins University Press, 2011.

Thomason, Andy. "Is College President 'the Toughest Job in the Nation'?" *Chronicle of Higher Education*, May 1, 2018. Accessed March 24, 2020. www.chronicle.com/article/is-college-president-the-toughest-job-in-the-nation/.

Tiede, Hans-Joerg, Samantha McCarthy, Isaac Kamola, and Alyson K. Spurgas. "Data Snapshot: Whom Does Campus Reform Target and What Are the Effects?" American Association of University Professors. Spring 2021. Accessed September 24, 2021. www.aaup.org/article/data-snapshot-whom -does-campus-reform-target-and-what-are-effects#.YWm9SxDMLuo.

Tinto, Vincent. *Completing College: Rethinking Institutional Action*. Chicago: University of Chicago Press, 2012.

——— "Dropout from Higher Education: A Theoretical Synthesis of Recent Research." *Review of Educational Research* 45, no. 1 (March 1975): 89–125.

——— *Leaving College: Rethinking the Causes and Cures of Student Attrition*. 2nd ed. Chicago: University of Chicago Press, 1993.

——— "Moving from Theory to Action: A Model of Institutional Action for Student Success." In *College Student Retention: Formula for Student Success*, 2nd ed., edited by Alan Seidman, 251–266. Lanham, MD: Rowman & Littlefield Publishers, 2012.

Tuberty, Jared T. "The Council of Student Personnel Associations in Higher Education: A Historical Analysis of Inter-Association Collaboration in Student Affairs." PhD diss., Bowling Green State University, 2018. Accessed March 4, 2021. http://rave.ohiolink.edu/etdc/view?acc_num =bgsu1539097186242367.

Tufts University. "Academics at Tufts." Accessed September 8, 2020. https:// admissions.tufts.edu/discover-tufts/academics/.

Tugend, Alina. "How Penn State Improved Conditions for Adjuncts." *Chronicle of Higher Education*, October 30, 2019. www.chronicle.com/article/how -penn-state-improved-conditions-for-adjuncts/.

Turner, H. Spencer, and Janet L. Hurley. "The History and Development of College Health." In *The History and Practice of College Health*, edited by H. Spencer Turner and Janet L. Hurley, 1–21. Lexington, KY: University Press of Kentucky, 2002.

Twenge, Jean M., A. Bell Cooper, Thomas E. Joiner, Mary E. Duffy, and Sarah G. Binau. "Age, Period, and Cohort Trends in Mood Disorder Indicators and Suicide-Related Outcomes in a Nationally Representative Dataset, 2005–2017." *Journal of Abnormal Psychology* 128, no. 3 (2019): 185–199. Accessed June 5, 2020. doi.org/10.1037/abn0000410.

Twenge, Jean M., Gabrielle N. Martin, and W. Keith Campbell. "Decreases in Psychological Well-Being among American Adolescents after 2012 and Links to Screen Time during the Rise of Smartphone Technology." *Emotion* 18, no. 6 (2018): 765–780. Accessed November 5, 2019. doi.org/ 10.1037/emo0000403.

Twenge, Jean M., Thomas E. Joiner, Megan L. Rogers, and Gabrielle N. Martin. "Increases in Depressive Symptoms, Suicide-Related Outcomes, and Suicide Rates among US Adolescents after 2010 and Links to Increased New Media Screen Time." *Clinical Psychological Science* 6, no. 1 (2018): 3–17.

United States Census Bureau. "School Enrollment in the United States: October 2017 – Detailed Tables." Table 5. December 11, 2018. Accessed August 16, 2019. www.census.gov/data/tables/2017/demo/school-enrollment/2017-cps .html.

United States Department of Agriculture, National Institute of Food and Agriculture. "The Hatch Act of 1887 (Multistate Research Fund)." Accessed February 17, 2021. https://nifa.usda.gov/program/hatch-act -1887-multistate-research-fund.

United States Department of Health and Human Services. "Summary of the HIPAA Privacy Rule." Accessed May 6, 2019. www.hhs.gov/hipaa/for-pro fessionals/privacy/laws-regulations/index.html.

United States Senate. "Sputnik Spurs Passage of the National Defense Education Act." Accessed February 17, 2021. www.senate.gov/artandhistory/history /minute/Sputnik_Spurs_Passage_of_National_Defense_Education_Act.htm.

Veysey, Laurence R. *The Emergence of the American University*. Chicago: University of Chicago Press, 1965.

Villlanova University. "From $60 to a College Education: Origins and Development of the GI Bill, The Servicemen's Readjustment Act of 1944 (GI Bill of Rights)", updated January 14, 2021, accessed February 4, 2022, www.villanovau.com/resources/military/origins-of-the-gi-bill/.

Wan, William. "The Coronavirus Pandemic Is Pushing America into a Mental Health Crisis." *Washington Post*, May 4, 2020, 12:57 p.m. EDT. Accessed June 5, 2020. www.washingtonpost.com/health/2020/05/04/mental-health -coronavirus/.

Washington Post. "Harvard Secret Court Expelled Gay Students in 1920." December 1, 2002. Accessed May 3, 2021. www.washingtonpost.com /archive/politics/2002/12/01/harvard-secret-court-expelled-gay-students-in-1920 /5633e721–67b4–426b-954f-4f25fc415c00/.

Weber, Max. *From Max Weber: Essays in Sociology*. Edited by H. H. Gerth and C. Wright Mills. London: Routledge, 2009.

Wegmans. "Company Overview." Accessed May 20, 2019. www.wegmans.com /about-us/company-overview.html.

Wellmon, Chad. "The Amoral University: How Professors Ceded Their Authority." *Chronicle of Higher Education*, November 30, 2018.

White-Lewis, Damani K. "The Facade of Fit in Faculty Search Processes." *Journal of Higher Education* 91, no. 6 (2020): 833–857. Accessed May 19, 2021. doi .org/10.1080/00221546.2020.1775058.

Whitford, Emma. "Tuition Discount Rates Reach New High." *Inside Higher Ed*, May 20, 2021. Accessed May 29, 2021. www.insidehighered.com/news /2021/05/20/private-colleges-cut-539-tuition-sticker-price-freshmen-average.

Williams, Damon A., Joseph B. Berger, and Shederick A. McClendon. *Toward a Model of Inclusive Excellence and Change in Postsecondary Institutions*. Washington, DC: Association of American Colleges and Universities, 2005. Accessed June 22, 2020. www.researchgate.net/publication /238500335_Toward_a_Model_of_Inclusive_Excellence_and_Change_in _Post-Secondary_Institutions.

Woods, Amanda. "Students Fear Dorm Mold Led to Freshman's Adenovirus Death." *New York Post*, November 23, 2018, 2:37 p.m. EST. Accessed August 22, 2019. https://nypost.com/2018/11/23/students-fear-dorm -mold-problem-led-to-freshmans-adenovirus-death/.

Wyckoff, Whitney Blair. "Jackson State: A Tragedy Widely Forgotten," *National Public Radio*, May 3, 2010, 12:00 a.m. EDT. Accessed February 17, 2021. www.npr.org/templates/story/story.php?storyId=126426361.

Young, Jeffrey R. "What Clicks from 70,000 Courses Reveal about Student Learning." *Chronicle of Higher Education*, September 7, 2016. www .chronicle.com/article/what-clicks-from-70-000-courses-reveal-about-student-learning/.

Zaloom, Caitlin. *Indebted: How Families Make College Work at Any Cost*. Princeton, NJ: Princeton University Press, 2019.

Index

Made in the USA
Middletown, DE
17 September 2022